आर्यललितविस्तरो नाम महायानसुत्रम्

།འཕགས་པ་རྒྱ་ཆེར་རོལ་པ་ཞེས་བྱ་བ་ཐེག་པ་ཆེན་པོའི་མདོ།

Lalitavistara

'Phags-pa rgya-cher-rol-pa
zhes-bya-ba theg-pa chen-po'i mdo

The Voice of the Buddha

Plate B

The Voice of the Buddha:
The Beauty of Compassion

Volume II

Translated into English from the French
by Gwendolyn Bays

Dharma Publishing

TIBETAN TRANSLATION SERIES

1. *Calm and Clear*
2. *Legend of the Great Stupa*
3. *Mind in Buddhist Psychology*
4. *Golden Zephyr*
5. *Kindly Bent to Ease Us, Parts 1–3*
6. *Elegant Sayings*
7. *The Life and Liberation of Padmasambhava*
8. *Buddha's Lions*
9. *The Voice of the Buddha*
10. *The Marvelous Companion*
11. *Mother of Knowledge*
12. *Dhammapada*
13. *The Fortunate Aeon*
14. *Master of Wisdom*
15. *Joy for the World*

Library of Congress Cataloging in Publication Data

Tripiṭaka. Sūtrapiṭaka. Lalitavistara. English.
The voice of the Buddha, the beauty of compassion.

(Tibetan translation series)
Includes index.
I. Title. II. Series.
BQ1582.E5B38 1983 294.3′823 83–15024
ISBN 0–913546–84–4 (v. 1)
ISBN 0–913546–85–2 (v. 2)
ISBN 0–913546–86–0 (pbk. : v. 1)
ISBN 0–913546–87–9 (pbk. : v. 2)

Typeset in Fototronic Baskerville with Bookman Light and Dutch Initials.
Printed and bound in the United States of America by Dharma Press, California.

9 8 7 6 5 4 3 2

Dedicated to
the Masters of the Buddhist tradition
and to Western students of the Dharma

Table of Contents

The Voice of the Buddha

Volume II

Plate 16

बिम्बिसारोपसंक्रमणपरिवर्तः

།གཟུགས་ཅན་སྙིང་པོ་འོངས་པའི་ལེའུ།

The Visit with Bimbisāra

O MONKS, TO ALLAY THE SORROW of King Śuddhodana and Gopā of the Śākyas, and to comfort the women attendants and all the other Śākyas, Chandaka, through the blessings of the Bodhisattva, told them about the circumstances surrounding the Bodhisattva's departure.

O monks, the Bodhisattva, after giving his silk garments woven with gold and silver to the devaputra who had taken the form of a hunter, then donned the saffron-colored garments to become a wandering monk, out of sympathy for the world, out of compassion for all beings, and to bring about their complete development.

The Bodhisattva then approached the hermitage of a brāhmin, who invited him to rest and partake of a meal. He was welcomed, too, at the brāhmin Padma's hermitage and at the hermitage of the brahmārṣi Raivata. Rājaka, who was the son of Datṛmadaṇḍika, also made the Bodhisattva welcome.

Thus, O monks, traveling by stages, the Bodhisattva finally arrived at the great city of Vaiśālī. It was here in this city that Ārāḍa Kālāma had established his dwelling, staying together with a great assembly of Śrāvakas and three hundred disciples, to whom Ārāḍa taught the doctrines that entail strenuous austerities associated with the various formless meditations. When Ārāḍa saw the Bodhisattva approaching from afar, he was filled with wonder and said to his disciples: "Look at the one who approaches! How beautiful he is!" The disciples replied: "We see him. He is indeed wonderful to behold!"

Then, O monks, approaching Ārāḍa Kālāma, I spoke to him thus: "Ārāḍa Kālāma, I wish to practice brahmacarya with you." And he answered: "O Gautama, practice this teaching, for through its practice a son of good family who possesses faith can acquire complete knowledge with little difficulty."

O monks, I considered thoughtfully: "Being endowed with intention, courage, mindfulness, deep meditation, and wisdom, with these qualities I can obtain this teaching. To manifest this teaching, I will dwell apart and practice alone with firmness and diligence." And so, monks, calm and diligent, I stayed in solitude and soon understood and manifested this teaching.

Then, O monks, I went to Ārāḍa Kālāma and said to him: "You have understood and made manifest this doctrine, O Ārāḍa." And he replied: "That is true, Gautama." I said to him: "I also have understood and manifested this teaching." He replied: "O Gautama, just as I know this teaching, so also do you know it; and everything which you know about it, I know as well. Now both of us can communicate it to the assembly of disciples."

And Ārāḍa Kālāma showered me with the greatest honors and established me at the head of his disciples for the mutual benefit of all.

Then, O monks, I considered: "Ārāḍa's doctrine is not liberating; it does not completely destroy suffering. I must search for a higher doctrine."

Therefore, O monks, after dwelling in Vaiśālī as long as I needed, I traveled to the land of Magadha. Nearing the city of Rājagṛha, I reached the region of Pāṇḍava, the king of mountains. There I lived on the slope of the king of mountains, alone and without companions, guarded by many hundreds of millions of gods.

One morning at dawn, wearing the robes of a monk and carrying the alms bowl, I entered the great city of Rājagṛha, through the Gate of Warm Waters. Looking to all sides, I advanced with a fine stride, wearing the light cloak, the garment of a monk, and carrying the alms bowl. As becomes a man transformed, my senses were unagitated, my mind was not directed outward. Walking like one who carries a bowl of oil, not gazing farther ahead than the length of a yoke, I went forth to seek alms.

Upon seeing me, the people of Rājagṛha were filled with astonishment. "Who can this be? Could he be Brahmā or Śakra, the lord of the gods? Could he be Vaiśravaṇa? Or perhaps he is some god of the mountains?" Such were their thoughts.

Concerning this it is said:

Possessing infinite and spotless splendor,
the Bodhisattva becomes a wandering monk.
His mind calm, his actions well-controlled,

he lives alone on the slope of Pāṇḍava,
the king of mountains.

Seeing that the night has passed,
the Bodhisattva, dressed in monk's robes,
humble in spirit, takes up his alms bowl.
Beautiful to behold, he enters Rājagṛha, seeking alms.

Crowds of men and women
behold the one who is like pure gold.
His self-mastery is complete;
he is marked with the thirty-two signs.
And no one tires of gazing upon him.

Sprinkling the streets before him with water,
adorning them with jewels and banners,
following behind as he passes,
the multitude asks: "Who is this being?"
Never before has such a one been seen,
one who makes the city shine with splendor.

Thousands of women, desiring to see
the most outstanding of men,
leave their houses empty; they stand on the rooftops,
in doorways, at windows, and in the streets
to gaze upon him.

The merchants stop doing business;
in the houses and the streets,
all drinking and revelry cease,
so intent are the people on watching
the most remarkable of men.

Quickly a citizen goes to the palace,
seeking out King Bimbisāra:
"Sire, the greatest of blessings is yours today.
Brahmā himself is here in the city, asking for alms.

"Some say it is Śakra, the king of the gods,
or the devaputra Suyāma or a Tuṣita god in disguise.
Others say one of the Sunirmita gods has arrived.

"Still others say it is Candra or Sūrya
or Rāhu or Bali or Vemacitri.
And there are those who say
it is the one who dwells on Pāṇḍava,
the king of mountains."

These words fill the king with the greatest joy,
and he goes to the window
to look upon the most excellent being,
the radiant Bodhisattva shining like the purest gold.

King Bimbisāra says to the citizen:
"Give him alms, and watch carefully where he goes."
And the man reports back to the king:
"Sire, he has gone to the side of the mountain."

When the night has passed, King Bimbisāra,
surrounded by a great entourage,
travels to the foot of Pāṇḍava and sees
the king of mountains shining with light.

Descending from his chariot,
the king climbs Mount Pāṇḍava.
There he looks with respect upon the Bodhisattva,
steadfast as Mount Meru,
sitting cross-legged on a cushion of grass.

The king bows his head respectfully
to the Bodhisattva's feet,
and they speak of many things,
until at length the king says:
"I will give you half my kingdom!

Enjoy here all you could of desire!
Do not go off as a wanderer!"

The Bodhisattva replies in a soft voice:
"Lord of the land, may you have a long life!
I have given up a beautiful kingdom;
and thus detached, I have embraced the religious life
to obtain peace."

The King of Magadha replies:
"You are in the flower of your youth!
Your complexion is brilliant; you are clearly robust.
Accept from me abundant riches and women.
Stay here in my kingdom and enjoy yourself!

"I feel the keenest joy from having seen you.
Pray, be my friend and companion.
I will give you my kingdom,
and everything you could desire.

"Stay no longer in the wilderness.
Stay no longer on this seat of grass.
While your body is in the bloom of youth,
stay here with me and enjoy the objects of desire."

The Bodhisattva, compassionate and helpful,
answers him softly, with kind but honest words:
"May blessings always be with you,
O protector of the land!
But I am no longer attracted by the qualities of desire.

"Desires are like poison, bringing endless harm—
through desire beings fall into hell
and into the animal and preta realms.
Through desire and base concerns, the wise are brought low.
I have expelled all such things like snot from the nose.

"Desires fall like fruits from trees;
they pile up like rain clouds in the sky;
changing and inconstant as the wind,
they are deceivers and destroyers of all that is good.

"He who does not obtain the object of desire
is sorely distressed, but so is he who does.
Neither finds contentment.
If violent desires are not mastered when they arise,
they produce great suffering.

"O King, even if one satisfies all desires—
be they human or divine,
even those desires worthy of praise,
complete satisfaction is not obtained;
for still one seeks for more.

"But those, O King, who are calm and restrained,
content because they are instructed by wisdom,
their perceptions filled with the venerable faultless Dharma,
such beings are truly fulfilled.
None of the qualities of desire
give them the slightest satisfaction.

"O King and protector of the land,
the more one serves desire,
the more things to desire limitlessly appear.
Just as drinking salt water increases thirst,
so he who serves his desires increases those desires.

"Further, O King, consider this body—
unstable, without essence, a mass of suffering,
always secreting impurities through its nine apertures.
O King, no longer do I have any impulse of desire.

"I abandoned all that is desirable
and gave up thousands of beautiful women.
Finding no joy in the things of the world,
I renounced them all to gain supreme Enlightenment,
the greatest happiness."

The King of Magadha says:
"From where have you come, O wandering monk?
Where were you born and where are your parents?
Are you kṣatriya, brāhmin, or king?
Speak, O monk who bears no burden."

The Bodhisattva replies:
"My father is Śuddhodana.
You have heard, O King, of Kapila,
the rich and flourishing Śākya city.
It is there I became a wandering monk,
in order to acquire virtue."

The King of Magadha replies:
"We are fortunate to have had you in our sight
and proclaim ourselves disciples of your source.
Pray, be patient in your heart with one
who desires to be free from all desire
and thus invites you here.

"When you have attained Enlightenment,
may you share your teachings with me,
O Master of the Dharma.
I have gained already the greatest benefit
since you have lived here in my kingdom,
O Naturally-realized Being."

And bowing again to the feet of the Bodhisattva,
and humbly circumambulating him three times,

the king, surrounded by his entourage,
returns to Rājagṛha.

Thus, having entered the land of Magadha,
and dwelling there peacefully as long as he wished,
attending to the needs of gods and men,
the Protector of the World goes forth
toward the banks of the Nairañjanā River.

The Sixteenth Chapter
The Visit with Bimbisāra

Plate 17

दुष्करचर्यापरिवर्तः

།དཀའ་བ་སྤྱད་པའི་ལེའུ།

The Practice of Austerities

AT THAT TIME, O MONKS, a son of Rāma named Rudraka had withdrawn into the city of Rājagṛha, where he was dwelling with an assembly of seven hundred disciples. He taught them a teaching which used ascetic practices to reach the samādhi in which there is neither perception nor non-perception.

O monks, the Bodhisattva saw that Rudraka, the son of Rāma, the guide of the assembly, the preceptor of multitudes, was well-known, was sought after, venerated, and esteemed by scholars. After seeing him, the Bodhisattva thought: "This Rudraka, the guide of the assembly, the preceptor of multitudes, is known, sought after, venerated, and esteemed by scholars. If I do not approach him myself, if I do not deliver myself over to austerities and ascetic practices, he will not respect me, or consider me as different from his other disciples. Unless I manifest this knowledge, I will not be able to refute his teachings—although his meditations and samādhis are transitory and limited in application. Therefore, I will practice according to instructions and manifest his meditations. I will demonstrate the samādhis which give worldly powers. After becoming a disciple of Rudraka, I will demonstrate the superiority of my meditation; I will also demonstrate the essential meaninglessness of the samādhi which is limited."

O monks, the Bodhisattva went to Rudraka, the son of Rāma for this purpose, and spoke thus: "Friend, who is your preceptor? Who teaches this doctrine which you know so completely?" Rudraka replied: "I have, my friend, no teacher, and it is solely by myself that I have understood this." The Bodhisattva replied: "What is it that you have understood?" Rudraka answered: "The way of acquiring calmness and the samādhi in which there is neither perception nor non-perception." The Bodhisattva said: "May I obtain from you this precept, the rule, and the way of this meditation?" Rudraka replied: "Let it be so. I will give this teaching as you have asked."

Then the Bodhisattva, having gone off by himself, sat down with his legs crossed. He was hardly seated when, because of the superiority of his virtue, the superiority of his knowledge, the superiority of the fruits of his previous practice of good works, and the superiority of his experience with all the meditations beginning with all the worldly and transworldly contemplations, the hundreds of types of calmness appeared to him directly in all their forms and with all their characteristics—all because he showed himself as master of his mind.

Then with mindfulness and knowledge the Bodhisattva arose from his seat and approached Rudraka, the son of Rāma. He spoke to him thus: "Friend, above the path of acquiring calmness and the samādhi where there is neither perception nor non-perception, is there a higher level of samādhi?" Rudraka said: "There is not."

Then the Bodhisattva thought: "Rudraka is not the only one with faith, effort, mindfulness, meditation, and wisdom. I too have faith, effort, mindfulness, meditation, and wisdom." Therefore, the Bodhisattva spoke to Rudraka, the son of Rāma: "Friend, I also have understood this doctrine; whatever you have understood, I also have realized."

Rudraka said: "Well, then, come. You and I will together teach this assembly." And so for the mutual benefit of all, he proclaimed the Bodhisattva as a teacher.

Then the Bodhisattva told Rudraka: "Friend, this way which you teach leads neither to distaste for the world nor the absence of desire, nor to the cessation of rebirth, nor to calm, nor to superior knowledge, nor to perfect Enlightenment, nor to being a śramaṇa, nor to Nirvāṇa." And the Bodhisattva left Rudraka, the son of Rāma, and his disciples, saying to himself: "So much for that. That is enough for me."

At that same time, five men of good family who were practicing brahmacarya under Rudraka considered: "The end for which we have been working and seeking for such a long time, and which we still do not understand, has been grasped and has been understood with little difficulty by the Śramaṇa Gautama. And yet it does not satisfy him; he is looking beyond it. Without any doubt, he will be the teacher of the world, and what he will understand will satisfy us." With such reasoning, the five men left Rudraka and attached themselves to the Bodhisattva.

Thus, monks, the Bodhisattva, having dwelt as long as he pleased at Rājagṛha, left the city to travel the country of Magadha, attended by the five men of good family.

At that time, a large group was having a celebration in a place between Rājagṛha and Gayā, and the Bodhisattva and his five followers were invited to take part in the feast. Continuing on, O monks, the Bodhisattva traveled through Magadha until he reached the peak of Mount Gaya, where he stayed for a time, practicing renunciation. And while he dwelt there, three examples concerning desire, previously unknown and unheard of, presented themselves to him. What were these three?

"There are śramaṇas and brāhmins who have not kept their bodies isolated from desire, who have not kept their minds isolated from desire, and who take pleasure in desire. They are attached to desire, are drunk with desire, long for desire, are consumed with desire, and are faint with desire. Since they do not calm their desire, they experience painful feelings, sharp, burning, and cruel, which torment their bodies and minds. They are therefore incapable of seeing or manifesting the highest wisdom, which is so much greater than the highest human knowledge. It is like a man who is looking for light and desires to make fire who takes a piece of green wood and then rubs it against another piece of green wood he has first put into water. He will not be able to produce a flame.

"So it is with these śramaṇas and brāhmins who have not kept their bodies and minds isolated from desire, who take joy in desire, are attached to desire, are drunk with desire, long for desire, are consumed with desire, and are faint with desire. Since they do not calm their desire, they experience painful sensations, sharp, burning, and cruel, which torment their bodies and minds. They are therefore incapable of seeing or manifesting the highest wisdom, which is so much greater than the highest human knowledge." This was the first example, previously unknown and unheard of, which came to the Bodhisattva.

And again the Bodhisattva considered: "There are other śramaṇas and brāhmins who have kept their bodies and minds isolated from desire, but take joy in desire. They are attached to desire, are drunk with desire, long for desire, are consumed with desire, and are faint with desire. Since they do not calm their desire, they experience painful feelings, sharp, burning and cruel, which torment their bodies and minds. They are therefore incapable of seeing or manifesting the highest wisdom, which is so much greater than the highest human knowledge. It is like a man who desires to make fire who takes a piece of green wood and, having placed it in a hollow, rubs it against another piece of green wood. He will not be able to produce a fire.

"So it is with these śramaṇas and brāhmins who have kept their bodies and minds isolated from desire, but take joy in desire, are attached to desire, are drunk with desire, long for desire, are consumed with desire, and are faint with desire. Since they do not calm their desires, they experience painful sensations, sharp, burning, and cruel, which torment their bodies and minds. And they are therefore incapable of seeing or manifesting the highest wisdom, which is so much greater than the highest human knowledge." This was the second example, previously unknown and unheard of, which came to the Bodhisattva.

And again: "There are śramaṇas and brāhmins who keep their bodies and minds isolated from desire, who find pleasure in desire. These are attached to desire, are drunk with desire, long for desire, are consumed by desire, and are faint with desire. But they calm their desire. They also experience painful feelings, sharp, burning, and cruel. They, however, are capable of seeing and manifesting the highest wisdom, which is so much greater than the highest human knowledge. It is like a man who desires to make fire and light who takes two pieces of dry wood and rubs them together in a dry hollow: he will be able to make flame burst forth and light shine.

"So it is with these śramaṇas and brāhmins who keep their bodies and minds isolated from desire, who find pleasure in desire, are attached to desire, are drunk with desire, long for desire, are consumed by desire, but who calm their desire. They also experience painful feelings, sharp, burning, and cruel, but they are capable of clearly seeing and manifesting the highest wisdom, which is so much greater than human knowledge." This is the third example, previously unknown and unheard of, which came to the mind of the Bodhisattva.

Then, O monks, the Bodhisattva considered: "I certainly keep my body isolated from desire, and my mind isolated from desire. Although I have found pleasure in desire, and been attracted by desire, have been drunk with desire, have longed for desire, and been consumed by desire, I have calmed all these. And although I have experienced painful feelings, sharp, burning, and cruel, I am certainly capable of seeing and manifesting the highest wisdom, which is so much greater than any human knowledge."

O monks, having dwelt as long as he pleased at Gayā, on Mount Gayāśirṣa, the Bodhisattva went by foot toward Uruvilvā. Near this village he caught sight of the river Nairañjanā with its pure water and beautiful waterfalls, its shores lined with branching trees and pleasant woods, surrounded on all sides by pasture lands and villages. There, the mind of the Bodhisattva was extremely content. "In truth, this corner of the world is level, pleasant, and hospitable; it is just right for a son of good lineage intent on renunciation. As I am truly desirous of renunciation, here I will remain."

Then, O monks, the Bodhisattva reflected: "In this time of the five degenerations, I have descended into the land of Jambu among beings with base inclinations, into a land full of tīrthikas imbued with various different views and doctrines. Many yearn wholeheartedly for a fine body in their future lives, but in their ignorance, they teach and search for purity by means of various penitences and mortifications. There are those who rely on magic spells, who lick their hands after eating, who do not stand up, who do not speak; there are those who eat only roots and neither flesh nor fish, who do not travel in the rainy season, who abstain from alcohol, rice gruel, and water.

"There are those who believe they should take their nourishment at the homes of one, three, five, or seven families; those who eat roots, fruits, valisneria, kuśa grass, leaves, cow dung, cow urine, milk, curds, butter, molasses, or unground seed; those who wash and take as food what geese and pigeons have tasted and rejected. There are those who look for their subsistence only in villages or deserts; those who live like cows, gazelles, dogs, sheep, monkeys, or elephants; those who only stand; those who do not speak; those who eat only one mouthful of food, or else up to seven mouthfuls; those who eat once a day, once in a day and a night, or else four, five, or six times a day; those who fast for half a month, regulating their fasts by the moon.

"Then there are those who wear the feathers of vultures and owls, and make loincloths of muñja grass, asana bark, darbha grass, or valvaja grass; those who wear blankets of camel's hair, blankets of goat's hair, blankets of horsehair or leather; and those who wear wet cloth.

"There are those who sleep on stools, or in puddles of water, on cinders, on gravel, on rocks, on boards, on thorns, on grass; those who sleep on slabs of wood, those who sleep with the head down or sleep squatting; those who sleep on bare ground; those who wear one, two, three, four, five, six, seven garments or more; those who go naked; those who take as a rule to bathe or not to bathe; those who grow their hair, their nails, or their beards; those who wear their hair in a knot; those who eat a single juniper berry or grain of sesame or rice; those who smear their bodies with cinders, with blacking, with flower essences, with dust, dung, or mud. There are those who wear human hair, human skin, human skulls, and fingernails; those who wear loincloths of hair, who cover themselves with mud, and wear bones; those who drink warm water, filtered rice water, or boiled water. Some carry coals, some mark themselves with daubs of color, some wear dark red garments. Some carry tridents, others shave their heads. Some carry a water pot, others a human skull and a club.

"In all these ways do these foolish ones understand purity! They inhale smoke, they inhale fire; they gaze at the sun; they perform the five austerities; they stand on one foot; they stay with one arm uplifted; they bury one foot; they stay in one spot. Thus do they pile up austerities.

"They walk on burning straw and other burning substances. They walk on hot coals, burning vases, burning stones; they walk into flaming fire. Some take no food and live in deserts or under waterfalls. They search for the desired path by means of courting death. They pursue purity by saying OṀ; by saying VAṢAṬ; by saying SVADHĀ; by saying SVĀHĀ. By reciting mantras, and by reading the sacred books and the Dhāraṇa, they pursue purity.

"Believing themselves pure, they go for refuge to such as Brahmā, Indra, Rudrā, or Viṣṇu, Devī, Kumāra, Mātṛ, Kātyāyanī, Candra, Āditya, Vaiśravaṇa, or Varuṇa; to the vāsus, the aśvins, the nāgas, or the yakṣas, the gandharvas, the asuras, the garuḍas, the kinnaras, the mahoragas, the rākṣasas, or the pretabhūtas; to the kumbhāṇḍas, the pārṣadas, the gaṇapatis, the piśācas, the devarṣis, the rājarṣis, or the brahmarṣis; to all these they render homage. All these things they find meaningful.

"They also take refuge in earth, water, fire, wind, or ether; in mountains, valleys, rivers, fountains, lakes, ponds, and reservoirs; in the sea, basins, wells, or ditches; in trees, bushes, ivy, grasses, or trunks of trees; in enclosures, cemeteries, crossroads, public squares, lanes, or doors. They render homage to houses, pillars, and rocks, to pestles, swords, bows, axes, arrows, spears, and to three-pointed weapons. They accept as signs of benediction curdled milk, clarified butter, mustard seeds, barley, garlands, darbha grass, jewels, gold, silver, and other such substances.

"These are the things done by tīrthikas. Tormented by fear of rebirth, these are the things to which they have recourse. And some among them think: 'We will achieve the highest states of being and deliverance by these means.' And by saying that to themselves, they travel on a false road, conceiving as refuge that which is not a refuge, conceiving as a blessing that which is not a blessing; they take for pure what is impure.

"And so I myself will undertake with purity that which will confound and convert all these opponents. I will make meaningful the time and actions of those whose time and actions have been meaningless. I will demonstrate the meditations of the gods of the realm of both form and meditation by performing great austere practices."

O monks, having thus reflected, the Bodhisattva for six years practiced terrible austerities, those most difficult to practice, the most difficult among the most difficult. And so he has been called Duṣkaracaryā, the One who has Done the Difficult. No one among all the myriad beings, human or non-human, is capable of practicing such difficult austerities except a Bodhisattva in his last existence, who has entered the space-like meditation known as the Āsphānaka.

What is this meditation called Āsphānaka? The first time the Bodhisattva entered into the fourth profound meditation, he completely cut off all inhalation and exhalation; his meditation was non-investigative, non-conceptual, unshakable, free from perception, unchangeable; it penetrated everywhere and was independent of everything. Such a meditation had never previously been achieved by anyone, not by those in the stage of learning or by those who had finished learning, not by Pratyekabuddhas or Bodhisattvas who have entered the path of action. From this comes the name Āsphānaka.

This meditation is called 'the sky', for it is like space—all-encompassing, without extending anywhere. It cannot be dispersed and is all-inclusive. Because it is like ākāśa, space, it is called Āsphānaka.

O monks, the Bodhisattva caused marvelous actions to be seen in the world. He sat thus to reduce the pride of the tīrthikas, to confound all opponents, to accord with the wishes of the gods, to counter and guide the nihilists, the eternalists, and the materialists, to indicate the results of meritorious actions and the genuine fruits of knowledge, to show the various stages of meditation, to demonstrate the strength and energy of the body, and to produce true heroism of the mind. For all of these reasons the Bodhisattva sat with crossed legs on the unswept earth; and having seated himself, he put his body and mind through great torment.

O monks, for eight winter nights I subdued and tortured my body. Sweat ran from my armpits, ran from my forehead, and fell to the ground in brilliant droplets so warm they evaporated like smoke. Like a strong man who seizes a weak man by the neck and overpowers him, so, monks, did I subdue my body with my mind and force it, until sweat ran from my armpits and from my forehead, falling to the ground in brilliant droplets so warm they evaporated like smoke.

Then, monks, it occurred to me: "I will apply myself to Āsphānaka contemplation." And as I did so, inhalation and exhalation through both the mouth and nose ceased. Great loud noises came forth from the two openings of my ears, loud noises, great noises like those made when one works a bellows. Monks, this loud noise, this great noise, came forth from the two openings of my ears because inhalation and exhalation through both nose and mouth had stopped.

Next, monks, I thought again to devote myself to the Āsphānaka contemplation. O monks, my nose, my mouth, and my ears were stopped up, so that the breath hit the top of my skull. O monks, since my mouth, my nose, and my ears were stopped up, inhalation and exhalation being obstructed, the breath hit the top of my skull, striking it as would a man who sought to pierce the skull with a sharp lance.

A devaputra saw this condition and spoke thus: "Alas, in truth the young Siddhārtha has gone to his death!" Others said: "No, it is not the time for his death. Arhats who dwell in meditation proceed in this way." And they recited these two verses:

"No, truly, this prince of the Śākyas
will not die here in this wilderness
without having fulfilled his purpose.
He will not leave the three worlds
in misery and without a protector;
he will not depart without having achieved his goal.

"Ah! Heart of living beings whose promise is firm!
In times past, O Protector, you invited us
joyfully to serve the holy Dharma!
Where, O Guide, is the firm promise
which you, the Pure One, made in Tuṣita?"

Then these gods entered the realm of the Thirty-three gods, and sent this news to Māyādevī: "The young prince has reached the hour of death." At midnight Māyādevī, surrounded by a host of apsarases, went to the bank of the river Nairañjanā, where she saw the Bodhisattva, his body wasted. On seeing him thus like a corpse, she began to weep. Choked by sobs, she recited these verses:

"When you were born in the garden called Lumbinī,
O my son, like a lion, you took seven steps forward
all by yourself, and after gazing in the four directions,
you pronounced these beautiful words:
'This is my last birth.'
Now these words will go unfulfilled.

"When Asita declared:
'He will be a Buddha in the world,'
his prophecy proved false.
He had not seen the instability of fate.

"Nor have you tasted the splendor
which delights the heart of Cakravartin kings.
O my son, without obtaining supreme Enlightenment,
you have gone to your death in the forest!

"What a great affliction this is for me!
To whom can I now turn for help?
Who will give the breath of life back to my son?"

The Bodhisattva replied:
"Who is this woman weeping bitterly,
tearing her hair and destroying her beauty?

Who is this so sorely afflicted,
lamenting so greatly over her son?"

Māyā replied: "For ten months
I carried you like a diamond in my womb.
O my son, the one so miserable is your mother."

Then the Bodhisattva consoled her: "Do not fear; you shall have your son again. I will return to you your fruitful labor: the renunciation of a Buddha is always productive. I will clearly fulfill the prediction of Asita and make the prediction of Dīpaṁkara come true. The earth could be torn into hundreds of pieces; the peak of great Meru could be turned upside down; the multitude of stars could fall to earth; yet should a single human being remain, I would not die! So you have no cause to give yourself over to sorrow. The time is not far distant when you will see the Enlightenment of a Buddha!"

As soon as Māyā heard these words, she shivered with delight. She covered the Bodhisattva with māndārava flowers, and after circumambulating him three times, withdrew to her abode amidst the sound of heavenly instruments.

Then, O monks, there came to my mind this thought: "There are śramaṇas and brāhmins who believe that by eating only a very little food, one is pure." And so I thought: "I also must apply myself to the practice of eating only a very little food."

And I recognized, monks, that I must eat but a single juniper berry and not a second one. And if you think, monks, that the juniper berry of that time was larger, you are certainly wrong. In truth, at that time, the juniper berry was the same size as it is today. And my body which took for food only a single berry became extremely thin and weak. O monks, like the knots of the āsītakī plant or the knots of the kālika plant were my limbs and their joints. Like the sides of the crab, so also were my sides. My rib cage was like an old stable with its sides caved in, so that light shines through—so likewise, you could see light shine through my body. The vertebrae of my spine were like the uneven contours of a braid of hair—high and low, uneven. So were the vertebrae of my spine. Like a gourd cut too young which has withered and finally dried up completely, my head withered until it looked old and wrinkled and dry. Like the reflections of the stars in a well during the last month of summer when the water is so low the reflections are difficult to see, so also my eyeballs sank in, becoming difficult to see. Like the foot of the goat or the hoof of the camel were my shoulders, my stomach, my chest, and the rest.

And, monks, when I thought I was touching my stomach with my hands, it was my spine that I was feeling. When I tried to get up, I was so bent over that I fell backwards. When with difficulty I again got up, and rubbed my limbs with dust, all the hairs came away from my body. Through the rough self-abasement I was undertaking, my former beautiful and delicate complexion disappeared. And the people who dwelt in the neighboring village thought: "Ah, truly, he is black, the Śramaṇa Gautama! Ah, truly, he is dark blue, the Śramaṇa Gautama! Ah, truly, the Śramaṇa Gautama is the color of the madgura fish! His former beautiful and clear complexion has disappeared!"

This came to my mind, monks: "I must apply myself more and eat even less." And I knew that I needed only a single grain of rice and not a second one. Monks, if you think that the grain of rice of that time was larger, put the thought out of your mind. A grain of rice of that time was the same as that of the present. O monks, sustained only by one single grain of rice in a day, my body became even thinner and weaker, and the people thought: "Ah, truly, the Śramaṇa Gautama is the color of a madgura fish. His former beautiful and clear complexion has disappeared!"

Monks, this came to my mind: "I must attempt to eat still less." And I knew that I needed only one grain of sesame seed and not a second one. And as before, my body grew thinner still, and people said: "His beautiful and delicate complexion has disappeared."

Monks, this came to my mind: "There are śramaṇas and brāhmins who believe that purity comes from not eating. I will therefore apply myself to not eating at all."

And then, monks, my body, receiving no food at all, became excessively dry, thin, and weak. My limbs and their joints were two or three times, four times, five times, even ten times, thinner than the knots of the āsītakī plant or the knots of the kālika plant. My sides were like those of a crab. My rib cage was like a caved-in stable, my spine took on the contours of a braid of hair, my skull became like a dried-up gourd, my eyeballs like the stars reflected at the bottom of a well.

And monks, when I thought to myself, how good to get up and loosen the limbs, and bent over to do so, I fell down. When with difficulty I picked myself up and rubbed my limbs, all the hairs of my body fell out. Because of the rough self-abasement I had undertaken, my beautiful, clear, and brilliant complexion disappeared. And those people who dwelt in the neighboring village thought: "Ah! Truly, he is black, the Śramaṇa Gautama! Truly, he is dark blue, the Śramaṇa Gautama! Ah! Truly, the Śramaṇa Gautama is the color of the madgura fish! His beautiful, clear complexion has disappeared."

At that time, King Śuddhodana sent a messenger to the Bodhisattva every day.

Thus, monks, the Bodhisattva, in order to cause marvelous actions to be seen in the world, to guide the actions and karma of beings whose actions were defiled, to express his accumulation of merits, to show the virtues of great knowledge, to define clearly the stages of meditation, manifested for six years the practice difficult to accomplish, eating but a single juniper berry and a single grain of rice. His mind never dejected, the Bodhisattva remained for six years with his legs crossed, abiding just so and never deviating from the path of pure action.

When the sun fell on him, he did not move into the shade, and from the shade he did not move into the sun. He did not seek refuge from wind, sun, or rain; he did not chase away horseflies, mosquitos, or snakes. He did not excrete urine or excrement or spittle or nasal mucous; he did not get up or stretch; he did not lie down on his stomach or back or side. The great storms and tempests, the rain and hail of autumn, spring, and winter descended on the Bodhisattva, who at the end, did not even try to shelter himself with his hand. He did not fight his senses, nor did he welcome the objects of the senses.

The young men and young girls of the village who passed by—cowherds, grass or wood gatherers or collectors of cow dung—thought: "He is a dust demon!" and they made fun of him and covered him with dust. During those six years, the body of the Bodhisattva had become so weak, so feeble and thin that when they put grass and cotton in the openings of his ears, it came out through his nostrils; when they put stuff in his nostrils, it came out through his ears; when they put anything in his ears, it came out through his mouth; when they put anything in his mouth, it came out through his ears and his nose; when they put stuff in his nose, it came out of his ears, his nose, and his mouth.

And the gods, the nāgas, the yakṣas, the gandharvas, the asuras, the garuḍas, the kinnaras, and the mahoragas were witnesses of the virtues of the Bodhisattva. They remained near him day and night, giving homage to the Bodhisattva and praying.

By means of the Bodhisattva's practice of austerities, twelve complete niyutas of gods and men were brought to complete maturation in the three vehicles.

Concerning this it is said:

The Bodhisattva endowed with great qualities leaves home;
he generates skillful means
for the sake of aiding and fulfilling
the purpose of living beings.

At the time of the five degenerations,
when people are inclined toward
base and worldly doctrines,
he was born into the land of Jambu
where much karma is created.

"This land is filled with tīrthikas,
foolish ones who proudly put themselves on display.
Because of the tortures they practice on their bodies,
they believe they have attained pure minds.

"They walk into fire and throw themselves from cliffs;
naked, they cover themselves with dust and ashes.
To torment their bodies thoroughly,
they zealously practice the austerity of the five fires.

"Some repeat spells, some lick their hands after eating;
some refuse offerings from bronze vessels
or refuse to do rituals near pillars or gates.

"Some refuse offerings from a place with a dog,
or where they are told: "Wait!" or "Come!"
After receiving a single offering from a dwelling,
they believe they have become pure.

"Some reject ghee, sesame oil, honey, and molasses,
milk, curd, fish, and flesh,
eating only śyāmaka grain and vegetables.
Others eat only gardūlas and rice sprouts,
and the fibers of the lotus.

"Some eat only roots, leaves, and fruits,
and wear clothing of kuśa grass, skins, or felt;
others wander naked, saying foolishly:
'Here is truth, the rest is falsehood!'

"Some hold their hands uplifted
and wear their hair in a tangled knot.
Having completely lost their way,
they desire the path to happiness,
yet pursue a road that is wrong.

"They sleep on grass or ashes,
on piles of sticks or thorns, or sleep crouched over.
Some stand on one foot with faces lifted,
gazing at the sun and moon.

"Fountains, ponds and lakes, seas and rivers,
the moon and sun, trees, mountains, and clay—
these are some of the things they worship.

"By means of various mortifications,
they shrivel their bodies, those foolish ones!
Wrapped in false views,
they fall quickly into lower states of being.

"These terrible mortifications I practice
are surely a difficult course—
impossible for gods or men to do.

"And I will apply myself to Āsphānaka contemplation,
whose foundation is as solid as a diamond;
a contemplation which the Pratyekabuddhas
are incapable even of seeing.

"In this world there are gods and men
happy with miserable tīrthika practices;
in order to bring them to complete maturity,
I must practice rough and difficult austerities."

And the Bodhisattva, having crossed his legs,
remains seated on the exposed earth,
demonstrating the method of nourishing the body
with only a juniper berry, a sesame seed, a grain of rice.

Completely cutting off both inhalation and exhalation,
he is not shaken, he who is strong!

For six years, he applies himself
to the great contemplation, the Āsphānaka.

Without investigation or conceptualization,
this meditation is without change or vacillation,
and all-encompassing like space—
he applies himself to Āsphānaka contemplation.

And he does not move from sun to shade,
or from the shade into the sun.
Unshakable as Meru,
he applies himself to Āsphānaka contemplation.

Without shelter from the wind and the rain,
without protection against mosquitoes and scorpions,
snakes and crawling insects,
with unshakable practice,
he applies himself to Āsphānaka contemplation.

He strives not for himself alone
but applies himself out of compassion for others,
contemplating great benefit for the world.

And the young people of the village,
the cowherds, the grass and wood gatherers,
imagine that he is a dust demon
and cover him with dust.

They heap filth upon him
and do other malicious things.
But he is unperturbed; unconcerned,
he applies himself to the Āsphānaka contemplation.

He does not rise, nor does he lie down;
he makes no effort to shield himself.

He excretes neither excrement nor urine.
Unfrightened by noise, he does not look at others.

His flesh and blood dry out,
his skin wizens; tendons and bones stick out.
Through his stomach one can see his spine,
like the knots of a braid of hair.

And those who excel in all things—
the gods, asuras, nāgas, yakṣas, and gandharvas—
render homage day and night
to the one who possesses great virtues.

And they set forth this prayer:
"May we soon be like the one who,
with the all-embracing contemplation of openness,
applies himself to Āsphānaka meditation, the samādhi
which is the all-encompassing openness of space."

Not for his own happiness,
not to taste the sweetness of meditation
does he apply himself,
but out of compassion for the well-being of others,
out of concern for the troubles of the world.

Those with opposing views are overcome;
the tīrthikas with base minds are subjugated.
Where is the Enlightenment so difficult to obtain,
even over numerous kalpas?
The great actions and deeds are being demonstrated—
those which were told to Kāśyapa.

For the sake of the joy of all beings,
he applies himself to the Āsphānaka contemplation.

Twelve complete niyutas of men and gods
become trained in the three vehicles.
For this reason does the one with the great mind
apply himself to Āsphānaka contemplation.

The Seventeenth Chapter
The Practice of Austerities

Plate 18

नैरञ्जनापरिवर्तः

།ནཻ་རན་ཛི་ནརི་ཝརྟ།

The Nairañjanā River

O MONKS, DURING THE SIX YEARS that the Bodhisattva practiced austerities, the demon Pāpīyān followed behind him step by step, seeking an opportunity to harm him. But he found no opportunity whatsoever and went away discouraged and discontent.

Concerning this it is said:

There in the pleasant forests and woods,
among thickets lush with vines,
to the east of Uruvilvā
where the Nairañjanā river flows,

Namuci approaches the one
who applies himself to renunciation,
striving zealously for perfection, firm in his valor.

Namuci approaches, speaking sweetly:
"Śākya son, arise! What need have you to weary yourself?

Life is most valuable for the living;
in living, you will practice the Dharma.
The living can act in such a way
that their deeds do not bring sorrow.

"You are weak, discolored, defeated;
death approaches—death which has a thousand parts
while life has only one.

"Great merit comes from giving alms
and making fire offerings when one can.
What can you do by renunciation?

"Sorrowful is the path to renunciation,
difficult the submission of the mind."
This is Māra's discourse of the moment
addressed to the Bodhisattva.

The Bodhisattva replies to Māra:
"Pāpīyān, ally of those gone mad,
you have come out of self-interest alone.

"You have not the slightest concern for my merit.
O Māra, whoever is truly interested in virtue
would speak like this:

" 'I do not think of immortality,
for life assuredly has death as its end.
Yet I will not turn back
for I am practicing brahmacarya.

" 'The wind which dries up the river's flow
can easily dry up the body and blood of renunciates.
After the blood dries up, the flesh will certainly be next;
and when the flesh is diminished, the mind becomes clear.'

"And so I abide with purpose, effort, and contemplation,
and because I dwell like this,
I have obtained higher perceptions and feelings.

"I have no concern for my body or life.
See the pureness of my rigor!
Firm in my purpose and effort, I have wisdom as well.
In this whole world I see no one
who could move me from my endeavor!

"Death which steals the vital breath
is better than a miserable life in the town.
Death in combat is better
than the life of the vanquished.

"Though he takes no pride in the victory,
only the hero can conquer an army.
The timid do not succeed.
Soon, Māra, I will overcome you.

"Desires are your first army;
the second is discontent;
the third is hunger and thirst;
covetousness is the fourth.

"The fifth is laziness and indolence;
fear is said to be the sixth;
the seventh is doubt;
anger and hypocrisy make the eighth.

"Ambition, praise, and respect, falsely acquired renown,
self-glorification that puts others down:
such is the army of Māra,
allies of the dark and burning ones;
to them the śramaṇas and brāhmins succumb.

"Such is your army which subjugates
this world and that of the gods.
But my wisdom will destroy your army,
as water destroys the unbaked vessel of clay.

"I will act with understanding,
for my mind is established in mindfulness,
and I have meditated well on wisdom.
But your mind is set on wickedness;
so what can you accomplish?"

At these words, Māra Pāpīyān,
confused, humiliated, and full of resentment,
at once disappeared from that very place.

Then, monks, it occurred to the Bodhisattva: "There are śramaṇas and brāhmins who in times past, present, or future, harm themselves by tormenting their bodies, causing great misery and pain. The tortures and great sufferings they experience are not good."

And therefore, O monks, I further reflected: "Though their actions and attainments are much greater than the highest teachings of ordinary men, they do not bring the highest wisdom into view; they are not on the route to Enlightenment. This is not the path that will bring about the disappearance of future births, old age, and death. The path of Enlightenment, which brings an end to future births, old age, death, and suffering, is other than this."

And, monks, the thought came to me: "In my father's garden, seated in the shade of a jambu tree, detached from desire, free from that which is non-virtuous and debasing, I attained the first level of meditation, in which there is observation and reflection, a meditation endowed with joy and pleasure born of solitude. I proceeded on to the fourth contemplation, and this I sustained. This is the path of Enlightenment which will lead to the disappearance of the miseries of birth, old age, sickness, and death." This was my thought. And there followed for me the clear perception that this was the path of Enlightenment.

There came to me again the thought: "On a path where one becomes exhausted and weak, one cannot manifest complete Enlightenment. And if, moreover, I approached Bodhimaṇḍa, the Seat of Wisdom, with strength of knowledge and wisdom, but with a weakened body, I could not devote my last existence to compassion. And truly such is not the path of Enlightenment. Therefore, only after taking nourishment and regaining strength in my body will I approach Bodhimaṇḍa."

Then, monks, the devaputras, out of sympathy for a being so exhausted, understanding clearly my thoughts and my deliberation, came to me and said: "O Holy Being, do not partake of rough food, as you intend. We will insert strength into you through your pores."

O monks, the thought occurred to me: "If the devaputras, out of sympathy for my exhaustion, inserted strength into me through my pores, I could swear that I was not eating, and the people who inhabit the neighborhood could acknowledge that the Śramaṇa Gautama does not eat. But this would be on my part the greatest of falsehoods." And so to avoid this lie, the Bodhisattva did not heed the devaputras but maintained his intention of eating substantial food.

And so, O monks, after six years devoted to austerities, the Bodhisattva arose from his seat and spoke these words: "I will eat solid food, such as dal, molasses, and boiled rice."

However, monks, the five men of good family reflected: "By the achievements of this path, the Śramaṇa Gautama will never be able to manifest the saintly wisdom which is above the highest human knowledge. As he is now eating food in abundance, and as he is begging food, he is clearly an ignorant and stupid fellow." And with this thought, withdrawing from the presence of the Bodhisattva, they traveled to Vārāṇasī and took up residence at Ṛṣipatana in the woods of the Deer Park.

When the Bodhisattva had first begun to practice austerities, ten young village girls came to see him. They had continued to honor and to serve him, although it was the five men of good family who generally attended on him, giving him the juniper berry, grain of rice, or sesame seed. The names of the ten girls were: Balā, Balaguptā, Supriyā, Vijayasenā, Atimuktakamalā, Sundarī, and Kumbhakārī, Uluvillikā, Jātilikā, and Sujātā.

These young girls now prepared several kinds of food which they offered to the Bodhisattva. He partook of them and thereafter regularly sought alms in the village, so that he regained his color and his strength, and became known as the beautiful śramaṇa, the great śramaṇa.

O monks, from the first moment the Bodhisattva had begun to practice austerities, Sujātā, daughter of the head villager, offered food for eight hundred brāhmins, so that the Bodhisattva might end his ascetic practices and mortifications and regain his strength. "May the Bodhisattva, having received food from me, attain perfect and fulfilled

Enlightenment and become a Buddha!" This was the prayer that she uttered.

O monks, the saffron garments which I had worn for six years had become extremely worn. And, monks, this came to my mind: "How fine it would be if I were to find something with which to cover myself."

At that time, O monks, Rādhā, a girl who had served Sujātā, daughter of the head villager, had just died. After being wrapped in a hemp cloth, she was taken to a corner of the cemetery, where she was left. I noticed this dusty rag, and stepping close with my left foot, I stretched out my right hand and bent over to take the cloth away. At that motion the earth gods called out to the gods of the air: "What an astonishing thing, friends! How extraordinary! Here is the descendent of a great royal family, who not only has abandoned the sovereignty of a Cakravartin, but now stoops down for a dusty cloth!" The gods of the air, having heard these words from the gods of the earth, called out to the Four Great Kings, and word then passed from them to the Thirty-three gods; from them to the Yāmas, to the gods of Tuṣita, the Nirmāṇaratis, to the Parinirmita vaśavartins, and from them to the gods of the Brahma realm. And so, monks, in the same instant, in the same voice, these very words reached the gods of Akaniṣṭha: "What an astonishing thing, friends! How extraordinary! Here is the descendent of a great royal family, who not only has abandoned the sovereignty of a Cakravartin, but now stoops down for a dusty cloth!"

In the meantime, O monks, the Bodhisattva thought again: "I have found a dust-covered cloth. It would now be good to find some water!" At once the gods struck the ground powerfully with their hands and on the very spot, a pond appeared. Today this pond is still called Pāṇihatā, Struck with the Hands.

The Bodhisattva thought again: "I have found water. Would it not be fine to find a rock on which to wash this dusty cloth?" At once Śakra placed there a flat rock, and the Bodhisattva began to wash the dust-covered cloth. Śakra then said to the Bodhisattva: "Pure Being, pray give the cloth to me. I will wash it." But the Bodhisattva, in order to show the obligations of a wandering monk, did not give the cloth to Śakra, but washed it himself.

When the Bodhisattva, being quite weary, thought to step out of the pond, the demon Pāpīyān, out of envy, raised the edges of the pond by magic. But on the shore of this pond stood a large kakubha tree, and the Bodhisattva, as was the custom at that time, spoke to the goddess of this tree to propitiate her. He then asked her to bend down a branch of the tree, and when she had lowered the branch, the Bodhisattva pulled himself out of the water. Once out of the water, he sat under the kakubha tree and sewed the cloth, fashioning it into a monk's garment. Today, this place is still called Pāṁsukūlasīvana, The Sewing of the Dust-Covered Cloth.

Then a devaputra from the Śuddhāvāsa realm named Vimalaprabha offered the Bodhisattva various garments dyed with saffron such as are suitable to a śramaṇa. The Bodhisattva took these garments, and early in the morning, dressed in monk's garb, went toward the village near which he had lived during his mortifications.

In the middle of the night, the gods had spoken to Sujātā, the daughter of Nāndika, head of the village of Uruvilvā, saying: "Sujātā, the one for whom you have made many offerings has ceased the practice of mortifications, and is now ready to receive pure and abundant food. Formerly you prayed: 'After partaking of the food prepared by me, may the Bodhisattva attain perfect, supreme, and complete Enlightenment.' Now do what must be done."

O monks, upon hearing this, Sujātā, daughter of Nāndika the head villager, immediately took the milk of a thousand cows, drew from it seven times the purest cream, and poured this cream together with the freshest and newest rice into an earthen pot which she put on a new fireplace. And in the midst of this special food, as she prepared it, there appeared auspicious signs: a śrīvatsa, a svastika, a nandyāvarta, a lotus, a vardhamāna, and other signs of blessing.

Then Sujātā thought: "Since such signs appear, there can be no doubt: after taking this food, the Bodhisattva will obtain the perfect, supreme, and complete Enlightenment." Previously, a sage who knew the signs, who knew the rules for understanding the marks of the body, had come to the village and had prophesied that Immortality would be attained there.

Putting the soup on a prepared spot of ground, Sujātā covered it with flowers and perfumed it with scented water. She then asked a servant girl named Uttarā to request the presence of the Brāhmin while she herself watched over the soup of milk and honey. "Very well, mistress!" answered Uttarā, and she set forth. Going toward the east, she caught sight of the Bodhisattva. Likewise, when she went toward the south, the west, and the north, wherever she went, she always caught sight of the Bodhisattva. As for the tīrthikas, they had all been held back by the devaputras from the

Śuddhāvāsa realm, and not a single one appeared. Upon returning, Uttarā said to her mistress: "In truth, mistress, wherever I go, here or there, the handsome śramaṇa is the only one I see. I see no other śramaṇa or brāhmin."

Sujātā replied: "For that very śramaṇa has this food been prepared; please ask him to come here." "Very well, miss," replied Uttarā, and going to the Bodhisattva, she bowed to his feet and extended an invitation to him in the name of Sujātā.

Then, monks, the Bodhisattva went to the home of Sujātā, daughter of the head villager, and sat upon the seat prepared for him. O monks, Sujātā offered the Bodhisattva a golden bowl filled with milk and honey. At that moment, the Bodhisattva thought: "Now that Sujātā has offered such food to me, there can be no doubt: after partaking of it, I will attain the perfect, supreme, and complete Enlightenment of a Buddha."

As the Bodhisattva accepted the food from Sujātā, he asked her: "My sister, what should I do with the golden bowl?" and she replied: "Take it with you." To which the Bodhisattva replied: "I have no need of such a bowl." To this Sujātā answered: "Then do with it what you please. I do not give food to anyone without also giving a bowl."

So taking the bowl of food with him, the Bodhisattva left Uruvilvā, and later in the morning arrived near the Nairañjanā, the river of the nāgas. Placing the bowl and his garments to one side, he entered the river to refresh himself.

And, monks, while the Bodhisattva was bathing, several hundreds of thousands of devaputras rendered homage by filling the river with aloes and powders of sandalwood and tossing into the water heavenly flowers of many colors, so that the Nairañjanā grew thick with flowers and heavenly perfumes. Thousands of niyutas of koṭis of gods scooped up the water with which the Bodhisattva had bathed and took it away, each to his own abode, there to build a caitya and do homage to the Bodhisattva.

As for the hair and whiskers of the Bodhisattva, Sujātā, daughter of the head of the village, took them away as objects full of blessing, to build a caitya for them and to render homage to them.

Emerging from the water, the Bodhisattva looked for a place to seat himself along the shore, and a daughter of the nāgas who resided in the Nairañjanā river came from deep below and offered him a resplendent lion throne. Seating himself, the Bodhisattva ate his fill of the soup of milk and honey, thinking with kindness of Sujātā, the daughter of the head villager. When he had eaten as much as he needed, he threw the golden bowl into the river, without thought of attachment. No sooner had he thrown the bowl into the water than Sāgara, a king of the nāgas, feeling faith and respect arise within him, took up the bowl and carried it to his abode, saying: "This bowl is worthy of homage!"

Now, Indra, the destroyer of cities, took the form of a garuḍa with lightning in his beak, and sought to take the golden bowl from the nāgas, but did not succeed. He then asked for it courteously in his own form and carried it away to the abode of the Thirty-three gods to build a caitya for it and to pay it homage. There he established the Feast of the Begging Bowl, held on the autumn holy days. And even today, the celebration of the bowl takes place every year among the Thirty-three gods. As for the throne, it was taken away by the same daughter of the nāgas, who built a caitya in its honor.

O monks, as soon as the Bodhisattva had eaten, his body regained its former exceedingly beautiful color through the strength of his merits and the force of his wisdom. The thirty-two signs of a great man reappeared, as did the eighty secondary marks and the brilliant light that radiated from his body.

Concerning this it is said:

After passing through six years
of austerities and mortifications,
the Bhagavat considers:
"Though I have the strength of meditation,
of knowledge, and of wisdom,
if I go in this condition
to the foot of the bodhi tree, the king of trees,
and become an omniscient Buddha,
I will not be able to engender compassion
for the beings who follow.

"Gods and men have little merit
and seek for wisdom in misguided ways.
While my body is so weak, I am unable to achieve
immortal Buddhahood for these beings,
so I must eat sufficient food.
Only then will I go to the foot of the king of trees
and obtain the omniscience of a Buddha."

And the daughter of the head villager named Sujātā,
who in times past had done many good deeds,
made continual offerings, saying in her heart:

"May the austerity of the Guide of Beings bear fruit!"
When she hears the exhortation of the gods,
she joyfully carries a soup of milk and honey
to the edge of the Nairañjanā, where she stops.

And the One who for thousands of kalpas
has always practiced good conduct,
his senses calm, perfectly calm, goes to the Nairañjanā
surrounded by the gods, by hosts of nāgas, and by ṛṣis.
Having crossed the river,
the prince who has the desire of delivering all beings
has the thought of bathing in the river.
Pure and without defilement,
filled with compassion for all the world,
the Muni descends into the river and bathes.

With gladdened hearts, gods by the hundreds of thousands
fill the water with perfume and powder
to refresh the Highest of Beings.
When the Bodhisattva, pure and satisfied,
emerges onto the shore,
thousands of gods carry the water away
to pay homage to the Highest of Beings.

A devaputra gives the Bodhisattva
pure and spotless saffron cloth,
and there on the riverbank,
the Bhagavat dons this most suitable garb.

A daughter of the nāgas, her heart filled with joy,
prepares for the Bodhisattva a lion throne.

And upon this throne the being with calm mind—
the one who has the vision of all the world—takes his seat.

The mindful Sujātā bows to the feet of the Bodhisattva,
and serves him food in a golden bowl, saying joyously:
"Pray, partake of my food, O Charioteer of Beings."

After eating what food he requires,
the sage throws the bowl into the river
where Indra, master of the gods,
takes it up, saying: "I will render homage to it."

After the Jina eats his fill of the very best food,
the strength, splendor, and majesty
of his body return at once.
He gives a discourse on the Dharma
for Sujātā and the gods, bringing them great benefits.
And with the gait of the lion, the poise of the goose,
and the bearing of the king of elephants,
the Bodhisattva approaches the Bodhi tree.

The Eighteenth Chapter
The Nairañjanā River

Plate 19

बोधिमण्डगमनपरिवर्तः

།བྱང་ཆུབ་ཀྱི་སྙིང་པོར་བཞུད་པའི་ལེའུ།

The Walk Toward Bodhimaṇḍa

O MONKS, AFTER THE BODHISATTVA had bathed himself in the Nairañjanā river, after he had eaten and regained his strength and vitality, in order to triumph completely over Māra, he turned toward the foot of the great tree of Enlightenment, to the place on earth with the sixteen forms. He advanced with the stride of the great man: the untroubled stride, the stride like the caitya of the sages, the stride as firm as Mount Meru, the king of mountains. He advanced with the illustrious gait, the straightforward gait, the strong gait, unhurried and unhindered. He walked with the unagitated and unhesitating stride, the stride not going astray, surefooted, and not slowing down.

He advanced with the blessed stride, the spotless stride, the stride of virtue, the stride without anger, without ignorance, without desire.

He walked with the gait of the lion, the gait of the king of geese, the gait of the king of the nāgas, the gait of Nārāyaṇa, the gait which does not touch the earth.

He advanced with the stride which causes the image of a thousand-spoked wheel to appear on the earth, the stride of the one with copper-colored fingernails and fingers joined by a membrane.

He advanced with the stride which makes a whistling sound, the stride which sounds like rolling mountains, the tapping stride. He advanced with the stride of the one who touches beings with a ray of light that emanates from the space between his webbed fingers, leading them into bliss.

It was the gait which leaves the spotless lotus as its footprint, the gait which has the momentum of good works previously completed, leading toward the lion throne of the former Buddhas.

He walked with the stride of a firm mind, indestructible like the vajra, a stride destroying all the difficulties of beings on wrong paths, producing all happiness, showing the road of deliverance, annulling the strength of Māra, conquering the hosts of evil in accord with the Dharma, destroying the blemish of ignorance, clearing away the fettering passions, clearing away saṁsāra.

He proceeded with the stride which dominates Śakra, Brahmā, Maheśvara, and the Guardians of the World, the stride of the unique hero of the three thousand great thousands of worlds, the unsurpassable stride of the self-arising being, the stride which leads toward omniscience, the stride of mindfulness and intelligence, the stride leading to bliss and calm, the stride which causes old age and death to disappear without a trace, the stride of pure peace, the stride free from fear of Māra.

He proceeded with the stride which carries beings to the city of Nirvāṇa. With such a stride did the Bodhisattva advance toward Bodhimaṇḍa.

O monks, the road from the river Nairañjanā leading up to Bodhimaṇḍa was cleansed by the gods of the winds and the clouds; it was sprinkled with perfumed water by the devaputras of the rain clouds who strew flowers down upon it. Throughout the three thousand great thousands of worlds, the trees all bent their crowns toward Bodhimaṇḍa. And all the children born on that day turned their heads toward Bodhimaṇḍa as they slept. And in all the regions of the three thousand great thousands of worlds, all the mountains, beginning with Sumeru, also bent in the direction of Bodhimaṇḍa.

O monks, the road leading from the river Nairañjanā to Bodhimaṇḍa, for the distance of a krośa, had been made ready by all the devaputras of the desire realm. On each side of the road, to both right and left, altars composed of seven precious things had been magically constructed seven palm trees in height, sheltered above by jeweled nets, ornamented with royal parasols, standards, and banners. At the distance of an arrow's flight, palm trees formed of seven precious substances had been produced by magic, and on each palm tree was a dais.

All of the palm trees were connected by jeweled cords. Between each two palm trees appeared a pond lined with golden sand, brimming with perfumed water, and covered with blue, yellow, red, and white lotuses. Each jeweled dais was encircled by jeweled staircases of pearl and lapis lazuli. The calls of thrushes, cranes, and geese, of swans, herons, and peacocks enlivened the air. Eighty thousand apsarases sprinkled the road with perfumed water, and eight thousand apsarases cast down fresh flowers with divine scents. In front of each palm tree a jeweled platform was raised, and upon each platform stood eighty thousand apsarases carrying boxes of sandalwood powder and aloes, as well as cassolettes wafting the smoke of balsam through the air. And on each platform apsarases singing sweet melodies assembled into groups of fifty thousand and played concerts on divine instruments.

O monks, all the Bodhisattva-fields were quaking, and rays of light numbering hundreds of millions shone forth; hundreds of thousands of musical instruments played, while flowers rained down. Thousands of floating banners were waving in the breeze, and hundreds of thousands of drums resounded under repeated beats. Horses neighed, elephants trumpeted, and bulls roared, all while circumambulating the Bodhisattva three times. Parrots, jays, black cuckoos, nightingales, and jīvaṁjīvas, geese, mallards, herons, and peacocks by the hundreds of thousands called out to the Bodhisattva amidst hundreds of thousands of benedictions. On this road, prepared in so spectacular a manner, did the Bodhisattva advance toward Bodhimaṇḍa.

On the very night when the Bodhisattva determined to attain the perfect and complete Enlightenment, Brahmā Sahāṁpati, who is called Vaśavartin, the sovereign of the three thousand great thousands of worlds, spoke to the assembly: "Friends, the Bodhisattva Mahāsattva, having donned the great armor, the solid armor, has not put aside his great promise; he who never becomes discouraged has performed all the practices of a Bodhisattva and has succeeded in going beyond all the Pāramitās. He has mastered all the stages of the Bodhisattva and knows perfectly all the thoughts and actions of a Bodhisattva. He has penetrated the senses of all beings and has entered into all the secrets of the Tathāgatas.

"He has completely overcome all the devious ways of the demon. Virtuous in all things, he is independent of others and blessed by all the Tathāgatas. He teaches all beings the way of complete deliverance; he is the Leader of the great caravan. Destroyer of all the domains of the demon Māra, he is the unique hero of the three thousand great thousands of worlds. As the great King of Physicians, discoverer of the means of complete deliverance, he procures all the remedies of the Dharma. He is the great King of the Dharma who shines forth the great light of wisdom; he is the king bearing the great banner. Untainted by the eight worldly dharmas, the Bodhisattva is like a great lotus that sheds water from its leaves. He never forgets the dhāraṇīs, the great formulas of the Dharma.

"He is like the great ocean, free from desire and jealousy. He is like the great Sumeru, unchangeable, unshakable. Pristine, perfectly pure, with a well-enlightened intelligence, he is like a great precious jewel, exercising mastery over all the Dharma. He has every circumstance well in hand.

"The Bodhisattva, appearing like the great Brahmā, advances to Bodhimaṇḍa to assume the perfect and complete Enlightenment of a Buddha, to overcome completely the army of Māra. He proceeds to Bodhgayā to fulfill completely the ten strengths and the four fearlessnesses, to accomplish completely the eighteen pure Buddhadharmas. He proceeds in order to turn the Wheel of the Dharma, to utter the great lion's roar, to satisfy all beings with the Dharma, to purify the Dharma eye of all beings, to offer the aid of the Dharma to all opposed to the Dharma, to show the perfect fulfillment of a former promise, and to obtain supreme mastery over all the dharmas. Friends, make haste in offering the Bodhisattva your homage and your respects."

And on this occasion, the great Brahmā Vaśavartin uttered these verses:

"By his great virtue and splendor,
he reveals the path of the brahmavihāras—
the path of love, compassion, joy, and equanimity.
Manifesting meditation and clear knowledge,
having performed for thousands of kalpas
the actions of the Bodhisattva,
he walks toward the Bodhi tree.
Render offerings to the Muni as he achieves his goal!

"After taking refuge in him,
one has no fear of traveling lower paths
or of losing one's opportunity.
One will enter the vast dwelling of Brahmā,
obtaining the desired happiness among the gods.
Having accomplished for six years
things difficult to achieve,
he is going to the Bodhi tree.
Filled with the greatest joy,
may all beings render homage to him!

"He is the king of the three thousand worlds,
the powerful lord, the sovereign lord of the Dharma.
In the realms of Śakra, Brahmā, Sūrya, and Candra,
none is equal to him at whose birth
hundreds of millions of Buddha-fields quaked in six ways.

Today he advances toward the magnificent tree,
intent on conquering the armies of Māra.

"Even those who dwell in the lofty abode of Brahmā
cannot catch sight of his head.
Bearing the most excellent marks,
his body is adorned with the thirty-two signs;
his speech goes straight to the heart,
sweet, penetrating, and harmonious,
like the voice of Brahmā;
his mind is calm and without anger.
Let us proceed to offer him homage!

"May those who wish to taste the bliss of meditation
in the abode of Brahmā and Śakra;
those who wish to cut the vine of the fettering passions;
those who wish to attain the Enlightenment
of a peaceful, immortal Pratyekabuddha
who does not hear the Teachings from another;
those who desire to obtain the condition
of a Buddha in the three worlds—
may they all pay homage to the Guide of All!

"The earth and surrounding ocean
he has completely renounced;
he has given up innumerable precious things—
palaces with oval windows and pavilions,
horses and chariots,
the land adorned with brilliant masses of fresh flowers,
with ponds and gardens;
he has given up his hands and feet,
his head and eyes, his whole body;
such is the one making his way toward Bodhimaṇḍa."

O monks, at that moment the great Brahmā who presides over three thousand great thousands of worlds called for all to assemble in this world—in the region which was as smooth as the palm of the hand, free of rock and without gravel, covered with diamonds, pearls, crystal, and lapis lazuli, bedecked with conch shells, coral, gold, and silver, carpeted with smooth green grass that swirled to the right like a nandyāvarta and was soft to the touch as kācalindi down. To this one point in the three thousand great thousands of worlds Brahmā called all to assemble. And all the great seas were as calm as the surface of the earth, and no harm befell the beings who lived within them.

When Śakra, Brahmā, and the Guardians of the World saw this place on the earth thus adorned, they also carefully adorned the hundred thousand Buddha-fields in the ten directions in order to render homage to the Bodhisattva. With offerings and preparations surpassing those of gods and men, the Bodhisattvas also adorned the immeasurable Buddha-fields of the ten directions in order to render homage to the Bodhisattva. And all the Buddha-fields were as one, adorned with various ornaments and preparations. Mountains encircling the world—the Kālaparvatas, Cakravālas, and Mahācakravālas—had disappeared entirely, and all the Buddha-fields appeared bathed in the clear light radiating from the Bodhisattva.

Sixteen devaputras who had acquired the unswerving patience of irreversibility were standing vigilant in their role as guardians of Bodhimaṇḍa. They were Utkhali, Sūtkhali, Prajāpati, Śūrabala, Keyūrabala, along with Supratiṣṭhita, Mahindhara, Avabhāsakara, Vimala, Dharmeśvara, and Dharmaketu, Siddhapātra, Apratihatanetra, Mahāvyūha, Śīlaviśuddhinetra, and Padmaprabha.

In order to pay honor to the Bodhisattva, these sixteen vigilant devaputras decorated Bodhimaṇḍa. For eighty yojanas, Bodhimaṇḍa was encircled by seven altars made of seven precious materials; seven rows of tāla trees rimmed the altars, and beyond the trees were seven precious nets adorned with tiny bells, encircled by seven golden cords. Holy books were there, covered with cloths made of gold from the rivers of Jambu. Woven into the material were golden lotuses and the symbols of the seven precious things, made from thread of gold from the rivers of Jambu.

Bodhimaṇḍa was perfumed with the softest scents and sheltered by a jeweled lattice. All the different trees found in all the worlds of gods and men in all ten directions were seen at Bodhimaṇḍa. All the different flowers found in the ten directions, growing in the water or on the earth, were also seen at Bodhimaṇḍa. And the Bodhisattvas of the various worlds in all the ten directions adorned Bodhimaṇḍa with the arrangement of the accumulation of their knowledge and boundless virtue.

O monks, the devaputras who were the vigilant guardians of Bodhimaṇḍa also made similar supernatural displays at Bodhimaṇḍa. At the sight of these preparations, the gods, nāgas, yakṣas, gandharvas, and asuras compared their own abodes to cemeteries and expressed their admiration: "Ah! This is indeed the incomprehensible result of the complete maturation of merit!"

And all four goddesses of the Bodhi tree, Veṇu, Valgu, Sumanas, and Ojāpatī, out of respect for the Bodhisattva, beautified the tree of Enlightenment: its fabulous roots and trunk, its branches, leaves, flowers, and fruits, its remarkable height and breadth. The Bodhi tree was glorious to see and very imposing, rising to the height of seven tālas.

Wonderful and radiant, the Bodhi tree entirely delighted the mind. It was surrounded by seven jeweled altars which in turn were rimmed by seven rows of precious tālas; these were circled by seven nets, laced with tiny jeweled bells, and all was surrounded and linked by jeweled cords. The eye would never grow weary of seeing this tree, majestic as the coral tree and the kovidāra tree.

At this place where the Bodhisattva would sit to attain perfect and complete Enlightenment, here at the center of the three thousand great thousands of worlds, the earth was unchangeable, its essence immutable, its nature that of a diamond.

O monks, while the Bodhisattva was advancing toward Bodhimaṇḍa, a brilliant light shone forth from his body which emptied the unfortunate realms, destroyed all anxieties, and caused all bad feelings to disappear. All beings with imperfect senses had their senses entirely restored; those attacked by illnesses were cured; all the unhappy became joyful; those tormented by fear were reassured; those held in bondage were released; the poor received all their hearts' desires; beings tormented by the fettering passions were no longer assailed; the hungry had their stomachs filled; those desperate with thirst were relieved of thirst; pregnant women gave birth easily; those who were languishing and weak were endowed with vigor.

At that moment all beings were relieved of the pains of desire, hatred, and ignorance, anger, envy, meanness, and jealousy. At that moment no being died or was reborn in a lower realm. At that moment all beings were filled with the desire to be helpful to each other, with the benevolent feelings of a father or mother.

Concerning this it is said:

Even as far as the Avīci hell
where dwell underworld beings terrible to see,
suffering is relieved,
and all beings experience great joy.

All those born from the wombs of animals
who prey upon each other
are touched by the rays of the Muni
and feel sweetly benevolent toward each other.

All the hungry ghosts in the world of pretas,
tormented by hunger and thirst,
through the splendor of the Bodhisattva,
obtain food and drink.

Every obstruction to practice is removed,
and all the lower realms are emptied.
All beings in fortunate states of being
become as happy and as satisfied as the gods.

Those deprived of sight and hearing
and those with limbs imperfect are all completely cured.

All beings tormented by the fettering passions
or assailed by desire and hatred
or by other human miseries,
all have their emotionality appeased,
and all are filled with well-being.

The demented regain their senses;
the poor gain riches; the sick are cured;
prisoners are delivered from their bonds.

Hostility, envy, meanness, and quarrels all cease,
and people become benevolent, ready to help one another.

Like the tenderness of a mother and a father
for an only son, such is the affection
of beings for each other.

Immeasurable Buddha-fields in all the ten directions—
Buddha-fields as numerous as the sands of the Ganges—
are bathed in the rays of light
which are shining from the Bodhisattva,
light so bright the Cakravāla and Kālaparvata mountains
can no longer be seen,
and all the vast and varied fields appear as one.

Smooth as the palm of the hand,
the Buddha-fields are filled with precious things
as offerings to the Bodhisattva:
adorned and decorated, all the fields resemble jewels.

Sixteen gods attend to Bodhimaṇḍa,
adorning it to a distance of eighty yojanas.

And through the splendor of the Bodhisattva
all the great, endless ornamental array
in the tens of millions of fields
can be seen everywhere.

The gods, the nāgas, and the yakṣas,
the kinnaras and the mahoragas
reflect that their own airy abodes
are cemeteries in comparison.

On seeing this glorious array, gods and men are amazed,
and they cry to each other in wonder:
"Such a blessing is indeed the result of his virtue!"

Effortless in action, in word, and in thought,
all his affairs succeed! His wishes are attained.

Even the wishes of others are fulfilled by his former actions;
the prosperity produced here is the complete maturation
of all the Bodhisattva's actions.

Decorated by the four goddesses of the Bodhi tree,
Bodhimaṇḍa stands out
like a flower of the coral tree against the sky.

And the qualities of the display at Bodhimaṇḍa
arranged by the gods
cannot be completely described in words.

O monks, the light cast by the Bodhisattva completely illumined the abode of Kālika, the king of the nāgas. Pure and pristine was this light, which produced joy and delight, happiness and calm in the body and mind of all beings, clearing away all the fettering passions. Seeing this light, Kālika, the king of the nāgas, uttered these verses in the presence of his following:

"Brilliant rays stream forth,
flooding my abode with shining light,
like the light seen emanating from Krakucchanda
and also from Kanakāhvaya,
like the pure light seen streaming from Kāśyapa.

There can be no doubt:
the Muni, King of the Dharma, has been born,
a helpful being endowed with the best signs,
one possessing the light of wisdom.

"The shadows of previous evil actions
have kept from my dwelling the light
of sun and moon, of fire and stars,
the flash of lightning, and the sparkle of jewels.
Not even the light of Śakra or Brahmā,
or the light of the asuras has graced my home.

"But today the splendid light of virtue
shines within my dwelling like the sun,
causing joy to arise in the mind and well-being in the body.

"The limbs are refreshed;
the burning sands which fall upon the body have cooled.
Clearly, the one who has done his utmost
for tens of millions of kalpas
is now proceeding toward the Bodhi tree.

"Quickly, bring the lovely flowers of the nāgas,
fine perfumed garments, necklaces of pearls,
bracelets, sweet-smelling powders, and the best of incense.
Sing and play the instruments in harmony;
with drums and tambourines honor the helpful being,
worthy of homage from the entire world!"

And rising up, accompanied by his daughters,
he looks in the four directions
and sees the one who is like Mount Meru,
well-adorned with splendor,
surrounded by tens of millions of gods and dānavas,
brahmendras and yakṣas, who joyously offer homage
and show him the road, saying, "This way is good."

After making offerings to the Best One in the World,
the king of the nāgas, filled with joy,
bows down respectfully at his feet.
The daughters of the nāgas render joyful homage
to the Muni, tossing flowers, aloes, and perfumes,
and playing sweet music.

The king of the nāgas joins his palms
and gives praise to the Muni's true qualities:
"It is sweet to see you, O Guide,
O Greatest Being in the World,
you whose face is like the full moon.
I have seen the signs of the ṛṣis of old;
we see these signs in you as well.
Today, having conquered the demon Māra,
full of strength, you will obtain the highest state.

"For the sake of this moment
you upheld your discipline, your giving, and your vows;
you gave up all your possessions.
For the sake of this moment
you have meditated on the power of discipline,
on good conduct, on love, compassion, and patience;
for this purpose were you firm in effort.
Delighting in contemplation,
you became a torch of knowledge.
Your prayers have been completely fulfilled:
today you will be a conqueror.

"The trees with their leaves, their flowers and fruits,
bow to the Bodhi tree.
A thousand urns full of clear water surround you;
hosts of joyous apsarases sing their sweet songs;
geese and flocks of herons frolic in the sky,
joyously circling the Ṛṣi.

"Today you will be an Arhat.
Beautiful golden rays of light
penetrate hundreds of Buddha-fields;
all sufferings are relieved,
and all beings are delivered from lower realms.
Today, rain has fallen on the abodes of Candra and Sūrya,
and a soft wind blows.
O Driver of the caravan of beings,
you will be the one who delivers
the three worlds from birth and old age.

"The gods abandon the joys of desire
and come before you to render homage.
Brahmā and his priests as well as many gods
have interrupted a meditation full of sweetness;
all the powerful beings in the three worlds
have come here before you.
Today the King of Physicians will deliver
the three worlds from birth and old age.

"The gods have sprinkled and decorated the route
by which you advance—
the route used also by the blessed Bhagavats
Krakucchanda, Kanakāhvaya, and Kāśyapa.
Where your feet touch the ground,
perfect pure lotuses, spotless and beautiful,
push up through the earth.
You are full of extraordinary strength;
today you will become an Arhat.

"Myriads of millions of demons—
as numerous as the sands of the Ganges—
cannot move you or draw you from the Bodhi tree,
for you have made hundreds of thousands of offerings—

as numerous as the sands of the Ganges.
Your actions always aid the world.
Therefore does your light shine here in my realm.

"Though the planets and the moon, the stars and sun,
should fall from the sky to the earth;
though the greatest among the grandest of mountains
should move from its place;
though even the ocean should dry out;
though a sage who would be able to teach
should arise from each of the four realms;
once you have arrived at the foot of the king of trees,
you would not arise before gaining Enlightenment.

"Because I have seen the Charioteer of Beings,
great fortune and richness have become mine.
You have been given offerings,
your virtues have been proclaimed—
now I am full of ardor for Enlightenment,
as are my sons and daughters.
May we be delivered from birth!
Like a great elephant you advance;
may we proceed in the same way."

O monks, Suvarṇaprabhāsā, the wife of Kālika, king of the nāgas, now came forward and circumambulated the Bodhisattva, surrounded and preceded by a multitude of daughters of the nāgas. They carried jeweled parasols, musical instruments, and necklaces of pearls, gems, perfumes, and garlands, both human and divine. They bore urns filled with incense and played instruments while singing most sweetly. As they came before the Bodhisattva, they tossed heavenly flowers and praised him with these verses:

"You who are without error and without fear,
without timidity, fright, depression, or sadness,
you who are joyous and difficult to conquer,
free from desire, defilement, confusion, and envy,
you who have reached deliverance,
to you we bow down, O Great Ṛṣi!

"Physician who causes no pain,
you train those needing training.
Great doctor who cures all suffering,
knowing the unfortunate lack refuge and protection,
you were born into the three worlds where they dwell
in order to give them refuge.

"The hosts of the gods, eager and joyous,
let fall a great rain of flowers from the skies;
they float great numbers of banners in the wind.
Today you will be a Jina! Let happiness burst forth!

"Draw near the king of trees and sit down uprightly.
Shake off the nets of the fettering passions,
and the armies of Māra will be conquered.
Like the Jinas before you,
you will attain supreme Enlightenment,
complete and perfectly calm.

"For the purpose of securing the world's deliverance,
you have done things difficult to do
for several tens of millions of kalpas.

Now your intention is well-fulfilled;
the time has come to approach the king of trees,
and reach supreme Enlightenment!"

Then, O monks, the Bodhisattva reflected: "What did the former Tathāgatas sit upon when they assumed perfect and complete Enlightenment?" And he knew that it was upon a mat of kuśa grass.

Hundreds of thousands of gods of the Śuddhāvāsa realm appeared in the sky, knowing in their minds the thoughts of the Bodhisattva, and spoke thus: "So it was, Holy One; so it was. They attained supreme, perfect, and complete Enlightenment after seating themselves on a mat of kuśa grass."

And then, O monks, the Bodhisattva noticed on the right side of the road the kuśa grass seller, Svastika, who was cutting fresh rushes and braiding them so that they swirled to the right like the soft feathers of a peacock's neck. These grasses were soft to the touch like cloth made of kācalindi down, sweet-smelling, and of a color that delighted the eye. At this sight, the Bodhisattva left the road and, approaching Svastika, the kuśa grass seller, addressed a discourse to him in a soft voice. It was a discourse which made everything known, made it perfectly known, perfectly clear; a discourse not interrupted, producing affection, beautiful and worthy of being heard, sweet, and mellow; a discourse worthy of being retained, encouraging, satisfying, joyous, and friendly; a discourse without slackness, without hesitation, without harshness, without haste; soft, harmonious, agreeable to the ear, pleasing to the body and the mind; free from passion, hatred, ignorance, argument, and harshness.

This discourse was like the song of the nightingale and the sonorous voice of the kunāla and the jīvaṁjīvaka; like the sound of the drum; like melodies of sweet song; causing no harm, truthful, clear, exact; like the harmonious accents of Brahmā; like the sound of the billowing ocean; like the sound of colliding mountains.

This was a discourse worthy of praise from the master of the gods and the master of the asuras, profound, difficult to penetrate; a discourse rendering Māra powerless, reducing the opposition to silence; a discourse like the formidable roar of a lion; like the neighing of the horse and the trumpeting of the elephant; resounding like the voice of a nāga; thundering like storm clouds filling all the Buddha-fields of the ten directions.

This was a discourse consoling to beings needing discipline; not harsh, neither precipitous nor slow; well-bound, suitable, appropriate to the time, and wholly opportune; well-formed of a hundred thousand dharmas; subtle and unhindered; with a persistent energy.

It was a discourse emitting all voices with a single voice, making all of his purposes known, producing well-being, teaching the path of deliverance, indicating the multiplicity of ways; a discourse not passing from the assembly, delighting the whole assembly, and conforming to what has been uttered by all the Buddhas. With such a discourse the Bodhisattva addressed Svastika, the gatherer of kuśa grass:

"Listen, Svastika! Quickly, give me your kuśa grass.
I have great need of such grass today.
After overcoming great Māra and his army,
I will attain Enlightenment's great calm.
For this purpose have I carefully practiced giving
for thousands of kalpas;
for this purpose have I carefully practiced
mastery over the self, discretion, renunciation,
good conduct, fidelity to vows, and austerities;
today complete Enlightenment will come to pass.

"The strength of patience and the strength of effort;
the strength of contemplation and wisdom;
the strength of merit and knowledge of liberation:
today will I fulfill all these.

"The strength of wisdom and the strength of means;
supernatural power and the strength
of love without grasping;
the strength of correct understanding
and the strength of truth:
today will I fulfill all these.

"By giving me a bundle of kuśa grass,
you will gain the strength of boundless merit.
No troubles will ever beset you,
and you yourself will become a teacher without equal."

Having received this most beautiful blessing full of sweetness from the Guide of the World, Svastika was joyous, transported, delighted, and full of contentment. He took a bundle of new rushes, soft to the touch, tender and beautiful, and standing before the Bodhisattva, addressed to him this speech, his heart filled with joy:

"If with a few bundles of kuśa grass
one can attain the path of the former Buddhas,
so difficult to see, so calm, the greatest Immortality,
and the highest state of Enlightenment,
then pray accept this grass.
You are already a greatly renowned Ocean of Virtues;
let me be the first to become a Buddha,
attaining the highest state of Immortality."

The Bodhisattva replied:
"This Enlightenment, O Svastika, is not obtained
by sitting on a seat of the softest grass
without having first practiced for numerous kalpas
austerities and actions difficult to accomplish.
When a sage has been lifted by wisdom, merits,
and the knowledge of means,
the Victorious Munis will make a prediction, saying:
'You will be faultless.'

"O Svastika, if this Enlightenment
could be given to others like a ball of boiled rice,
there would be no hesitation in giving it
to great gatherings of living beings.

When I obtain Enlightenment,
know that I will share Immortality.
In times ahead, come listen to the Holy Dharma,
and you will become faultless."

The Guide took up the soft, sweet-smelling grass
and departed with the gait of a lion
and the beautiful bearing of a swan.
The earth trembled strongly.
The gods and nāgas, their palms pressed together,
their hearts full of joy, said:
"Now he will conquer the army of Māra
and attain Immortality."

O monks, while the Bodhisattva was approaching the Bodhi tree, eighty thousand Bodhi trees were adorned by the devaputras and the Bodhisattvas, who thought: "Here, after seating himself, the Bodhisattva will obtain Enlightenment and will become a perfect and complete Buddha." Some of the Bodhi trees were formed of flowers and were a hundred yojanas high; others were formed of incense and reached the height of a thousand yojanas; there were also Bodhi trees of sandalwood a hundred thousand yojanas high; Bodhi trees of cloth which were five hundred thousand yojanas high; Bodhi trees of jewels a million yojanas high; other Bodhi trees of jewels tens of millions of niyutas of koṭis of yojanas high. At the feet of all these Bodhi trees stood lion thrones, prepared in suitable form, covered with various kinds of heavenly cloths. At the feet of other Bodhi trees were prepared lotus thrones, thrones of incense, or thrones of various precious jewels.

The Bodhisattva entered into the contemplation called Lalitavyūha, the great Playful Arrangement, and at that very instant, the Bodhisattva, well-adorned with the thirty-two signs and the eighty secondary marks, appeared to be seated on each one of the lion thrones at the feet of all the Bodhi trees.

The devaputras and the Bodhisattvas all thought: "It is on my own seat that the Bodhisattva sits and enters into meditation, and not on that of the others." And in the same way that the devaputras had this idea through the power of the Bodhisattva's Lalitavyūha contemplation, all the beings of hell, all the beings born in animal realms, all those in the world of Yāma, all gods and men born in whatever condition, all beings saw the Bodhisattva seated on a throne at the foot of a Bodhi tree.

And still more—in order to delight the minds of beings who are attracted to earthly things, the Bodhisattva, taking a bundle of kuśa grass, approached the Bodhi tree and circumambulated it seven times. He himself laid out the mat of grass, excellent in every respect, with the tips of the grass to the inside and the roots to the outside. Then, like a lion, like a hero, like a strong being, like a firm being, like a courageous being, like a vigorous being; like a wisdom holder, like a nāga, like a possessor of the supreme power; like one freely arising, like a being without equal, like an eminent being, like an elevated being, like a glorious being, like an illustrious being; like one accustomed to giving, like a being endowed with good conduct, with patience, effort, and meditation; like a knowledgeable one, like a being endowed with all virtues; like a being who has destroyed the opposition of Māra; like all of these, the Bodhisattva sat down upon the mat of kuśa grass, holding his body erect in the cross-legged posture, his face toward the east. Manifesting great mindfulness, he made this vow in a firm voice:

"Here on this seat my body may shrivel up,
my skin, my bones, my flesh may dissolve,
but my body will not move from this very seat
until I have obtained Enlightenment,
so difficult to obtain in the course of many kalpas."

The Nineteenth Chapter
The Walk Toward Bodhimaṇḍa

Plate 20

बोधिमण्डव्यूहपरिवर्तः

།བྱང་ཆུབ་ཀྱི་སྙིང་པོར་བགོད་པའི་ལེའུ།

The Displays at Bodhimaṇḍa

O MONKS, DURING THE TIME the Bodhisattva was seated at Bodhimaṇḍa, six gods of the desire realm remained in the eastern region to protect the Bodhisattva from obstacles. The southern, western, and northern regions were also guarded by the gods.

O monks, during the time the Bodhisattva was seated there at Bodhimaṇḍa, he cast forth the rays of light called Exhortation of the Bodhisattva. Immeasurable and innumerable light rays spread out in all directions, illuminating all of the Buddha-fields of boundless space in the vast open sphere of the Dharma.

From the eastern region, from Vimala, from the Buddha-field of the Tathāgata Vimalaprabhāsa, the Bodhisattva known as Lalitavyūha was drawn by the light from the Bodhisattva. Surrounded and preceded by a great host of Bodhisattvas whose number surpassed all calculation, he approached Bodhimaṇḍa where the Bodhisattva was seated. And as a token of homage to the Bodhisattva, Lalitavyūha manifested a great supernatural power that made all the Buddha-fields of boundless space in all ten directions visible as a single circle of pure, deep lapis lazuli.

At the same time, Lalitavyūha caused the Bodhisattva at Bodhimaṇḍa to be visible to all beings born into the five conditions of existence. And beings everywhere pointed out the Bodhisattva to each other, wondering: "Who is this one with such an auspicious form, the most gracious of all? Who is this one with such an auspicious form, who shines so brightly?" And in the presence of all of these beings, the Bodhisattva caused other Bodhisattvas to appear, who pronounced this verse:

"From the body of the one who has destroyed
all inclinations toward desire, hatred, or impurity,
rays of light stream forth,
eclipsing all other light in all the ten directions.
The treasure of his knowledge, contemplation, and merit
has increased during a multitude of kalpas;
now Śākyamuni, holiest of the great Munis,
glorifies all points of space."

Then, from the south, from Ratnavyūha, from the world realm of the Buddha-field which belongs to the Tathāgata Ratnārcis, the Bodhisattva Mahāsattva who is known as Ratnacchattrakūṭa-saṁdarśana was drawn by the light of the Bodhisattva. Surrounded and preceded by a great multitude of Bodhisattvas which surpassed all calculation, he approached Bodhimaṇḍa where the Bodhisattva was seated. And as a token of homage, he gave shelter to the entire assembly with a single jeweled parasol.

Then Śakra, Brahmā, and the Guardians of the World said to each other: "Of whose merit is this the fruit? What brings about this display of a jeweled parasol?" And from the precious parasol, this verse was heard:

"With a loving mind, he has given
millions of perfumed and jeweled parasols
to incomparable beings now in Nirvāṇa;
the one who gives aid,
the one with the strength of Nārāyaṇa,
the one who is marked with the best signs
and filled with virtues,
the one who has approached the Bodhi tree:
to him this homage is given."

Then from the western region, from Campakavarṇa, from the world realm of the Buddha-field of the Tathāgata Puṣpāvali Vanarāji Kusumitābhijñā, a Bodhisattva Mahāsattva named Indrajāli was drawn by the light from the Bodhisattva. Surrounded and preceded by Bodhisattvas surpassing calculation, he approached Bodhimaṇḍa where the Bodhisattva was seated. And as a token of homage to the Bodhisattva, he gave shelter to the whole assembly with a single jeweled net.

The gods, nāgas, the yakṣas, and the gandharvas of the ten directions said to each other: "Why then is there such a display of light?" And from within the jeweled net, this verse came forth:

"I honor the mine of precious gems,
the exalted banner, joy of the three worlds,

first among precious jewels, greatly renowned,
the one joyous in the Dharma,
zealous in striving ceaselessly for the Three Jewels,
the one who will obtain Enlightenment."

Then from the northern region, from Sūryāvartā, from the world realm of the Buddha-field of the Tathāgata Candra-sūrya Jihnī Karanaprabha, a Bodhisattva Mahāsattva named Vyūharāja was drawn by the light from the Bodhisattva. Surrounded and preceded by an incalculable multitude of Bodhisattvas, he approached Bodhimaṇḍa where the Bodhisattva was seated. As a token of homage, he displayed within the circle of the assembly all the qualities of the Buddha-fields of all the world realms in all the ten directions. At this some of the Bodhisattvas asked: "For whom are these displays?" And from the midst of the displays, this verse came forth:

"We honor the chief of the Śākyas,
the one who has come before the king of trees,
the one who has purified his body by merit and wisdom;
the one who has purified his speech by vows and austerities,
and by the truthfulness of the Dharma;
the one who has purified his mind by modesty,
devotion, love, and compassion."

Then from the southeastern region, from Guṇākarā, from the world realm of the Buddha-field which belongs to the

Tathāgata Guṇarājaprabhāsa, the Bodhisattva Mahāsattva who was named Guṇamati was drawn by the light from the Bodhisattva. Surrounded and preceded by a great multitude of Bodhisattvas surpassing all calculation, he approached Bodhimaṇḍa where the Bodhisattva was seated. As a token of homage, he manifested within the circle of the assembly a many-storied palace possessing every wonderful quality. And from this palace came forth this verse:

"The one by whose virtues
gods, asuras, yakṣas, and mahoragas shine,
possessor of the qualities of the Guṇarāja family,
the ocean of virtue is seated in front of the Bodhi tree."

From the southwestern region, from Ratnasambhavā, from the world realm of the Buddha-field belonging to the Tathāgata Ratnayaṣṭī, a Bodhisattva Mahāsattva who was known as Ratnasambhava was drawn by the light from the Bodhisattva. Surrounded and preceded by an incalculable multitude of Bodhisattvas, he approached Bodhimaṇḍa where the Bodhisattva was seated. As a token of homage, he manifested within the circle of the assembly immeasurable and innumerable celestial temples. From these holy temples this verse came forth:

"The one who has renounced both earth and ocean,
who has given up precious things in great number—
beautiful palaces with turrets and oval windows,
horse-drawn chariots and celestial temples,

gardens covered with garlands of flowers,
even his feet, his hands, his head, his eyes:
this one is seated at Bodhimaṇḍa."

From the northwest, from Meghavatī, from the world realm of the Buddha-field of the Tathāgata Megharāja, the Bodhisattva Mahāsattva Meghakūṭābhigarjiteśvara was drawn by the light from the Bodhisattva. Surrounded and preceded by a multitude of Bodhisattvas surpassing all calculation, he approached Bodhimaṇḍa where the Bodhisattva was seated. As a token of homage to the Bodhisattva, he manifested a cloud of balm and sandalwood and caused a fine dust composed of the essence of Uraga sandalwood to rain down upon the assembly. And from within the circle of the cloud of balm, this verse came forth:

"He extends the cloud of the Dharma,
shining with the rays of deliverance and realization,
into the three worlds.
Free from attachment, he rains down the holy Dharma
and the attainment of Immortality and Nirvāṇa.
He cuts away the vines of desire and the fettering passions,
with all their tendencies which bind so completely.
The flowers of meditation, the supernatural abilities,
the ten powers and strengths open
through the power of faith."

Then from the northeast, from Hemajālapratichannā, from the world realm of the Buddha-field belonging to the Tathāgata Ratnacchatrābhyudgatāvabhāsa, a Bodhisattva Mahāsattva named Hemajālālaṁkṛta was drawn by the light from the Bodhisattva. Surrounded and preceded by a host of Bodhisattvas which surpassed all calculation, he approached Bodhimaṇḍa where the Bodhisattva was seated. As a token of homage to the Bodhisattva, he caused figures of Bodhisattvas completely adorned with the thirty-two signs to appear in all of the storied palaces and temples, each figure holding garlands of divine and human flowers. Bowing toward the Bodhisattva, each Bodhisattva hung these garlands of flowers about Bodhimaṇḍala and uttered this verse:

"I bow my head to the one
praised by hundreds of thousands of previous Buddhas,
to the one who has produced great faith and humility,
the one who speaks with the melodious voice of Brahmā,
who now has arrived at Bodhimaṇḍa."

From the lower region, from Samanatavilokitā, from the world realm of the Buddha-field belonging to the Tathāgata Samantadarśin, the Bodhisattva Mahāsattva Ratnagarbha was drawn by the light from the Bodhisattva. Surrounded and preceded by an incalculable multitude of Bodhisattvas, he approached Bodhimaṇḍa where the Bodhisattva was seated. And as a token of homage, he caused golden lotuses which grows in the water of Jambu to appear within the circle of lapis lazuli. In the hearts of the lotuses appeared radiant maidens revealing the upper half of their bodies, well-ornamented with jewelry, flower garlands, and golden cords, with many necklaces and bracelets on their wrists and arms. After hanging wreaths of silk and flowers around Bodhimaṇḍa, they bowed toward Bodhimaṇḍa and to the Bodhisattva and uttered this verse:

"Come, bow before this one so filled with virtue,
who himself has always bowed before spiritual teachers—
before the Buddhas, the Śrāvakas, and the Pratyekajinas;
the one joyful in mindfulness and conduct,
the one who lacks all pride."

From the higher region, from Varaganā, from the world realm of the Buddha-field of the Tathāgata Ganendra, a Bodhisattva Mahāsattva named Gaganagañja was drawn by the light from the Bodhisattva. Surrounded and preceded by a host of Bodhisattvas surpassing all calculation, he approached Bodhimaṇḍa where the Bodhisattva was seated. As a token of homage, he stood in the sky and from the Buddha-fields of the ten directions manifested all sorts of things never seen before: heavenly flowers, incense, perfume, flower garlands, ointments, perfumed powders, religious robes, clothing, ornaments, parasols, standards, streamers, banners, jewels, precious stones, gold, silver, pearl necklaces, horses, elephants, chariots, infantrymen, vehicles, flowers, trees, fruits, young men, young women, gods, nāgas, yakṣas, gandharvas, asuras, garuḍas, kinnaras, and mahoragas, as well as Śakra, Brahmā, and the Guardians of the World, humans and non-humans. From the middle of the sky, they all rained flowers down, producing joy in all beings and causing fright or harm to none.

Concerning this it is said

From all the ten directions
all the sons of the Jinas have come
to pay homage to the Enlightenment
which will benefit all beings.
Listen to the measure, the symmetry, the order,
the swiftness, the beautiful display of the sons of the Jinas.

Some come like storm clouds in the sky,
draping garlands by the hundreds of thousands.
Some come with precious diadems in their flowing hair,
revealing crystal palaces of flowers in the sky.

Some come roaring like lions,
proclaiming emptiness which is signless and wishless.
Some come bellowing like bulls,
tossing beautiful flowers never seen before.

Some come crying out like peacocks,
their bodies shimmering with thousands of colors.
Some come like full moons in the sky,
reciting the qualities of the son of the Jinas—
a garland of virtues.

Some come like suns emitting light,
eclipsing the abodes of Māra.
Some carry staffs with banners like Indra's;
having amassed the treasures of merit,
they have come to Bodhimaṇḍa.

From the height of heaven they toss jeweled nets
decorated with shining candras and sucandras;
they toss garlands and bouquets of māndārava,
sumana, jasmine, and magnolia flowers
to the perfect Bodhisattva,
seated in front of the king of trees.

Some come shaking the earth with their stride,
bringing joy to all people.
Some come carrying Mount Meru
in the palm of their hands;
from the sky they toss down baskets of flowers.

Some approach carrying the four seas on their heads,
sprinkling perfumed waters on the earth.
Some come carrying jeweled staffs,
pointing out the perfect Bodhisattva from a distance.

Some approach in the tranquil form of Brahmā,
calm in mind, perfectly calm, abiding in meditation.
From their pores comes a delightful voice,
expressing the immeasurables:
love, compassion, joy, and equanimity.

Others come in the form of Indra,
preceded by gods by the hundreds of thousands;
after approaching the Bodhi tree,
they bow with joined palms, and toss precious gems
like those of Indra.

Some come in the form of the Four Guardians,
surrounded by gandharvas, kinnaras, and rākṣasas;
they rain down brilliant flowers like flashes of lightning
and praise the Hero with the voices
of gandharvas and kinnaras.

Others come carrying flowering and fruit-bearing trees,
whose blossoms perfume the air;
showing the upper half of their bodies amidst the foliage,
they bow toward Dhāraṇīmaṇḍa and throw flowers.

Some come bearing ponds filled with lotuses,
yellow, blue, and white.
In the heart of each lotus stands one who bears
the thirty-two signs of a great man—
one who praises the Bodhisattva,
the sage whose mind is completely detached.

Some manifest bodies as immense as Meru:
they appear in the sky,
then hurl themselves toward the earth,
their falling bodies turning into garlands of fresh flowers,
which fill the three thousand fields of the Jinas.

Some approach with eyes flaming
like the conflagration at a kalpa's end
when the world is destroyed and reborn.
From their bodies issue voices,
teaching numerous doors of the Dharma,
freeing hundreds of millions from envy.

Some who approach are beautiful,
with lips as red as the bimba
and voices as resonant as the kinnaras';
some appear as young girls,
adorned with beautiful necklaces,
entrancing to the assembled gods.

Some appear with bodies indestructible as the diamond,
wading through the deepest waters of the ocean floors.

Others appear like the sun or with full faces like the moon,
their light and brightness destroying the fettering passions.

Some come adorned with jewels,
holding precious gems in their hands.
For the joy, the benefit, and happiness of many beings,
they rain down the most beautiful jewels
and flowers of sweetest perfume,
which cover tens of millions of fields.

Some approach reciting the collections
of great and precious dhāraṇīs;
hundreds of thousands of Sūtras issue from their pores.
With energy, wisdom, and intelligence,
they awaken the proudest of the proud.

Some approach carrying Mount Meru like a drum;
struck loudly, it resonates throughout the heaven realms,
through tens of millions of Buddha-fields,
announcing in the ten directions:
"The Teacher, who is still to obtain Immortality,
today will become a Buddha!"

The Twentieth Chapter
The Displays at Bodhimaṇḍa

Plate 21

मारधर्षणपरिवर्तः

།བདུད་བདུལ་བའི་ལེའུ།

The Defeat of Māra

SUCH, O MONKS, were the numerous displays which the Bodhisattvas manifested at Bodhimaṇḍa as homage to the Bodhisattva. And the Bodhisattva himself made visible at Bodhimaṇḍa all the displays of ornaments in all the fields of the Bhagavats, past, present, and future, in all of the ten directions.

Then, O monks, while the Bodhisattva was seated at Bodhimaṇḍa, the thought occurred to him: "The demon Māra is lord of this realm of desire—the master who wields the power; it would not be right to become a Buddha, to attain perfect and complete Enlightenment, without first informing him. I shall therefore summon Māra Pāpīyān. When he is conquered, all the gods of the desire realm and all others will be subdued as well. Moreover, among the entourage of the demon Māra are devaputras of his realm who have previously generated the root of virtue. When these devaputras have seen how the lion sports, they will then turn their thoughts toward perfect and complete Enlightenment."

O monks, when the Bodhisattva had so reflected, he emitted from the tuft of hair between his eyebrows a ray called Sarvamāra-maṇḍalavidhvaṁsanakarī, That Which Destroys All the Domains of the Demon. As soon as this ray appeared, all the abodes of Māra in the three thousand great thousands of worlds grew dim and shook severely. The three thousand great thousand worlds were filled with a great light, and Māra Pāpīyān heard these words coming from within the light:

"Today the completely pure being
who has performed pure actions for numerous kalpas,
who gave up his position as the son of King Śuddhodana
in order to benefit the world,
who set forth with the desire to manifest Immortality,
approaches the tree of wisdom.
May he now make great effort!

"May he help others cross over after he himself crosses over.
May he deliver others as he himself is delivered.
Having taken breath, he will give breath to others;
having entered into complete Nirvāṇa,
he will help others enter also.

"He will empty the three lower realms,
leaving behind not a single sentient being;
he will fill to overflowing the cities of gods and men.
He is the great Benefactor; having obtained Immortality,
he will bestow on others the great bliss
of contemplation, omniscience, and Immortality.

"O Ally of Evil, upon his Enlightenment
he will cause the great rain of the Dharma to fall;
he will empty all your cities.
Without using force, he will weaken your army
and render it powerless.
Deprived of your army, O Māra,
you will be a partisan without partisans;
you will not know where to turn or what to do."

O monks, agitated by these challenges, Māra Pāpīyān dreamed a dream with thirty-two aspects. What were the thirty-two?

He saw his abode enveloped in shadows. Dreaming, he saw his dwelling covered with dust and filled with sand and gravel. He saw himself running in all directions, overcome by fear and anger; in his dream he was without diadem or earrings. He dreamed that his lips, his throat, and his palate were parched and dry. He saw himself with heart tormented. In his dream his gardens had all been stripped of leaves, flowers, and fruits; the ponds, whose waters had drained away, were left cracked and dry. He dreamed that the flocks of geese, storks, peacocks, nightingales, the kunālas, jīvaṁjīvas, and other birds, all had had their wings clipped.

He saw drums, conch shells, tambourines, kettle drums, lutes, guitars, theorbos, cymbals, and all other imaginable musical instruments broken in pieces and scattered over the ground. He saw himself, Māra, dejected and somber, abandoned by his following and by those he loved. He saw his favorite wife, adorned with garlands, fallen from her couch onto the ground, beating her head terribly with her fists. And he dreamed that he saw the most valiant, the strongest, the most brilliant, the wisest of the sons of Māra bowing before the Bodhisattva, who had come to the holy place of Bodhimaṇḍa.

He saw his daughters weeping and shouting: "O father! O father!" He dreamed his body was covered with a soiled garment, and that his head was covered with dust. His face was pale, he was without strength, and his splendor was gone. He saw his palaces with their galleries, oval windows, and arcades crumbling and covered with dust. In his dream the captains of his armies of yakṣas, rākṣasas, kumbhāṇḍas, and gandharvas were in flight, and were holding their heads in their hands, weeping and crying out. He saw the great leaders of the gods of the desire realm, Dhṛtarāṣṭra, Virūḍhaka, Virūpākṣa, Vaiśravaṇa, and Śakra, Suyāma, Santuṣita, Sunirmita, Vaśavartin, and the others as well, turn their faces toward the Bodhisattva, ready to serve him.

He dreamed that in the midst of combat, his sword would not come out of the scabbard. He saw himself uttering cries of misfortune; he saw himself abandoned by his following. He dreamed that the urns of benediction at his door had overturned. He saw the brāhmin Nārada uttering curses, and the doorkeeper Ānandita wailing in despair. He saw the canopy of the heavens enveloped in shadows, and saw the goddess of fortune, Śrī, who lives in the realm of desire, crying great tears. He dreamed that his supreme empire had been overturned, that he had become powerless, that the nets of pearls and precious gems had been broken into pieces and had fallen to earth. In his dream he saw the entire abode of Māra shaken hard. He saw trees cut down, walls fallen, and the whole army of Māra put to rout.

Such, O monks, were the thirty-two aspects of the dream of the demon Pāpīyān. Awakening trembling and frightened, he assembled all his men: his army, his attendants, his captains, and gatekeepers. When they had assembled, he addressed them in verse:

The demon Namuci is stricken
when he sees these things in a dream.
He summons his sons and his attendants
and the demon captain Siṁhahanu,
and addresses these allies of darkness:

"Last night I heard some verses in the air,
announcing that one born among the Śākyas,
the one bearing the excellent signs,
who for six years practiced austerities
most terrible and difficult to do,
has now arrived before the Bodhi tree.
It is time for us to make great effort!

"When the Bodhisattva awakens,
he will awaken hundreds of millions of others.
When he obtains Immortality
and enters the cool of Nirvāṇa,
he will empty my abode of every being.

"With a vast army we must go forth.
We will strike the śramaṇa who sits alone
at the foot of the king of trees.

Quickly assemble the four divisions of troops.
If you want to please me, act quickly!

"Though the world is full of Pratyekabuddhas and Arhats,
my strength is not diminished when they enter Nirvāṇa.
But if he becomes a Jina, King of the Dharma,
there will be countless Buddhas,
their numbers immeasurable."

Then, O monks, a son of the demon named Sārthavāha addressed this verse to the demon Pāpīyān:

"Why, O father, is your face so sad and pale?
Why is your heart beating so fast?
Why are your limbs trembling so?
What have you heard? What have you seen?
Tell us at once! Having looked at the problem,
we will decide what to do."

Māra put aside his pride and answered:
"Listen to me, dear son.
I have seen terrible things in a dream,
sights most frightening. If I told you the whole of it,
you would all faint in terror!"

Sārthavāha said:
"If the time of combat has arrived,
there is nothing wrong with winning,
but losing brings great harm!

If you have seen bad omens in a dream,
there may be virtue in standing aside,
rather than being destroyed in battle!"

Māra said:
"For one with an agile mind, success in combat is certain.
If we are firm and act with skill, the victory will be ours.
Where is there a man who would not bow to my feet
at the sight of my army?"

Sārthavāha said:
"However large the army, if it lacks sufficient strength,
it will fall to a single powerful hero.
Though fireflies filled the three thousand worlds,
the sun alone would eclipse their light
and plunge them into obscurity."

And he added:
"The one who acts unskillfully
through pride and ignorance, without reasoning,
will surely be destroyed."

O monks, the demon Māra Pāpīyān did not listen to Sārthavāha. He proceeded to deploy his great army of four divisions of troops, strong and valiant in combat, so formidable that it made the hair stand on end, an army such as gods and men had never seen or even heard of before.

Māra's soldiers were endowed with the ability to change their faces into many different shapes and to transform themselves in a hundred million ways. Around the hands and feet and bodies of the demons were coiled snakes by the hundreds of thousands; in their hands they held swords, bows and arrows, axes, hammers, hatchets, tridents, clubs, staffs, chains, bludgeons, discuses, and lightning bolts; their bodies were protected by fine coats of armor.

The demons' heads and their hands and feet were twisted and distorted; their bellies were distended; their heads and faces and eyes were flaming, shining with a terrible fierceness; their eyes shone red and flashing like those of the venomous black serpent; their canine teeth stuck out, enormous and frightful; their tongues hung from their mouths, thick and rough like matting.

Some of the demons spewed forth venom; others, like garuḍas, grasped sea-snakes in their hands. Some were eating human flesh and blood, gnawing on hands and feet, heads, livers, entrails, and bones. Their bodies were of different colors: greenish, dark blue, reddish brown, blue, red, and yellow. Some had crooked eyes or eyes hollow like wells, eyes inflamed or torn out and hanging; eyes slyly squinting or twisted; eyes flashing and deformed.

Some of the demons approached proudly, carrying fiery mountains and riding atop other fiery mountains. Others made their way toward the Bodhisattva grasping uprooted trees. Some had ears like goats, hogs, or demons; like the hanging ears of an elephant, or the ears of a boar. Some had no ears at all. Some looked like skeletons with emaciated bodies but stomachs distended. Others had stomachs like pitchers and feet like skulls. Their skin and flesh were shriveled, their ears, noses, hands, and feet, or eyes and heads were missing. Some in their desire to drink blood were cutting off each other's heads.

With raucous voices, ugly, harsh, and frightening, some of the demons were groaning: "Hu, hu, I come!" or calling out: "Hulu, hulu!" Some were screaming: "Grab him! Hit him! Strike him! Rip him to pieces! Tie, grab, cut, break, crush! Away with the Śramaṇa Gautama and the tree!"

Some of the demons had the faces of wolves or jackals; of swine, asses, oxen, of elephants, horses, camels, wild asses, water buffalo, onagers, or rabbits; of yaks, rhinoceroses, and śarabhas—deformed faces, inspiring terror. Some had the bodies of lions, tigers, rams, or bears; of monkeys, leopards, cats, or goats; of serpents, mongeese, fish, sea monsters, alligators, or turtles; of ravens, vultures, owls, garuḍas, and other creatures.

Some of the demons had strange forms, with one head or two or up to a hundred thousand heads while others had no head at all. Some had one arm or up to a hundred thousand arms while others had no hands. There were creatures with one foot or up to a hundred thousand feet while others had no feet.

Some of the demons had serpent venom dripping from the openings of their ears, their mouths, their noses, eyes, and navels. Some brandished swords, bows, arrows, lances, hatchets, axes, discuses, iron clubs, or javelins, lightning bolts, spindles, small javelins, and all sorts of other weapons as they threatened and taunted the Bodhisattva.

Some of the demons were wearing garlands of severed human fingers and garlands made of human bones and skulls. Some were smeared with serpent venom; others rode elephants, horses, camels, donkeys, bulls, and water buffalo, while spouting fire from their heads. Some were covered with hair like monkeys; others had hair like needles, or the hair of oxen, donkeys, boars, or mongeese; the hair of goats, rams, śarabhas, cats, monkeys, wolves, or jackals.

There were demons which vomited and swallowed iron balls, and breathed fire. They spread a rain of flaming copper and iron, a rain of lightning bolts, a rain of burning iron sand, and a rain of arrows, making black clouds arise. And in the great darkness, the demons rushed toward the Bodhisattva, calling out fiercely. Rattling chains, they made great mountains crumble. The demons stirred up the great seas and jumped over looming mountains, shaking Mount Meru, the king of mountains.

Pushing here and there, the demons threw their limbs from side to side, uttering great screaming bursts of laughter as they pierced and beat their chests. Jostling one another, shaking their heads, their hair standing on end or blazing with fire, their eyes like those of jackals, they attempted to frighten the Bodhisattva.

The forms of old women approached the Bodhisattva wailing to him: "Alas, my son! Alas, my son! Arise, quickly! Run! Save yourself!" Creatures in the shape of rākṣasīs, of piśācas, and one-eyed pretas, lame, weak, and hungry, rushed up to the Bodhisattva with their arms raised, their mouths distorted, uttering fearful cries.

With such an army of demons was the attack carried out. For twenty-four yojanas on all sides, the demons by the hundreds of millions converged on the Bodhisattva. Māra's army spread out and filled the air, occupying entirely the three thousand great thousands of worlds.

Concerning this it is said:

Creatures in the forms of yakṣas and kumbhāṇḍas,
mahoragas, pretas, and piśācas—
everything most disagreeable and frightful in the world,
all appear by magic.

There appear yakṣas with one head,
two heads, three heads, a thousand heads;
with one arm, two arms, three arms, a thousand arms.

There are many with one foot, two feet,
three feet, up to a thousand feet;
there are those with dark blue faces and yellow bodies,
with yellow faces and dark blue bodies.

Some have faces of one kind and bodies of another:
white faces with black bodies, black faces with white bodies.

And so the whole army of demons approaches
with the faces of tigers and snakes and swine,
with the faces of elephants, horses, insects, and camels,
with the faces of monkeys, lions, and bears:
the army with demonic faces advances.

Fearsome yakṣas with heads like sheep
are covered with horrible growths
and sticky with human blood.
So the yakṣa demons advance—with feet like antelope,
with eyeballs like monkeys, teeth like elephant tusks:
such are the faces of the demon army advancing.

Bodies like crocodiles, ears like goats',
eyeballs hollow and shining with fire:
such are the faces of the demons advancing.

Some brandish sticks and others, axes and lances;
some are carrying great mountains:
such are the fearful forms of the yakṣas advancing.

Some, with eyes swirling, brandish wheels of fire
or carry great mountain peaks in their hands,
while hurling iron balls and stones amidst hurricane winds:
such are the frightful yakṣas advancing.

They make the wind blow fiercely and the rain to fall;
lightning flashes follow one on another
by the hundreds of thousands.

Thunder crashes, and trees overturn,
but not a leaf on the tree of wisdom quivers.
Rain pours down, the streams fill to overflowing;
the earth is covered with water.

In the midst of all these numerous terrors,
night falls imperceptibly.
All around trees crash to the ground,
and the most frightful of forms are everywhere seen.

Yet, even as he views these shocking forms,
the mind of the one with the signs of virtue,
shining in his glory like Mount Meru, remains unmoved.
Like magic, like a dream, like clouds:
thus he regards all things.

Reflecting that all substances are thus,
he sits still and meditates, abiding in the Dharma.
The thought comes to his mind:

"Those who think 'I' and 'mine'
are attached to themselves and to other things.
The wise who see this condition of grasping
become intent on breaking free."

But the son of the Śākyas realizes
that all things come forth dependently,
that their nature is without substance.

Endowed with a mind like great space,
he remains untroubled at the sight
of the deceiver with his army.

O monks, among the thousands of sons of the demon Pāpīyān were some who were partisans of the Bodhisattva. Led by the demon Sārthavāha, they stood on the right side of Māra, while those who took the side of Māra Pāpīyān stood on his left. Then Māra Pāpīyān spoke thus to his sons: "With what sort of army shall we subdue the Bodhisattva?"

And on his right side, Māra's son Sārthavāha
addressed this verse to his father:
"Would you want to wake the sleeping king of the nāgas,
or the sleeping king of the elephants?
Or arouse the sleeping king of the beasts?
Yet you want to stir up the most powerful of men
who is abiding there at ease."

From the left side, the son of Māra named Durmati
spoke thus: "Look here!
I can cause hearts to break! I can fell great trees!
No one alive can keep his strength
when struck by the deathblow of my glance."

From the right side, one named Madhuranirghoṣa said:
"Because you can destroy great trees,
you think that you can take on this man?
Where is your sense?
Even if your glance could destroy Mount Meru,
you could not even open your eyes in his presence.

"You might take up the ocean in your hands
and even drink down its waters,
but looking such a pure one in the face
would bring you great suffering!"

On the left, one named Śatabāhu said:
"I have a hundred arms and can shoot
one hundred arrows at one time.
I will make holes in the body of the śramaṇa.
O my father, do not worry! Advance without delay!"

On the right side, Subuddhi said:
"Though you have one hundred arms,
they will be like one hundred hairs against him.
Even your hundred arrows can do nothing.

"Why is this? The Muni has meditated on a love
that passes far beyond the world;
his body cannot be touched by poison, arrows, or fire;
all weapons hurled against him change into flowers.

"The strongest of the strong, be they men or yakṣas
from the sky, the earth, or water,
though armed with swords and hatchets,
will lose their strength
when they approach the master of men,
who arms himself with the strength of patience."

On the left Ugratejas said:
"I will enter his beautiful body, and I will burn it,
as a forest fire burns dead trees, from trunk to twigs."

On the right, Sunetra said:
"Even if you could penetrate and burn Mount Meru,
the likes of you could never burn this one,
who has the diamond mind,
though your numbers equaled the sands of the Ganges.

"Though all the mountains crumble,
and the great oceans dry up,
though the sun and the moon fall to the earth,
and the earth itself should be destroyed,

"The one who has undertaken to help the world,
who has made a solemn vow,
would never arise from beneath the great tree
without having obtained supreme Enlightenment."

On the left side, Dīrghabāhugarvita said:
"With my hand I can crush
the abodes of Candra and Sūrya;
I can crush the stars as if they were right here before me;

"I can part the waters of the four oceans in sport.
O father, I will seize the śramaṇa
and throw him to the other side of the sea.

"Have the army stand ready, O father!
Do not be disheartened.
I will tear him to pieces,
and the tree of wisdom as well,
and scatter the bits to the ten directions."

From the right side, Prasādapratilabdha said:
"Even if you could crush to powder
the earth, the seas, and the mountains,
together with the gods, asuras, and gandharvas,
you and thousands like you,
equal in number to the sands of the Ganges,
could still not move one hair of the Bodhisattva,
the one who is the wisdom-holder."

From the left side, Bhayaṁkara said:
"Why, O father, are you so afraid
while you stand in the midst of your army?
He has no army, and where are his allies?
What reason is there to fear him?"

On the right side, Ekāgramati said:
"Moons and suns, Cakravartins and lions,
all have no armies in this world.
True, the Bodhisattva has no army—
but alone he can conquer Māra."

On the left side, Avatāraprekṣi said:
"He has no lances, no spears, no clubs or swords,
no elephants or horses, no chariots or soldiers.
Fear nothing, father! I will kill him—
this worthless śramaṇa who sits there alone."

On the right side, Puṇyālaṁkāra said:
"Like Nārāyaṇa, his body is indestructible.
Armed with the strength of patience,
wielding the solid sword of valor
and the bow of knowledge,
he rides the triple vehicle of complete deliverance.

O father, by the strength of his merit,
he will overcome the army of Māra."

On the left Anivartin said:
"The forest fire does not spare the grass;
the archer's arrow does not return;
the lightning from the sky does not turn aside;
nor will I rest until I conquer the son of the Śākyas."

On the right side, Dharmakāma said:
"Encountering damp grass, fire draws back;
hitting a rock, the arrow rebounds;
striking the earth, the lightning is buried below.
Until he has obtained peaceful Immortality,
he will not rest. And why?

"O my father, even if one could draw figures in the air,
or unite all sentient beings in a single thought;
even if one could bind with a cord
the sun, the moon, or the wind,
still one could not move the Bodhisattva
from Bodhimaṇḍa."

On the left side Anupaśānta said:
"By the great venom of my glance,
I can burn Mount Meru and dry up the oceans.
Watch, dear father, how I pierce with my gaze
the Bodhi tree and the śramaṇa;
see how today I reduce them both to ashes."

On the right side the devaputra Siddhārtha said:
"Even if the three thousand worlds
were filled with poison and aflame,
a glance from the one who is a source of virtues

would drain all the poison away.
The three worlds are full of terrible poisons:
desire, hatred, and ignorance.
Yet, in his body and mind they are nowhere to be found.
no more than mud or dust are found in the heavens.

"His body, his speech, his mind are perfectly pure;
he is filled with love for all beings
and neither weapons nor poison can harm him.
For this reason, dear father, sound the order to withdraw!"

On the left side, the one who was named Ratilola said:
"By exciting his desires
with a thousand musical instruments
and a hundred thousand well-adorned apsarases,
I will lead him into the finest of cities.
Overcome with desire, he will be in your power!"

On the right side, Dharmarati said:
"His pleasure is in the Dharma and in contemplation,
in the meaning of Immortality, in love,
and in delivering all beings.
He finds no pleasure in the joys of passion!"

On the left side the one named Vātajava said:
"With my all-consuming power,
I could devour the sun and moon
and the wind which blows from the sky.
This very day, O my father, I will seize the śramaṇa
and break him into pieces,
as the wind scatters a handful of straw!"

On the right, the son of Māra named Acalamati spoke thus:
"However formidable your speed and power,

even if it equaled that of gods and men together,
it could do no harm to this unequaled man."

On the left side, Brahmamati said:
"Even if your strength were that great,
your self-esteem is weak; never would you win.
Every enterprise succeeds through numbers;
he is alone: what could he possibly do?"

On the right side Siṁhamati said:
"Lions never move in herds,
nor do beings who kill with their looks;
glorious beings, the first among men,
who conquer with the truth,
also do not group together."

On the left side, Sarvacaṇḍāla said:
"Thus do your sons speak to you with heated words,
words full of courage, impetuosity, and strength—
let us go and kill the śramaṇa quickly!"

On the right side, Siṁhanādi said:
"In the winding paths of the forest,
the jackals bark when the lion is not near,
but they flee in terror at the sound of his roar,
scattering in all directions.

"The ignorant sons of Māra shout proudly
when they do not hear the voice of the best of men;
but as soon as the Lion of Men speaks out,
they will run."

On the left side, Duścintitacinti said:
"What I have in mind will be quickly done.
This idiot knows nothing;

does he not see our legions?
Why does he not rise promptly and flee?"

On the right side, Sucintitārtha said:
"Neither stupid nor easy to conquer is he;
it is you who are harmless and stupid.
You do not understand his strength.
By the power of his wisdom, he will conquer all!

"Even if the number of Māra's sons
were equal to the sands of the Ganges,
with all your strength you could not move
even a single hair on his head.
How could you think to kill him?
Have no thought of harm and calm your mind;
fill it with faith and respect; withdraw without fighting;
here in the realms of existence, he will be king."

And so in this way all the sons of Māra,
forming a full thousand,
those on the light side and those on the dark,
each in his turn, addressed verses to the demon Pāpīyān.

Then Bhadrasena, the captain of Māra's armies,
said to Māra: "All who have marched in your ranks—
Śakra, the Guardians of the World, the kinnaras,
the most powerful of the asuras, the lords of the garuḍas—
all join their palms and bow before him.

"And the more so those who have not followed you—
the devaputras of Brahmābhāsvara
and the gods of Śuddhāvāsa—all have bowed before him.

"And even here, the wise among your sons,
the intelligent and strong,

unite their hearts with the Bodhisattva
and also bow before him.

"He looks upon this army of demons,
yakṣas, and other terrors,
an army extending for eighty-four yojanas,
and his mind is wholly tranquil;
for he lacks completely all moral fault.

"Having seen this fearsome army,
terrible, monstrous, terrifying,
he is neither astonished nor overcome.
Certainly the victory today will go to him.

"Everywhere this army of owls and jackals stops,
they make their cries heard:
when the crow and the donkey raise their voices,
the time to retreat is at hand.

"Look at Bodhimaṇḍa: the patakuntas, swans,
kokilas, and peacocks circle him, doing homage.
Certainly the victory today will go to him.

"Where your army stops, ink and dust rain down;
at Mahimaṇḍa, there is a rain of flowers.
Do as I say, withdraw your forces!

"Where your army stops, the ground is unlevel,
rocky, and covered with thorns;
the ground of Mahimaṇḍa is spotless gold.
The wise would quickly withdraw.

"Withdraw, unless you wish your dream to come true.
Withdraw, or he will reduce you to ashes,
as the land of the ṛṣis was razed.

"On his royal walk, a great ṛṣi
was irritated by Brahmadatta,
and for many years thereafter
no grass grew in the burned out forest of Daṇḍaka.

"Yet this one is superior to the greatest of ṛṣis
the whole world over—ṛṣis of good conduct,
who fulfill their vows and are devoted to austerities—
for he truly does no harm to any being.

"Have you not heard it said in former times:
'When the one who bears the beautiful, striking signs
leaves his family, he will be a Buddha,
a conqueror of the fettering passions'?

"The sons of the Jinas have manifested a great display,
and today they come to honor him;
the first of beings accepts
this first among all offerings.

"The perfectly pure ūrṇā between his brows
shines in tens of millions of Buddha-fields.
Alas! Surely we shall be eclipsed!
The army of Māra will be destroyed!

"Since his head cannot be seen even by the gods
who dwell in the uppermost worldly realms,
he will surely obtain omniscience
without being instructed by others.

"Meru and the Cakravālas, the sun and moon,
Indra, Brahmā, and the trees and highest mountains
all bow before Mahimaṇḍa.

"Without any doubt, through the strength of his virtue,
the strength of his wisdom, the strength of his knowledge,

the strength of his patience, and the strength of his valor,
he will render powerless the demon's allies.

"Like an elephant smashing an earthen pot,
or a lion conquering a jackal;
like the sun outshining a glowworm,
the Sugata will conquer this army."

After hearing this speech, another son of Māra,
his eyes aflame with anger, said:
"You pronounce words of exaggerated praise
for that one all alone.
What can he do by himself?
Do you not see this great and frightful army?"

Then, from the right side,
a son of Māra named Mārapramardaka said:
"The sun needs no companion in this world,
nor does the moon, a lion, or a Cakravartin king.
Certainly the Bodhisattva,
well-seated and greatly strengthened by wisdom,
has no need of other companions."

Meanwhile, in order to weaken the forces of Māra, the Bodhisattva shook his head like a hundred-petaled lotus in full bloom. Seeing this, the demon fled, for he thought that he saw his army vanish within the Bodhisattva's mouth. From a safe distance, he reconsidered, thinking that this could not be, and so turned back.

Returning to his followers, he hurled projectiles at the Bodhisattva; but even when he threw mountains like Meru, they were transformed into a canopy of flowers and celestial palaces. From the attackers' eyes came the venom of serpents, from their breath came poisons and flames. But the flames hovered over the Bodhisattva like a circle of light.

The Bodhisattva touched himself on the forehead with his right hand, and Māra fled toward the south, thinking: "The Bodhisattva has a sword in his hand!" But then he thought: "There was nothing!" and again turned back.

Māra aimed at the Bodhisattva all sorts of frightening weapons: swords, arrows, lances, javelins, stones, spindles, axes, rammers, sharp lightning bolts, clubs, discuses, hammers, uprooted trees, boulders, chains, and iron balls. But no sooner did he throw these weapons than they changed into garlands and canopies of flowers. Flowers covered the ground and hung as ornaments for the tree of wisdom. So magnificent were these displays made for the Bodhisattva that Māra Pāpīyān was devoured with anger and envy. He cried to the Bodhisattva: "Arise! Arise, youthful prince! Go and enjoy your kingdom! Through what merit will you gain deliverance?"

Then the Bodhisattva in a deep firm voice, solemn, sweet, and pleasant, answered Māra Pāpīyān in these words: "Pāpīyān, through a single offering freely made you have become head of the empire of desire; but I have freely made hundreds of millions of offerings. I have cut off my hands, my feet, my eyes, and my head as gifts for those who wished them; ardently desiring the deliverance of beings, I distributed houses, riches, seeds, beds, garments, gardens, and parks to all who asked."

Then Māra Pāpīyān addressed the Bodhisattva with this verse:

"In a previous existence,
I freely made an irreproachable offering;
to this you are the witness;
but you have no witness to offer evidence in your support,
and so you will be conquered!"

The Bodhisattva replied: "Pāpīyān, this earth is my witness." And then the Bodhisattva enveloped Māra and all his following with a thought proceeding from love and compassion. He was like a lion, without distress or fear, terror or weakness, without dejection, without confusion, without agitation, without the dread which makes the hair stand on end.

With his right hand, which had on its palm the designs of a conch, a banner, a fish, a vase, a svastika, an iron hook, and a wheel; this hand which had the spaces between the fingers joined by a membrane; which was beautifully adorned with fine softly polished fingernails the color of red copper; which had the graceful form of youth; which during innumerable kalpas had accumulated great masses of virtue; with this hand he touched all parts of his body, and then gently touched the earth. And at that moment he uttered this verse:

"This earth, the home of all beings,
is impartial and free of malice
toward everything which moves or does not move.
Here is the guarantee that there is no deception:
take the earth as my witness."

And as the Bodhisattva touched the great earth, it trembled in six ways: it trembled, trembled strongly, trembled strongly on all sides; resounded, resounded strongly, resounded strongly on all sides. Just as the bronze bells from Magadha ring out when struck with a stick, so this great earth resounded and resounded again when touched by the hand of the Bodhisattva.

Then the goddess of the earth that is in this world realm of the three thousand great thousands of worlds, the goddess named Sthāvarā, surrounded by a following of a hundred times ten million earth goddesses, shook the whole great earth. Not far from the Bodhisattva, she revealed the upper half of her body adorned with all its ornaments, and bowing with joined palms, spoke thus to the Bodhisattva: "Just so, Great Beings. It is indeed as you have declared! We appear to attest to it. Moreover, O Bhagavat, you yourself have become the supreme witness of both the human and god realms. In truth, you are the purest of all beings."

Having frustrated the guile of Māra with these words, the great earth goddess Sthāvarā honored and praised the

Bodhisattva and showed in several ways her own power; then with her following she disappeared.

Having heard the voice from the earth,
the deceiver and his army, terrified and broken,
begin to flee. Like foxes in the woods
who hear the lion's roar,
like crows at the fall of a clump of earth,
all suddenly dispersed.

The demon Pāpīyān was angered and worried, crushed and humiliated; but dominated by pride, he did not move, did not retreat; he did not flee. Looking back at his army, he spoke: "All of you together, let us stop for a while until we determine if he can ever be budged. The destruction of such a jewel among beings cannot take place without careful consideration!"

Then Māra Pāpīyān said to his daughters: "Now go, my girls, and when you come to Bodhimaṇḍa, investigate the Bodhisattva. Determine if he is susceptible to desire or free from passion. Is he ignorant or wise? Is he blind, or is he well-acquainted with all things? Does he have followers? Is he weak or strong?"

Upon hearing these words, the apsarases approached Bodhimaṇḍa and, in the presence of the Bodhisattva, they manifested the thirty-two kinds of feminine wiles. What are these thirty-two? Some of the goddesses veiled half their faces; some showed off their firm round breasts; some with half-smiles flashed their pearl-like teeth; some stretched out their rounded arms while yawning; some showed their lips, which were red like the fruit of the bimba; some gazed at the Bodhisattva with half-closed eyes, glancing at him, and then quickly looking away; some were showing their half-covered breasts; with garments which were loosely belted, or in fitted, transparent garments, they revealed the curve of their waists. Some made their anklets jingle; some were wearing garlands of flowers on their breasts; some were baring half their thighs; some were parading parrots and jays on their shoulders and their heads.

Some of the goddesses were throwing sidelong glances at the Bodhisattva; some, although in good clothing, appeared disheveled; some shook the golden girdles at their waists; others, like wanton women, moved flirtatiously here and there; some were dancing and singing. Some flirted shamelessly; some were moving their hips like palm trees shaken by the wind; some were sighing deeply; others, dressed in finery, strolled about, tapping the bells that adorned their belts; some were shamelessly tossing their clothes and ornaments onto the ground; some were displaying the secret ornaments of guhyaka women; some were displaying their arms, rubbed with perfumed ointments; some were showing their painted faces and wore dangling earrings; some wore artful veils on both body and face, and unexpectedly revealed themselves.

Some of the goddesses were laughing together, reminding each other of their pleasures and their games, and then stopping as if ashamed. Some had the bodies of young girls;

some the bodies of young women who have not been mothers; some the bodies of mature women. Some, filled with desire, called out to the Bodhisattva. Some showered the Bodhisattva with flowers and stood before him, examining his face, seeking to guess his thoughts: does his look reveal that his senses are aroused, or is he gazing into the distance? Is he agitated or not? Questioning each other in this way, they looked at the pure, spotless face of the Bodhisattva, like the disk of the moon delivered from Rāhu, like the sun rising at first dawn, like the golden pillar of sacrifice, like a hundred-petaled lotus in full bloom, like the sacramental fire sprinkled with ghee; immovable like Mount Meru; noble like the Cakravāla mountains; with perfectly guarded senses; like an elephant with a well-controlled mind.

Then, in order to excite the desires of the Bodhisattva, the daughters of Māra sang these verses to him:

"Springtime has come, the most beautiful of the seasons,
and all the trees are in flower.
Come, friend, let us enjoy ourselves.
Your body is beautiful and graceful,
well-adorned with the signs of a Cakravartin king.

"We are well-born, well-made to give pleasure
to gods and men—for this do we exist.
Arise, enjoy your beautiful youth.
Supreme wisdom is difficult to attain;
dismiss it from your thoughts.

"These daughters of the gods have come for you—
they have come to you beautifully adorned
and ready for pleasure.
What man, having seen such beauty,
would not yield to passion, be drawn on by passion,
even were he as dried out as a piece of wormy wood?

"Framed by diadems and earrings,
their faces, beautifully painted,
are like flowers in full bloom.
Their silky hair is scented with the softest perfumes.
Their brows are beautiful,
their eyes as large and lovely as lotus petals.

"Their lips are like the ripe fruit of the bimba;
their beautiful teeth are as white as conch shells,
white as jasmine and snow;
their faces resemble the full moon.
Look at them! How beautiful they are,
and they dream only of pleasure.

"Look, Lord, upon their firm breasts, high and round.
The three folds at their waists are charming;
their hips are broad with graceful contours;
truly they are very lovely.

"Their thighs are as shapely as an elephant's trunk;
their arms are covered with bracelets,
their waists adorned with golden girdles.
Look at them, Lord! They are your slaves.

"They have the bearing of a swan, swaying as they walk;
they speak with grace the language of love,
the language that touches the heart;

they are beautiful and finely adorned;
they are skilled as well in the joys of the gods!

"They know the arts of music,
singing, playing instruments, and dancing.
They are ruled by love, they live to give pleasure.
If you disdain these great beauties,
you will truly be robbing yourself.

"These maidens are here of their own accord,
driven by desire—enjoy yourself with them!
Only a fool, not realizing the worth of a precious gem,
would run away on seeing a treasure."

O monks, the Bodhisattva remained there calmly, not moving so much as an eye, smiling, his senses calm, his body unaffected and glorious; free from all passion, hatred, and confusion, unshakable as the king of mountains, neither despondent nor anxious, without weakness, his mind perfectly firm. Having renounced emotionality, he had entered the gate of wisdom, and now with a voice as soft and pleasant as the song of the nightingale, a voice which surpassed Brahmā's, beautiful and heart-touching, he answered the demon's daughters:

"Desires collect much suffering;
desires indeed are the root of suffering.

They corrupt the contemplations, the supernatural powers,
and the austerities of those who do not take care.
The wise speak well: there is no satisfaction
to be found in the quality of desiring women.
By means of knowledge, I will satisfy the ignorant.

"Like the man who has drunk salty water,
the one who nourishes desires
finds his thirst increasing endlessly;
indulging in the passions, he is useful
neither to himself nor to others.
But I have the wish to be useful to both myself and others.

"Your bodies are like foam or water bubbles;
like illusions; they appear and disappear at will.
Like the pleasures found in dreams,
desires are neither permanent nor lasting.
Only fools are caught in such a mire.

"Eyes are like water bubbles covered by a film;
like round pimples swollen with clotted blood;
or like the germs of disease.
The belly is a filthy and disagreeable receptacle
for urine and excrement.
The body is a machine of suffering,
arising from karma and the fettering passions.

"The foolish and confused imagine
the body to be beautiful;
the wise know better.
Those who are confused turn round and round
in the world of rebirth, the root of suffering,
and experience the inconceivable suffering of beings in hell.

"From the belly a stream of filth
and disagreeable odors escapes;
the thighs, the legs, and the feet
are joined together like the parts of a machine.
Truly, you are like an illusion; you come forth
from the cause and circumstance of falsehood.

"The characteristics of desire lack all virtue;
they are bereft of virtue, like poison ivy, like fire,
like great and furious serpents.
The falsehood of desire turns beings
from the path of noble wisdom—
considering this, how foolish are the ignorant
to take desires for happiness.

"The man who through desire becomes a slave of women
abandons the pleasures of the Dharma;
he leaves the path of good conduct.
Longing for pleasure and the joys of desire,
he leaves the path of contemplation;
deprived of judgment, he dwells far from wisdom.

"I do not dwell with either passion or hatred;
I do not see anything of permanence, attraction, or self;
I do not dwell with what is pleasant or unpleasant;
like the wind in the sky, my mind is completely free.

"Were this world entirely filled with beings such as you,
were I to live with demons for a kalpa,
still no anger, desire, or ignorance would arise in me,
for Jinas abide in equanimity— their minds are like the sky.

"Although the gods and apsarases,
having neither blood nor bones,
are very pure and beautiful,

still they dwell in very great fear:
because their lives are not eternal,
and their nature is impermanent."

Meanwhile, the illusory daughters of the demon Māra, carefully adorned and completely intoxicated with passion, arrogance, and pride, continued to look for ways to excite the Bodhisattva, using feminine wiles as their father had instructed.

Concerning this it is said:

The most seductive of women have come in haste;
they bring desire and the pleasures of desire.
Sent by the demon to display their charms,
they sway and dance like the branches and leaves
of young trees in the wind;
they seek to seduce the prince,
seated at the tree of wisdom.

The time is spring,
most beautiful and charming of seasons,
when joy springs up in men and women,
when darkness and dust disappear.
The air rings with the cries of the cuckoo,
the goose, and the peacock; birds flock everywhere.
It is the time to taste the joys of the qualities of desire.

For a thousand kalpas
he has taken pleasure in good conduct,
accomplishing his vows and austerities,
unshakable as the king of mountains.
His body is like the rising sun,
his voice thunders like a storm cloud,
or like the lion's melodious roar.
Speaking words full of meaning,
he comes to the aid of all beings.

The wise avoid, the ignorant foster
whatever increases desires and quarrels,
hostility, rage, the fettering passions, and fear.
The time has come–
the Sugata will now obtain Immortality.

Today, having overcome the demon,
he will be an Arhat endowed with the ten strengths.
Yet, illusory beings show themselves to him, saying:
"Pray, listen, you with the lotus face:
you will be king, the greatest of lords,
a powerful master of the earth.

"While hosts of beautiful women
are playing a thousand instruments,
what are you doing in the garb of a Muni?
Leave it all behind–enjoy yourself!"

The Bodhisattva says:
"Yes, I will be king,
honored in the three worlds by gods and men,
a powerful master, endowed with ten strengths,
traveling with the Wheel of the Dharma,
greeted everywhere by millions of disciples
and by those with no more to learn.

My pleasure is in the Dharma;
my mind is not delighted with the objects of the senses."

The daughters of Māra say:
"While you are in the prime of your life,
before youth completely passes you by;
while you still possess beauty and vigor,
before sickness and old age have touched you;
while we are your friends,
with a smiling face taste the joys of desire!"

The Bodhisattva replies:
"I have now obtained the best of quietudes,
which is imperishable;
I have left behind the sorrows of unrest
found in the realm of the gods and the asuras;
I do not fear the enemies: old age, sickness, death.
Today I will attain the excellent path
which leads to the city free from fear."

The daughters of Māra say:
"Taste the joys of desire in the abode of the gods,
surrounded by apsarases as is the master of the Tridaśas.
Possess the joys of Yāma, Suyāma, or Santuṣita,
praised by the best of the greatest of gods.
Submit to the power of women in the city of Māra;
play with us and give us great pleasure!"

The Bodhisattva says:
"Inconstant are desires,
like the dewdrop on the grass, like autumn clouds.
Fearsome are desires,
like the anger of the daughters of the nāgas.
Even Śakra and the king of the Suyāmas
and the Tuṣita gods come under the sway of Namuci.

The ignoble are filled with the misery of desire;
who could find true pleasure in the abode of the gods?"

The daughters say:
"Behold the trees in bloom–
how beautiful their swaying young branches
where nightingales and the jīvaṁjīvakas sing,
surrounded by the buzzing of bees;
here on the ground where green grass has spread,
soft, rich, and thick, here in the woods alive with kinnaras,
give yourself over to pleasure with beautiful maidens!"

The Bodhisattva replies:
"By the power of time have these young branches bloomed;
hungry and thirsty, the bees approach the flowers.
In time, whatever is born from the earth
will wither under the sun.
But here I will certainly taste Immortality,
experienced by all preceding Jinas."

The daughters of Māra say:
"You whose face is like the moon,
look upon those with faces like the new lotus.
Their voices are soft and sweet;
their teeth as white as snow or silver.
Women like these are difficult to meet,
even in the abode of the gods–
the highest devaputras again and again
make them the object of their desire.
In the abode of men, their like cannot be found!"

The Bodhisattva says:
"I see the body as unclean and impure,
filled with worms, easily destroyed,
fragile, and enveloped in suffering.

I will obtain the imperishable state revered by the sages
who have produced the supreme happiness
of all sentient and non-sentient beings."

The daughters of Māra
show the sixty-four kinds of desire;
they shake their golden girdles and their anklets,
their clothing in artful disarray.
Struck by the arrows of desire, smiling proudly,
they ask the Bodhisattva:
"Lord, what wrong have we done you that you disdain us?"

The Bodhisattva replies:
"Beings who understand wrongdoing
will surely be set free.
Desires are like swords or javelins,
like spears or a razor smeared with honey;
like the head of a serpent or a furrow of fire:
this I understand well.
I have given up the company of women,
whose tendencies are to captivate."

Even with hundreds of thousands of feminine wiles,
they could not seduce the king of the Sugatas,
who has the bearing of the young elephant.
And now the daughters of Māra are ashamed.
They bow to the feet of the Muni;
gladdened, respectful, and gentle,
they praise the one who comes to aid the world:

"You are like the spotless calyx of the lotus;
your face is like the autumn moon.
You equal in splendor the flame of the offering lamp;
you are like a mountain of gold.

May your purposes and your prayer be accomplished.
You have passed through hundreds of lives;
having delivered yourself,
may you free this world enveloped in misery!"

The daughters of Māra praise in many ways
the one like the karṇikāra and magnolia flowers,
and having circumambulated three times
the one unshakable as a mountain,
they return to their father.
Bowing to his feet, they speak these words:
"O father, neither fear nor anger exist
in the Teacher of gods and men.

"He watches with a smiling face,
with eyes like lotus petals;
he does not gaze at anyone
with desire or with frowning brows.
Mount Meru could tremble, the sea could dry up,
even the sun and the moon could fall,
but the one who has seen the errors of the three worlds
would not fall into the grasp of a woman!"

The demon Pāpīyān, on hearing these words, was overcome with great sorrow and distress; dejected and full of bitterness, he spoke to his daughters: "He is ignorant and foolish not to appreciate the perfection of your beauty. How is it that you cannot lead him away from Bodhimaṇḍa?" Then the daughters of the demon addressed these verses to their father:

"He speaks soft and gracious words,
and there is no desire in him at all;
he sees what is most hidden and has no bitterness at all;
he sees the pure path and has no delusions at all.
He knows the true nature of the body;
his thoughts are profound.

"Clearly he knows the numerous faults of women;
his mind, completely free from desires,
remains unmoved by passion.
Neither god nor man, in heaven or here below on earth,
could match his mind and conduct.

"We showed him the deceptions of women, O father;
accompanied by passion,
they should have softened his heart.
Yet he saw and did not waver even an instant;
like the king of mountains, he remained unmoved.

"Filled with the splendor of hundreds of virtues,
full of brilliance from austerities accomplished,
he has practiced good works and discipline
for many millions of kalpas.
The gods and Brahmā, beings glorious and pure,
have fallen at his feet and made obeisance.

"After overcoming Māra and his army,
he will surely obtain the supreme wisdom
attained by all the previous Jinas.
Dear father, he does not seek combat
or a quarrel with us. Even for strong beings,
such combat would be a difficult enterprise.

"Behold, O father, in the sky—
hundreds of thousands of realized Bodhisattvas,

wearing diadems of precious stones,
have appeared out of respect for him.
Each is a jewel mine of precious things;
each is adorned with garlands of flowers;
each is possessed of the ten strengths;
and all have arrived to pay him homage.

"Beings sentient and otherwise—
trees, mountains, powerful gods,
kings of the garuḍas, asuras, and yakṣas—
all are prostrate before the one
who is a mountain of virtues.
O father, it would be best to turn your back on him today.

"No one who has not gone completely beyond
could ever wear him down;
no one who has not cut off the root of passion
could ever uproot him.
He is always patient and never disturbed;
no way can be found to upset him."

O monks, at this same time, the eight goddesses of the tree of wisdom—Śrī, Vṛddhi, Tapā, Śreyasī, Vidus, Ojobalā, Satyavādinī, and Samanginī—honored the Bodhisattva in sixteen ways, praising, exalting, and glorifying him:

"You are brilliant, Pure Being,
like the clear full moon;
you shine, Pure-minded Being, like the rising sun.

"You sparkle, Pure Being,
like the lotus in the midst of the waters;
you roar, Pure Being, like the lion
who strides like a monarch through the forest.

"You shine, Pure Being,
like the king of mountains in the midst of the ocean;
you manifest nobility, Pure Being, like Mount Cakravāla.

"You are difficult to fathom, Pure Being,
like the sea which is filled with jewels;
your intelligence extends, Protector of the World,
as far as the boundless sky.

"Your heart is firm, Pure Being,
like the soil of the earth which nourishes all beings;
you are endowed with a mind untroubled, First of Beings,
like Lake Anavatapta, which is always calm.

"Your mind is without fixed abode, Pure Being,
like the wind which is constantly shifting;
you are difficult to approach, Pure Being,
like the glorious monarch who shuns all conceit.

"You are strong, Pure Being,
like Nārāyaṇa, who is difficult to overcome;
you are firm in the observance of practices,
Protector of the World,
for you do not arise from Bodhimaṇḍa.

"O Pure Being, like the lightning bolt
hurled by the hand of Indra, you will not turn back.
You have obtained what is fine to obtain.
Soon you will come to possess the ten strengths."

In this way, O monks, the goddesses of the tree of wisdom exalted the Bodhisattva by glorifying him in sixteen ways.

In addition, O monks, the devaputras of the Śuddhāvāsa realm spoke words to weaken Māra Pāpīyān in sixteen ways. What were these sixteen ways? They are as follows:

"Conquered by the Bodhisattva, Pāpīyān,
you are like an old heron with little understanding.
You are without strength, Pāpīyān,
like an old elephant sunk in a swamp.

"You are alone, Pāpīyān,
like one who boasts of his valor after being conquered.
You have been deserted, Pāpīyān,
like a sick person abandoned in the woods.

"You are without strength, Pāpīyān,
like a young bull laboring under a burden.
You are overthrown, Pāpīyān,
like a tree uprooted by the wind.

"You are on the wrong path, Pāpīyān,
like a traveler who has lost his way.
You are the most miserable of the miserable, Pāpīyān,
like a poor and debt-ridden man.

"You chatter, Pāpīyān,
like an insolent crow.
You are overcome by pride, Pāpīyān,
like one who has forgotten his subjugation.

"Today you will be put to flight, Pāpīyān,
like a jackal frightened by the lion's roar.
You will be shaken, Pāpīyān,
like a bird tossed by the wind.

"You do not know the proper time, Pāpīyān,
like a mendicant whose merits are exhausted.
Today you will be abandoned, Pāpīyān,
like a broken pot full of dirt!

"Today you will be seized, Pāpīyān,
like a serpent hypnotized with a charm.
You are deprived of your powers, Pāpīyān,
like a man with his hands and feet severed."

O monks, thus did the gods of Śuddhāvāsa seek to weaken the demon Pāpīyān in sixteen ways. Also, O monks, the gods who honored the Bodhisattva attempted to dissuade the demon Pāpīyān in sixteen ways. What were these sixteen? They were as follows:

"Today, Pāpīyān, the Bodhisattva will overcome you,
in the same way a hero conquers an enemy army.

"Today, Pāpīyān, the Bodhisattva will seize you,
in the same way as a powerful wrestler grips a weakling.

"Today, Pāpīyān, the Bodhisattva will eclipse you,
in the same way the glowing orb of the sun
outshines a firefly.

"Today, Pāpīyān, the Bodhisattva will break you to pieces,
in the same way a great wind disperses chaff.

"Today, Pāpīyān, the Bodhisattva will frighten you,
in the same way a lion terrifies the jackal.

"Today, Pāpīyān, the Bodhisattva will overthrow you,
like a great śāla tree cut down at the roots.

"Today, Pāpīyān, the Bodhisattva will bring you to ruin,
in the same way a great king destroys a hostile city.

"Today, Pāpīyān, the Bodhisattva will entirely drain you,
in the same way great heat dries up a puddle of water.

"Today, Pāpīyān, the Bodhisattva will pursue you,
in the same way the law tracks down an escaped criminal.

"Today, Pāpīyān, the Bodhisattva will make you turn back,
in the same way the heat of a fire
turns aside a swarm of bees.

"Today, Pāpīyān, the Bodhisattva will condemn you
to be like a Dharmarāja stripped of his kingdom.

"Today, Pāpīyān, the Bodhisattva will ground you,
like an old heron whose wings have been clipped.

"Today, Pāpīyān, the Bodhisattva takes everything
from you, and you will be like one deep in the forest
without any provisions.

"Today, Pāpīyān, the Bodhisattva will compel you to groan
like one whose boat breaks up on the ocean.

"Today, Pāpīyān, the Bodhisattva will consume you,
like grass and trees flaming
in the conflagration at the end of a kalpa.

"Today, Pāpīyān, the Bodhisattva will reduce you to dust
in the same way a great bolt of lightning
destroys the top of a mountain."

In this way, O monks, those devaputras who honored Enlightenment attempted to dissuade the demon in sixteen ways. But the demon Pāpīyān would not be turned aside.

Concerning this it is said:

After hearing a sensible exhortation
from multitudes of gods,
the demon does not turn away, but cries:
"Kill! Strike! Tear him to pieces!
Do not let him live! If he delivers himself,
he will deliver others from my realm!
If the śramaṇa hopes for salvation,
he must arise, he must depart."

The Bodhisattva replies:
"Mount Meru, the king of mountains,
could wander from its base;
all beings could cease to exist;

the multitude of stars, the moon, and the planets
could fall from the sky to the earth;
all beings could be united in a single thought;
and the great ocean could dry up
before a being such as I,
once arrived at the foot of the king of trees,
would turn aside."

The demon says:
"I am the lord of desire,
lord of the entire world, master of the gods,
master of the dānavas, of men and beasts—
all act according to my will.
Arise, for you are in my realm.
Do what I say!"

The Bodhisattva says:
"If you are the lord of desire,
then you are not the lord of the light.
Look at me. It is I who am master of the Dharma.
If you are the lord of desire,
do not engage yourself on the lower path.
Powerless, you will watch as I obtain Enlightenment."

The demon says:
"What are you doing all alone in the forest, Śramaṇa?
What you seek is, in truth, not easy to attain.
Bhṛgu, Aṅgiras, and others,
even after great effort in austerities,
did not obtain this supreme dignity.
How could you, a mere man, obtain it?"

The Bodhisattva says:
"The austerities practiced by the ṛṣis
were not preceded by knowledge of the truth.

Their practices were meaningless;
the ṛṣis' minds were dominated by anger
and desire for the realm of the gods;
they persisted in the idea
that the self is both permanent and impermanent;
they persisted in the idea that liberation
is a place where beings go.

"Some say that life lacks a genuine purpose.
Some have no definite beliefs;
others believe in narrow dogma, and others in eternalism.
Some say that one who has a body is without a body.
Some believe in virtue, some in non-virtue.
Some believe in a creator, others believe there is no creator.

"Here today, upon this seat,
after having vanquished you,
conquered you, your pride, and your army,
I will obtain pure Enlightenment.
Then to all beings now and in the future,
I will show Nirvāṇa,
the cool nature of peace and tranquility,
free from all suffering."

Angered, furious, and worried,
Māra again utters a spiteful speech:
"Seize this monk seated here alone in the forest!
Seize him in my presence, and quickly take him off;
keep him under your power.
Quickly, guardians of the gate, take him to my abode,
and put him in bonds of wood and iron.
I will see him overcome by suffering,
uttering all sorts of groans, the slave of the gods."

The Bodhisattva says:
"Even if one could trace pictures in the sky,
drawing figures here and there,
or chain the rapidly shifting wind,
or obscure the sun and the moon,
and throw them from heaven to earth—
these things would come to pass more easily
than you and your kind could draw me from this tree,
though your numbers surpassed all calculation."

The powerful army of the demon
then arose with cries of 'Ha, ha!'
and the sounds of conches, drums, and gongs.
"Ah, my son! Dear child, are you not frightened
at the sight of Namuci's formidable army?

"You gleam with the golden hue of the rivers of Jambu
and the calyx of the magnolia;
you are in the flower of youth, praised by gods and men,
and worthy of homage.
But today you will fall to your destruction
in this great combat!
You will fall into the power of Māra
as Indra fell into the grip of the asuras."

The Sugata speaks to the troops of yakṣas and rākṣasas
with a voice like Brahmā's, like the nightingale's:
"You trying to frighten me from the tree of wisdom
is like a fool trying to frighten the sky!

"While I sit beneath this tree, no one can harm me:
not even one who could pulverize
the three thousand great worlds
and count the grains of their dust;

not even one who could make the water of the ocean
pass through a pore of his skin;
not even one who could crush in a moment
a mountain of diamond."

Frustrated and enraged, Māra draws a sharp dagger
from its sheath and says:
"Get up quickly, monk. Do what I say,
or I will cut you down like the green stem of a reed!"

The Bodhisattva replies:
"Were the three thousand worlds filled with demons,
each holding swords as large as Meru,
they could not touch even a single hair of my head;
they could not harm me. Let them oppose me:
they shall remind me of my firm resolve."

The demons attack,
some throwing mountain tops the color of flames;
some throwing uprooted trees and shafts of copper and iron;
some throwing camels and elephants with frightening eyes,
snakes and dreadful reptiles with venomous glances,
and other demons with heads of oxen.

Clouds thunder in the four directions,
hurtling down tongues of lightning and iron balls.
Spears and swords, javelins, sharp axes,
and poisoned arrows pierce the earth and destroy the trees.

Demons with hundreds of arms hurl spears;
they vomit up serpents and flames;
they pull makaras and other monsters out of the sea;
and others, transformed into garuḍas, hurl nāgas.

Furiously, they throw iron balls as large as Mount Meru,
and mountain peaks the color of flames.

Covering the earth, they disturb the land
and cause the subterranean waters to overflow.

Some fall forward, others backward;
they jump to left and right, crying: "Ah, my son!"
Their feet and hands are put on backwards;
their heads in flames, their eyes emitting sparkling flashes.

Seeing the frightful transformations of Māra's army,
the Pure Being recognizes them all as a product of illusion.
There is no demon, no army, no beings;
there is not even a self.
Like the image of the moon in the water,
the cycle of the three worlds is misleading.

There is no eye, no man, no woman, and no self;
no ear, no nose; likewise, no tongue and no body.
Substances arise by depending on each other,
free from a creator or one who perceives.
They are empty within and empty without.

With words of truth, he declares the truth
that all substances are empty.
And all the yakṣas who have submitted
and conformed to discipline
now see garlands of flowers
in the hands of those who had weapons.
This is the truthful discourse given by
the one whose words are always truthful.

The palm of his right hand
is adorned with beautiful membranes
and glossy fingernails the color of red copper;
it is embellished with a thousand-spoked wheel

as brilliant as gold from the rivers of Jambu.
He is strengthened by merit and good works,
and anointed with dignity from head to foot.

Extending his arm like a lightning flash into the sky,
he says: "This earth is my witness.
Formerly I made hundreds of thousands of offerings:
for there has never been reason to deny those who asked.

"Water, fire, and wind are my witnesses;
so too are Brahmā, lord of conditioned beings,
and the sun and the moon, together with the stars.
My witnesses are the Buddhas of the ten directions;
my witnesses are my good conduct, my austerities,
and the venerable branches of awakening.

"Giving is my witness, as are good conduct and patience;
effort is a witness, and also contemplation and wisdom.
The four immeasurables are witnesses,
along with omniscience;
all the stages of the Bodhisattvas' practice are my witness.

"Even if one could count the merits, strength,
and good conduct, the knowledge, and the offerings
of all the beings in the ten directions,
they would not attain in number
the hundredth part of my activities."

The Bodhisattva touches the earth gently with his hand,
and the earth resounds like a vase of bronze.
Having heard the sound,
Māra is thrown down on the ground
and he hears these words:
"Strike! Seize the ally of darkness!"

Māra's body is covered with sweat,
all his splendor is gone;
his face discolored, Māra sees old age overtake him.

He beats his chest and cries out;
spurred on by fear, he is without a protector.
His thoughts whirl about,
and madness touches his mind.

The army of horses and elephants
and chariots is over-turned.
Rakṣas, kumbhāṇḍas, and piśācas flee in fright;
bewildered, they can no longer find their way.
Without a place of refuge or protection, they scatter
like birds that see the forest suddenly ablaze.

Fathers, mothers, sons, sisters, and brothers ask each other:
"What have you seen? Where will you go?"
They debate their condition among themselves:
"We have fallen into misfortune;
we have no means to save ourselves!"

The unshakable army of Māra, great and powerful,
is scattered in disarray; it does not rally.
Seven days will pass
before they meet again and hoarsely say:
"You are alive, my friends. I am glad!"

The goddess of the tree of wisdom, moved with pity,
takes water and sprinkles the ally of darkness, saying:
"Arise quickly! Depart without delay.
Thus does it come to pass for those who do not listen
to the words of a spiritual teacher."

Māra replies:
"For not listening to the gentle and wise words of my sons,
for having offended a pure being,
I have today obtained great suffering,
fright, misfortune, sorrow, and ruin."

The goddess says:
"When foolish people harm those
who have not done them harm,
they will meet with calamity, suffering,
ruin, and misery, cursing, bad treatment,
imprisonment, and multiplied evils."

The gods, the asuras, the masters of the garuḍas,
the kinnaras, Brahmā as well as Śakra,
and the gods of the Parinirmita realm,
along with the gods of the Akaniṣṭha realm,
hail the triumph: "Victory to you, Hero of the World!
Māra's army has been put to rout!"

They offer garlands of pearls, parasols,
standards, and victory banners;
they rain down flowers, aloes, tagara,
and sandalwood powder. Musical instruments play,
and these words sound forth: "They surrounded your tree,
O Hero, but the enemy troops have been conquered.

"O Hero, having gently overcome by your love
the forces of the crafty demon,
here on the best of seats you will today
obtain incomparable Enlightenment.
You will obtain the ten powers, the pure Buddhadharmas,
the realizations and all the domain of a Buddha.

"In order to subdue Māra, you entered into battle;
thirty-six koṭis and twenty-four niyutas of beings
have seen the powers and skills of a fully Enlightened Being,
and their minds have been directed toward
the supreme wisdom of a Buddha."

The Twenty-first Chapter
The Defeat of Māra

Plate 22

अभिसंबोधनपरिवर्तः

། མངོན་པར་རྫོགས་པར་བྱང་ཆུབ་པའི་ལེའུ །

Attaining Perfect and Complete Enlightenment

O MONKS, IN SUCH A WAY did the Bodhisattva overcome the opposition of Māra. Having subdued the enemy and triumphed in battle, he remained seated, surrounded by parasols, standards, and unfurled banners, and entered into meditation.

After having attained the first level of meditation, which is detached from desire, accompanied by observation and reflection, free from non-virtue and wrongdoing, and endowed with joy and pleasure that are born from tranquility, he remained steady.

Letting go of observation and reflection, his purified concentration became one stream, and he attained the second level of meditation, which is accompanied by joy and pleasure, and which is produced from the samādhi that is free from observation and reflection. And the Bodhisattva remained steady.

Letting go of attachment to pleasure, he abided in the third level of meditation: equanimity accompanied by awakened awareness, consciousness, and great joy, called by the Āryas the equanimity which dwells in great joy and mindfulness. After having attained the third level of meditation, free from pleasure, he remained steady.

Letting go of joy, so that all previous pleasant and unpleasant feelings abated, he abided in the fourth level of meditation where there is neither suffering nor pleasure, where equanimity and mindfulness are completely pure. And he remained steady.

Abiding thus in equanimity, the mind of the Bodhisattva was completely pure, perfect, luminous, free from emotionality, free from all the fettering passions, supple, perfectly balanced, unwavering. At the first watch of the night, the Bodhisattva prepared his mind well and directed it carefully in order to bring forth the vision of wisdom which comes from the divine eye.

With his perfectly pure divine eye, far surpassing the human eye, the Bodhisattva saw beings being born and passing away. He saw those of good birth, of bad birth, on good paths, on bad paths, the lowly and exalted, each proceeding according to the influence of his actions; and he understood it well: "Ah, truly, these beings obtain the fruit of their karma. By bad use of their bodies, their minds, and their speech, by disparaging the saints, and by having false views, beings fall into lower states at the time of their death and are reborn in the hells as a result of their karma. But those beings who make good use of their bodies, their speech, and their minds, those who show respect to the saints, and who have right views are reborn in the happy states of men and gods as a result of their karma."

And so, with the perfectly pure divine eye, far surpassing the human eye, the Bodhisattva saw beings born and passing away: from good births, from bad births, on good paths, on bad paths, the lowly and the exalted, each receiving the result commensurate with his actions.

This is how, O monks, in the first watch of the night, the Bodhisattva cleared away the darkness and produced direct knowledge and clarity.

Abiding thus in equanimity, the mind of the Bodhisattva was completely pure, perfect, luminous, free from emotionality, free from all the fettering passions, supple, perfectly balanced, unwavering. At the middle watch of the night, in order to bring about the disappearance of suffering, in order to bring forth directly the knowledge of the vision of wisdom which remembers former lives, the Bodhisattva prepared his mind and directed it.

He remembered his many previous lives, as well as those of other beings—in one birth, two births, three, four, five, ten births, in twenty, thirty, forty, fifty births, in a hundred births, a thousand births, a hundred thousand births, even in several hundreds of thousands of births, a koṭi of births, a hundred koṭis of births, a thousand koṭis of births, a hundred thousand koṭis of births, a hundred thousand niyutas of koṭis of births, many hundreds of koṭis of births, in many thousands of koṭis of births, many hundreds of thousands of koṭis of births, many hundreds of thousands of niyutas of koṭis of births, in births up to a kalpa of destruction, a kalpa of re-creation, a kalpa of destruction and of re-creation, several kalpas of destruction and re-creation, recalling:

I was such and such a person, my name was this, my race was this, my lineage this; my color was this, the food I ate was such and such, this the span of life, this the length of time that I remained there; this was the happiness and unhappiness which I experienced. And then after leaving that life, I was born such and such a person; having passed on, I was born such and such a person; having passed on, I was born here. He remembered exactly the places and circumstances of his own lives and those of all other beings.

The mind of the Bodhisattva abided thus in equanimity, completely pure, perfect, luminous, free from emotionality, free from all of the fettering passions, supple, perfectly balanced, unwavering. And in the last watch of the night when the dawn appears, at the moment when the drum is sounded, in order to vanquish suffering and the source of suffering, and in order to manifest the vision of knowledge which destroys corruption, the Bodhisattva prepared his mind carefully and directed it well.

There came to his mind: certainly this world is miserable, subject to birth, old age, sickness, and death, to change of existence and rebirth. No one knows the means to escape this cycle, which is a great mass of sufferings: old age, sickness, death, and the rest. Alas! What can put an end to this great mass of sufferings? No one knows!

Then this came to the mind of the Bodhisattva: what by its very existence gives rise to old age and death; what is the conditional cause of old age and death? Then there came to his mind: since birth exists, old age and death come forth; the conditional cause of old age and death is birth.

And this came again to the mind of the Bodhisattva: what by its very existence gives rise to birth; what is the conditional cause of birth? And there came to his mind: when existence exists, birth comes forth; the conditional cause of birth is existence.

Then it came to the mind of the Bodhisattva: what by its very existence gives rise to existence; what is the conditional cause of existence? And there came to his mind: when grasping exists, existence comes forth; the conditional cause of existence is grasping.

Then it came to the mind of the Bodhisattva: what by its very existence gives rise to grasping; what is the conditional cause of grasping? And there came to his mind: when craving exists, grasping comes forth; the conditional cause of grasping is craving.

Then it came to the mind of the Bodhisattva: what by its very existence gives rise to craving; what is the conditional cause of craving? And there came to his mind: when feeling exists, craving comes forth; the conditional cause of craving is feeling.

Then it came to the mind of the Bodhisattva: what by its very existence gives rise to feeling; what is the conditional cause of feeling? And there came to his mind: when contact exists, feeling comes forth; the conditional cause of feeling is contact.

Then it came to the mind of the Bodhisattva: what by its very existence gives rise to contact; what is the conditional cause of contact? And there came to his mind: when the six senses exist, contact comes forth; the conditional cause of contact is the six senses.

Then it came to the mind of the Bodhisattva: what by its very existence gives rise to the six senses; what is the conditional cause of the six senses? And there came to his mind: when name and form exist, the six senses come forth; the conditional cause of the six senses is name and form.

Then it came to the mind of the Bodhisattva: what by its very existence gives rise to name and form; what is the conditional cause of name and form? There came to his mind: when consciousness exists, name and form come forth, the conditional cause of name and form is consciousness.

Then it came to the mind of the Bodhisattva: what by its very existence gives rise to consciousness; what is the conditional cause of consciousness? And there came to his mind: when karmic dispositions exist, consciousness comes forth; the conditional cause of consciousness is karmic dispositions.

Then it came to the mind of the Bodhisattva: what by its very existence gives rise to karmic dispositions; what is the conditional cause of karmic dispositions? There came to his mind: when ignorance exists, karmic dispositions come forth. The conditional cause of karmic dispositions is ignorance.

And so, monks, it came to the mind of the Bodhisattva: ignorance is the conditional cause of karmic dispositions; karmic dispositions are the conditional cause of consciousness; consciousness is the conditional cause of name and form; name and form are the conditional cause of the six senses; the six senses are the conditional cause of contact; contact is the conditional cause of feeling; feeling is the conditional cause of craving; craving is the conditional cause of grasping; grasping is the conditional cause of existence; existence is the conditional cause of birth; birth is the conditional cause of old age, and of death, grief, lamentations, suffering, pain, and despair. Thus does the great mass of suffering come forth.

O monks, by fixing his mind on the source of suffering, on teachings never heard before, he produced wisdom, he produced vision, produced realization, great knowledge, prudence, and understanding. And light came forth.

Then the Bodhisattva thought: by the absence of what do old age and death not exist; by the cessation of what will the cessation of old age and death result? And there came to his mind: birth not existing, old age and death do not exist; by the cessation of birth, old age and death cease.

Then there came to the mind of the Bodhisattva: by the absence of what does birth not exist; by the cessation of what does the cessation of birth result? And there came to his mind: existence not existing, birth does not exist; by the cessation of existence, birth ceases.

And the Bodhisattva thought again: by the absence of what does existence not exist? and so forth in detail through the cessation of grasping, craving, feeling, contact, the six senses, name and form, consciousness, and up to the cessation of karmic dispositions. And from the cessation of what does the cessation of karmic dispositions result? And there came to his mind: ignorance not existing, karmic dispositions do not exist; from the cessation of ignorance, karmic dispositions cease. And furthermore: from the cessation of karmic dispositions, consciousness ceases; from the cessation of consciousness, name and form ceases; and so on through the cessation of the six senses, of contact, feeling, craving, grasping, and existence, up to: from the cessation of birth comes the cessation of old age and death, of grief, lamentations, suffering, pain, and despair. Thus there is the cessation of the great mass of suffering.

So, O monks, again and again, the Bodhisattva fixed his mind on teachings previously unknown, generating wisdom and vision, generating realization, great knowledge, prudence and understanding. And light came forth.

At this time, O monks, I recognized in accord with the truth the suffering of affliction; I recognized the source of affliction, the cessation of affliction, the way which leads to the cessation of affliction. In accord with the truth, I recognized: this is the affliction of desire, this is the affliction of existence, this is the affliction of contact, this is the affliction of view; it is here that afflictions cease without exception; it is here that afflictions disappear without leaving a trace.

This is ignorance, this the source of ignorance; this is the cessation of ignorance, and this is the way which leads to the cessation of ignorance. This did I recognize in accord with the truth. It is here that ignorance disappears, without a trace or reflection.

Here are karmic dispositions, here the source of karmic dispositions; here is the cessation of karmic dispositions, here the way which leads to the cessation of karmic dispositions. All this I recognized according to the truth.

This is consciousness, this the source of consciousness; this is the cessation of consciousness, and this is the way which leads to the cessation of consciousness. All this I recognized according to the truth.

Here are name and form; here the source of name and form; this is the cessation of name and form, this the way which leads to the cessation of name and form. All this I recognized according to the truth.

Here are the six senses, here the source of the six senses; here is the cessation of the six senses, and here is the way which leads to the cessation of the six senses. All this I recognized according to the truth.

This is contact; this the source of contact; this is the cessation of contact, this the way which leads to the cessation of contact. All this I recognized according to the truth.

This is feeling, this the source of feeling; this is the cessation of feeling; this the way which leads to the cessation of feeling.

This is craving, this the source of craving; this is the cessation of craving, and this is the way which leads to the cessation of craving.

This is grasping, this the source of grasping; this is the cessation of grasping, this the way which leads to the cessation of grasping.

This is existence, this the source of existence; this is the cessation of existence, this the way which leads to the cessation of existence.

This is birth, this the source of birth; this is the cessation of birth, this the way which leads to the cessation of birth.

This is old age, this the source of old age; this is the cessation of old age, this the way which leads to the cessation of old age.

This is death, this the source of death; this is the cessation of death, this the way which leads to the cessation of death. All this I recognized according to the truth.

This is sorrow, lamentations, suffering, pain, and despair. Such is the source of this great mass of suffering, and so forth, up to its cessation. This did I recognize according to the truth. This is suffering, this the source of suffering; this is the cessation of suffering, this the way which leads to the cessation of suffering. All this I recognized according to the truth.

O monks, during the last watch of the night, at the moment when the drum is sounded, in a single instant, the Bodhisattva, the Great Being, the Holy Being, the Superior Being, the Magnificent Being, Leader of Men, Elephant of Men, Lion of Men, Chief among Men, the Hero of Men, the Best of Men, the All-knowing Being, the Lotus of Men, the White Lotus of Men, the Being who Carries a Heavy Load, the Peerless Charioteer of Men, the one whose knowledge comes through the wisdom of the saints, the one who has gained understanding, attainments, and vision, and who has manifested whatever is suitable: through the wisdom that manifests all of those qualities in a single instant, the Bodhisattva attained Buddhahood, the complete, accomplished, unexcelled Enlightenment, and obtained the three knowledges.

Then, O monks, the gods called out: "Friends, throw down flowers! The Bhagavat is truly a perfect and complete Buddha." But the devaputras assembled who had seen the preceding Buddhas replied: "Friends, the preceding perfect Buddhas gave a sign; they showed a supernatural sign. Do not throw flowers before the Bhagavat gives such a sign."

O monks, the Tathāgata, knowing that the devaputras were uncertain, rose into the sky to the height of seven tāla trees and uttered these joyous words: "The chain is broken, the emotions stilled. The stream of impurities is dry and runs no more. Since the chain is destroyed, suffering is ended. Thus has it been said." It was then that the devaputras covered the Tathāgata with heavenly flowers up to the knees.

O monks, when the Tathāgata became a perfect Buddha, the darkness and the shadows disappeared, craving was purified, views changed, and fettering passions were shaken. The thorn was withdrawn, the knot untied; the banner of pride was overturned; the banner of the Dharma was unfurled. The inclinations were uprooted; the nature of the Dharma was understood. He reached the true end, entering reality, and understood well the sphere of the Dharma.

The realms of beings were restored to proper balance; all positive things were praised; all lower things were rejected; all things not so established were understood. The character of all beings was observed, and the conduct of all beings was perfectly known. The remedy for the sickness of beings was well understood; the nectar of immortality was applied; the King of Physicians manifested. The freedom from all suffering was set forth, establishing beings in the happiness of Nirvāṇa. The Tathāgata himself was seated on the great throne of the King of the Dharma, for the means of arriving at complete deliverance was obtained; he entered into the city of omniscience; indivisible from the knowledge of the sphere of the Dharma, he joined with the truth and with all the Buddhas.

In the week that followed, O monks, the Tathāgata remained seated at Bodhimaṇḍa—there I brought an end to the beginningless suffering of birth, old age, and death.

O monks, at the very moment that the Bodhisattva obtained omniscience, at that very instant, all the sentient beings in all the worlds in the ten directions experienced great bliss. In all the ten directions, a great splendor illumined all the world-realms, and even the sinister hellish regions, enveloped in darkness, were bathed in light. In all directions the earth shook in six ways; it shook, shook hard, shook hard on all sides; it trembled, trembled hard, trembled hard on all sides; it quaked, quaked vigorously, quaked vigorously on all sides; it was disturbed, was greatly disturbed, was greatly disturbed on all sides; it reverberated, reverberated loudly, reverberated loudly on all sides; it resounded, resounded loudly, resounded loudly on all sides.

And all of the Buddhas gave their approval to the One who had become a perfect and complete Buddha. They sent many gifts to the Pure One of the Dharma; the three thousand great thousands of worlds were covered with jeweled parasols. From these parasols networks of light shone forth, illuminating the innumerable and immeasurable regions of the earth in all the ten directions.

In all of the ten directions of space the Bodhisattvas and the devaputras uttered cries of gladness: "He has appeared, the Lotus of Beings, born from the ocean of knowledge! He comes forth untouched by the worldly dharmas. Embracing the sphere of the Dharma, he is the great and noble Cloud of Mercy, which will rain down the medicine of the Dharma for beings capable of being trained. From all the seeds of virtue, tender shoots will sprout forth and grow strong; in time the fruits of liberation will come forth and will fall like rain.

Concerning this it is said:

Having overcome the demon with his army,
the Lion of Men, the Teacher,
manifests the joy of meditation.
With the ten strengths, he takes pleasure
in the three realizations,
and the tens of millions of Buddha-fields tremble.

Desiring the Dharma, the Bodhisattvas come before him,
bowing at his feet and speaking thus:
"Are you not weary?
So fearsome was the army that appeared.
It has been broken by the strength
of your merit, wisdom, and valor."

From hundreds of thousands of Buddha-fields,
the Buddhas have sent parasols, saying:
"Good and Great Being, the army of Māra
has been overcome. You have obtained
the immortal abode free from sorrow.
Quickly pour down the rain of the Dharma
upon the three worlds!"

Extending their arms,
the Buddhas of the ten directions,
the Hearts of All Beings,
speak with the voice of the nightingale:
"As butter is similar to ghee, so, Pure Being,
you, like us, have attained Enlightenment."

Then, O monks, the apsarases of the desire realm learned that the one seated at Bodhimaṇḍa was the Tathāgata: the Omniscient One who has fulfilled all his intentions, the Victor in combat, Conqueror of the opponent Māra, the one with the parasol, the standard, and the unfurled banner, Hero uplifted by victory.

He is a Being, a Great Being, the Best of Physicians who pulled out the great thorn of craving; fearless like a lion, free from exasperation, having the well-controlled mind of the elephant, free from the three defilements and spotless; the Learned One with the three knowledges, who has crossed the four currents and arrived at the other shore.

He is the Kṣatriya who carries the parasol decorated with jewels; the Brāhmin of the three worlds who has abandoned wickedness; the Monk who has broken out of the shell of the egg of ignorance; the Śramaṇa who has gone beyond all attachment, the one now pure, free from all emotionality; he is the Hero whose banner has never been lowered, the strongest of all, possessing the ten strengths; he is the jewel mine filled with all the jewels of the Dharma.

Turning their faces toward Bodhimaṇḍa, the apsarases praised the Tathāgata with these verses:

"Sitting in front of the king of trees,
he conquered the army of Māra.
Unshakable and fearless like Mount Meru,
he did not flee from the army of Māra.

"For tens of millions of kalpas,
he practiced giving, discipline, and self-control,

until he achieved Enlightenment.
This is the reason today he shines.

"For tens of millions of kalpas
while he was searching for supreme wisdom,
Śakra and Brahmā were outshone by his good conduct,
his vows, and his ascetic practices.

"For tens of millions of kalpas,
armed with the strength of patience,
he endured suffering.
This is the reason today he sparkles like gold.

"For tens of millions of kalpas,
by his energy and strength of effort,
he left the others far behind—
and so the army of Māra is conquered.

"For tens of millions of kalpas,
he has greatly honored the Munis
through wisdom, omniscience, and meditation.
This is the reason today he is honored.

"For tens of millions of kalpas,
accumulating knowledge and learning,
he has helped tens of millions of beings;
and so he has quickly obtained Enlightenment.

"He has conquered the demons of the aggregates,
the lord of death, and the demon of emotionality.
He has conquered the god Māra; and so he has no sorrow.
He is the god of the higher gods,
worthy of being honored by the gods themselves,
worthy of homage in the three worlds.
Intent on virtue, he pours forth
the nectar of immortality, the fruit of amṛta.

"He is the one most worthy of offerings:
the merit from giving to him will never be lost
and will lead as well to gaining supreme Enlightenment.

"The tuft of hair between his eyebrows shines
and lights up tens of millions of Buddha-fields;
even the sun and the moon are eclipsed
as his light shines for all beings.

"He is well-endowed with a shining form,
with the most beautiful form, an excellent form,
marked with the best signs;
desiring only to be of aid,
he is worthy of the three worlds' homage.

"His vision is pure, he is the Self-arising One—
he sees many things: the Buddha-fields
and the masses of sentient beings,
as well as their thoughts and intentions.

"With the purest of ears he hears
an infinity of voices: the divine and the human,
the voices of Jinas, the voice of the Dharma.

"He has a broad tongue
and the beautiful voice of the nightingale;
let us listen to him teach the Dharma,
which leads to perfect and unending calm.

"When he saw the army of Māra,
his heart was not distressed;
when he saw the troops of the gods,
the Great Sage felt no relief!

"He conquered Māra's army using neither arms nor arrows;
with truth, fulfilled vows, and austerities,
he overcame the vindictive champion.

"Not shaken from his seat, his body quite unharmed,
he faced the situation bound by neither desire nor hatred.

"Benefits, great benefits will flow to the gods and men
who, seeking attainments, hear you teach the Dharma.

"By the merit of praising all your merit,
may we soon be like you, O Moon of Men,
possessor of the splendid virtues of the Jinas."

When the great leader of beings obtained
the Enlightenment of Buddhahood,
hundreds of thousands of Buddha-fields were shaken;
and after he had conquered the demon Māra,
the Guide of Men uttered these verses
with the voice of Brahmā,
with the voice of the nightingale:

"The maturation of merit brings happiness
and clears away all suffering.
All the aims of one with merit are accomplished.
Having conquered Māra,
he will quickly attain Enlightenment.
He will obtain the cool nature of peace, Nirvāṇa.

"Who then could have enough of doing good works?
Who could have his fill of the ambrosia of the Dharma?
Who could grow weary of staying in a lonely forest?
Who could have enough of benefiting mankind?"

Stretching out his hand, the Tathāgata says
to the Bodhisattvas: "You have given homage;
now return each of you to your own field."
Respectfully, they bow to the feet of the Tathāgata
and depart in different groups,
each going to his own field of action.

And seeing the great attack of Namuci
and the blessed sport of the Sugata,
seeing Māra and his army conquered,
beings send forth a single, unequaled prayer
for Enlightenment: "May we attain Immortality!"

O monks, at the very instant the Tathāgata attained perfect and complete Enlightenment seated on the lion throne, at the foot of the tree of wisdom, there took place the immeasurable play of a Buddha, which could not be described even in the course of a kalpa.

Concerning this it is said:

The earth stretches out as smooth as the palm of the hand;
lotuses arise, and opening their blossoms, cast forth light;
gods by the hundreds of thousands
bow before Bodhimaṇḍa;
the first sign has been heard—the roar of the lion.

Hundreds of trees in the three thousand worlds
bow before Bodhimaṇḍa;
many mountains bow low, together with Meru, their king.
Brahmā and Śakra come to bow down
to the one endowed with the ten strengths;
this too is part of the marvelous play
of the Lion of Men at Bodhimaṇḍa.

Rays of light by the hundreds of thousands
escape from his body; they spread
throughout the great fields of the Jinas,
bringing peace to those in the three lower realms.

At this instant, at this very moment,
all worries are set aside;
suffering, pride, and hatred torment no one any longer.

And still the Lion of Men, seated on his throne,
engages in marvelous play.
The light from the tuft of hair between his brows
eclipses the heavenly lights of the sun and the moon,
and outshines the maṇi stone, fire, and lightning.
And no being in the world can see
to the top of the head of the Spiritual Teacher.

This, too, is the sport of the Lion of Men,
seated on his throne.
At the touch of his hand, the entire earth trembles.
Māra's army is tossed about like tufts of cotton;
and with an arrow, Māra traces pictures on the ground.

The Twenty-second Chapter
Attaining Perfect and Complete Enlightenment

Plate 23

संस्तवपरिवर्तः

།མངོན་པར་བསྟོད་པའི་ལེའུ།

Praise

WHILE THE BODHISATTVA was seated at Bodhimaṇḍa the devaputras of the Śuddhāvāsa realm circumambulated him three times. Raining down divine sandalwood powder, they praised him with these verses:

"The light of the world has appeared—
Protector of the World who brings the light—
you give to the blind world eyes free from emotionality.

"Conqueror in combat,
through your merit, all your wishes are fulfilled.
Rich with accomplishing every pure doctrine,
you will bring satisfaction to all beings.

"Having crossed the swamp of saṁsāra,
you are truly undefiled;
you, Gautama, seated firmly,
will help other beings to cross over—
those carried away by the great current.

"Unsullied by worldly dharmas,
like the lotus from which water slips away,
you are eminent, Great Sage:
a man unequaled in all the world.

"With the lamp of wisdom, you can awaken this world,
asleep for so long, enveloped in shadows.

"O King of Physicians, who has appeared in the world!
You will deliver the distressed,
those long tormented by the fettering passions.

"Since you have come, O Protector,
worries will vanish,
and men and gods alike will be filled with well-being.

"Those before whose eyes you pass,
O Excellent Chief of Men, will not fall
to the lower realms for thousands of kalpas.

"Learned and free from sickness
will be those who listen to the Dharma;
having exhausted every trace of suffering,
having exhausted the aggregates,
they will be without fear.

"Having cut the bonds of the fettering passions,
they will quickly be delivered;
they will never fall into lower rebirths
and will obtain the fruits of great virtue.

"They are worthy of being given gifts in the world,
worthy of receiving offerings;
no gift made to them will be insignificant:
each will be a cause of final deliverance, Nirvāṇa."

O monks, after the devaputras of the Śuddhāvāsa realm had praised the Tathāgata, they bowed to him with palms joined and stood to one side.

Then the devaputras of Ābhāsvara made offerings to the Tathāgata seated at Bodhimaṇḍa, offerings of heavenly flowers, incense, garlands, aloes, and scented powders, of clothing, parasols, victory banners, and standards. After circumambulating the Tathāgata three times, they praised him in chorus:

"Muni with the profound mind, with the sweet voice,
with the melodious voice of Brahmā, like a soft song—
you have passed to the other shore,
obtaining the best benefit of supreme Enlightenment;
we bow down before you.

"You are the Refuge, the firm earth;
you are the Defender, protecting the world
with love and compassion.
You are the Best of Physicians, relieving suffering;
you are the Doctor who applies the sovereign remedy!

"As soon as you saw the Buddha Dīpaṁkara,
you completed the wonderful cloud of love and mercy.
Pour down, O Protector, the rain of amṛta;
calm the sufferings of gods and men!

"In all the three worlds,
you are like the lotus from which water slips away;
you are like Mount Meru, unwavering, unshakable.
Like the diamond, your word is immutable;
like the moon, you are endowed with all great qualities."

O monks, after the gods of Ābhāsvara had praised the Tathāgata seated at Bodhimaṇḍa, they bowed to him with palms joined and stood to one side.

Then the gods of the Brahma realm, headed by the devaputra Subrahmā, created shade for the Tathāgata seated at Bodhimaṇḍa, offering him a net which was adorned with several hundred niyutas of koṭis of precious gems. After circumambulating the Tathāgata three times, they praised him with these verses, fit for the occasion:

"We bow down to the one who is indefatigable,
endowed with unblemished virtue
and the splendid light of wisdom;
who is marked with thirty-two most excellent signs,
and possesses mindfulness, knowledge, and wisdom.

"We bow down to the one with the three eyes of purity,
who bestows the eye of the three liberations;
who is spotless and pure, free from the three defilements;
possessor of the three knowledges,
honored in the three worlds.

"Noble one of mercy and compassion,
your mind is peaceful;
you have cleared away the sorrows of bad times;
you benefit all beings.
Muni, eminent in contentment and perfectly calm,
delighting in equanimity,
you deliver others from uncertainty.

"Eminent in austerities and ascetic practices,
you benefit all beings;
with perfectly pure action,
you have reached the perfection of action.
Teacher of the Four Truths,
you have the joy of complete deliverance;
Delivered One, you will deliver other beings.

"Strong and full of zeal, Māra came before you;
and you conquered him by wisdom, effort, and love.
You have obtained supreme and immortal holiness;
we bow down to you,
conqueror of the army of the deceiver!"

O monks, the gods of the Brahma realm, who were led by the devaputra Subrahmā, having praised the Tathāgata with these verses, bowed low with palms joined and stood to one side.

Then the sons of Māra who had been on the side of purity approached the Tathāgata. Having sheltered him with a jeweled parasol and silken canopies, they joined their palms and praised the Tathāgata with verses fit for the occasion:

"It was granted to us to see the powerful army of Māra
matched against your extensive strength.
It was granted to us to see
you conquer Māra's frightful army in an instant
without ever arising or speaking a word,
without even moving.
We bow down to the Muni Sarvāsiddhārtha,
honored by all the worlds!

"Hundreds of millions of daughters of the demon,
as numerous as the sands of the Ganges,
could not shake you or turn you away
from the tree of Enlightenment.
You have made hundreds of millions of offerings,
as numerous as the sands of the Ganges,
and so today you shine in splendor
at the foot of the tree of Enlightenment.

"Beloved wives, dear sons, servants, and women attendants,
pleasure gardens, cities, and provinces,
kingdoms, royalty, and elephants,
your head, your eyes, and your tongue—
all these you have given up
in performing the actions of a Bodhisattva;
and so today you are resplendent.

"You made a vow:
'I will be a Buddha, armed with contemplation,
with the faculties of supernatural power and wisdom;
I myself will carry beings by the millions
across the ocean of suffering;

I will free them by means of the vessel of the holy Dharma.'
And this vow is fulfilled: you shall free all sentient beings.

"Through the merit of praising you, Chief of Orators,
who gives vision to the world,
we are making joyful prayers for omniscience.
May we obtain the unequaled perfect Enlightenment,
well-praised by the former Buddhas;
may we conquer the army of Māra;
may we too attain the omniscience of a Buddha!"

O monks, after praising the Tathāgata, the sons of Māra bowed to him with palms joined and stood to one side.

Then a devaputra of the Paranirmita vaśavartin realm, who was surrounded and preceded by hundreds of thousands of devaputras, showered the Tathāgata with golden lotuses from the golden rivers of Jambu, and, in the Tathāgata's presence, praised him with these verses:

"Without deviation, error, or falsity are your words.
Delivered from darkness, you have realized Immortality.
Unequaled in heaven or earth,
you are worthy of glory and homage.
Possessor of the light of wisdom, we bow to you.

"Your joyful words delight both gods and men;
you have practiced great austerities

and cleared away the defilements and fetters.
By the light which radiates from your great body,
Master of gods and men, you conquer all the worlds!

"Your skillful action on behalf of others
overcomes the multitudes of adversaries
and clears the minds of all beings.
You are beloved by gods and men—
discerning the conduct of others,
you are learned and prudent.
O you who possess the ten strengths,
may we walk on your path.

"After breaking the bonds of existence and suffering,
you train well the minds of gods and men.
You traverse the four directions like the moon in the sky.
Pray, be our defender and protective eye
here in the three realms of existence.

"Beloved in the world of gods and men,
objects of the senses leave you unmoved;
you rejoice in virtue and dwell free from the joys of desire.
O Eloquent Speaker, you have no peer in the three worlds.
O Guide and Refuge, you are the protector
of all sentient beings as they mature."

O monks, after having praised the Tathāgata, the devaputras of the Paranirmita vaśavartin realm, who were led by the devaputra Vaśavartin, bowed with palms joined and stood to one side.

Then the devaputra Sunirmita, surrounded and preceded by a multitude of gods, sheltered the Tathāgata with silk canopies and praised him, in his presence, with these verses:

"Free from the three defilements,
you appear as the noble light of the Dharma;
you destroy confusion, false views, and ignorance.
You extend majesty and glory everywhere,
establishing in Immortality all sentient beings
accustomed to delighting in false paths.
Coming forth into the world, you are honored
by caityas in heaven and on earth.

"You are the skilled Healer
who gives the happiness of amṛta.
You ease the illnesses of all beings;
by means of the Path of the previous Buddhas,
you clear away the accumulated propensities
toward ignorance, emotionality, and false views.
O Guide traversing the earth,
you are the Greatest of Doctors!

"The sun and moon, the precious maṇi stone,
fire, and the shining gods Brāhma and Śakra
lose their radiance in your majestic presence.

"You produce the light and splendor of wisdom,
and make its glory extend in all directions.
To your majesty and wisdom, we bow our heads.

"O Spiritual Guide with the sweetest of voices,
you clearly show what is true and what is not;
your mind is controlled and calm,
your senses subdued, your heart at peace.
We bow to the Teacher of gods and men
who teaches what is to be taught—
we bow to Śākyamuni, the Great Guide,
worshipped by both gods and men.

"O Wisdom-holder, endowed with great wise words,
you bring knowledge to the three worlds.
You teach the three forms of liberation
and the three realizations,
and remove the three defilements.
You are the Muni, who has known for countless aeons
how to subdue the mind. We bow to you respectfully,
marvel of the three thousand worlds,
honored in heaven and on earth."

O monks, having praised the Tathāgata, the devaputra Sunirmita with his following bowed to the Tathāgata with palms joined and then stood to one side.

Santuṣita then approached the Tathāgata, together with the gods of Tuṣita, and with lacework of gossamer cloth sheltered the Tathāgata seated at Bodhimaṇḍa, praising him, in his presence, with these verses:

"When you dwelt in the Tuṣita heaven,
you taught the Dharma of great extent,

which even today the devaputras practice;
the stream of your teaching flows uninterrupted.

"We can never see enough of you,
and we can never hear our fill of the Dharma.
Ocean of Virtues, Lamp of the World,
we bow down to you respectfully, with head and heart.

"After dwelling in Tuṣita heaven, you came to earth.
The worries there you cleared away.
Seated in front of the tree of wisdom,
you removed all the fetters of sentient beings.

"Having sought and obtained Enlightenment
for the sake of all beings, you have overcome Māra.
Your prayer is fulfilled;
now quickly turn the Wheel of the Dharma.

"Thousands of beings delighted by the Dharma
beg to hear the Teachings again!
Quickly turn the excellent Wheel of the Dharma;
deliver thousands of sentient beings from saṁsāra!"

O monks, having thus praised the Tathāgata, the devaputra Santuṣita with his following bowed to the Tathāgata with palms joined and stood to one side.

Next, the devaputra Suyāma, preceded by the Yāma gods, approached the Bhagavat seated at Bodhimaṇḍa, making offerings to the Tathāgata of flowers, incense, perfumes, garlands, and aloes. Then they praised him, in his presence, with these fitting verses:

"Your good conduct, contemplation,
and wisdom are unequaled.
We bow to you, O Tathāgata, skilled in affection
and in causing complete deliverance.

"We have witnessed the beautiful ceremonies
performed in your honor by the gods
here at Bodhimaṇḍa. No one else
is worthy of such honor from gods or men!

"You have come and have achieved your purpose:
you have done what is difficult to do;
you have conquered Māra with his army;
you have attained unequaled Enlightenment.

"You have spread light into the ten directions,
illumining the three worlds with the lamp of wisdom.
You have cleared away the shadows
and given to the world the peerless vision.

"Your praises, sung for kalpas, are endless—
equal in number to the pores of your skin.
O Tathāgata, Ocean of Virtues,
celebrated by all the worlds,
we bow our heads to you."

Having praised the Tathāgata, the gods led by the devaputra Suyāma bowed respectfully with palms joined and stood to one side.

Next, Śakra, the master of the gods, accompanied by the Thirty-three gods, honored the Tathāgata with flowers, incense, aloes, perfumed powders, garments, parasols, standards, streamers, and displays of all sorts, and praised him with these verses:

"O Muni, you are infallible and irreproachable,
always firm like Meru.
The light of your knowledge
is celebrated in the ten directions,
for you are endowed with great splendor and merit.
O Muni, through having formerly honored Buddhas
by the hundreds of thousands,
in this realm you now have overcome
the army of Māra, here before the tree of Enlightenment.

"Source of good conduct, of revelation,
of contemplation and wisdom, you carry the banner
emblazoned with the emblem of knowledge.
Destroyer of old age and death,
you are the Best of Physicians,
who gives eyes to the world.
O Muni, your heart and senses are peaceful;
you have cast off completely the three defilements.
Chief of the Śākyas, we take refuge in you,
who are King of the Dharma for all beings.

"By the power of zealous effort,
you have practiced to the limits
the noble actions of the Bodhisattva.

You are endowed with the strength of wisdom,
the strength of love and skillful means,
and the strength of virtue.
O Bhagavat, abiding in Enlightenment,
you take these strengths to their limit;
possessor of strength, abiding at Bodhimaṇḍa,
you are now Master of the ten strengths.

"The gods were filled with fear
at the sight of the endless army
of beings arrayed against you,
wondering if the King of the Śramaṇas
would hold strong at Bodhimaṇḍa.
But you had no fear; you never even wavered.
Your hand struck like a heavy weight;
completely terrified, Māra's army was conquered!

"Just as the Buddhas of former times
obtained Enlightenment seated on a lion throne,
so you have become a Buddha as well.
You are their equal, their like;
equal in heart and equal in mind;
there is not the slightest difference.
By your own effort, you have obtained omniscience.
O Highest Being in the world, self-arising,
be the field of merit for all beings!"

O monks, when Śakra, master of the gods, along with the Thirty-three gods, had praised the Tathāgata, with joined palms they bowed respectfully to the Tathāgata and stood to one side.

Then the Four Great Kings together with the devaputras of their realm approached the Tathāgata, carrying garlands and bouquets of abhimuktaka, magnolia, sumana, jasmine, and dhanuṣkarī flowers. Surrounded by a hundred thousand apsarases, they rendered homage to the Tathāgata with heavenly music, praising him with these fitting verses:

"Muni, your sweet speech and your voice touch the heart.
Your mind is clear, your face smiling, your tongue broad.
You produce the best and greatest of joys,
and like the moon you bring tranquility.
O Muni, we bow to you!

"All the sounds and voices of the entire world—
sweet delights for gods and men—
disappear at the sound of your soft voice.

"Your voice calms desire, hatred, and ignorance;
it calms the fettering passions;
it produces pure and heavenly pleasure.
Those assembled will hear the Dharma
with an untroubled mind
and obtain the highest deliverance.

You are not inflated with pride in your knowledge,
and so you do not disdain the ignorant.
Neither haughty nor meek, you are solid,
like a mountain in the midst of the ocean.

"The birth of such a being in the world
brings great benefit to mankind.
Like the goddess of fortune who gives the greatest riches,
so will you give all the world
the great offering of the Dharma."

The Four Great Kings together with the gods of their realm praised greatly the Tathāgata seated at Bodhimaṇḍa, and bowing respectfully with palms joined, they stood to one side.

Then the gods of the sky came into the presence of the Tathāgata, in order to render homage to the perfect and complete Enlightenment. They adorned the entire sky with jeweled nets festooned with tiny bells, and offered the Tathāgata jeweled parasols, jeweled standards, precious earrings, pearl necklaces, and garlands of flowers. And the gods were almost completely covered by these offerings of flowers. The gods of the sky offered flower arrangements to the Tathāgata and praised him, in his presence, with these verses:

"O Muni, from our place in the sky
we see the conduct of all beings in the universe.
We have examined your conduct, Pure Being,
and we find no weakness in your heart.

"The Bodhisattvas have come to render homage to you;
the sky is filled with them, O Guide of Men.
As they have the nature of space,
no harm can touch them or their palaces of crystal.

"Streams of flowers fall from the sky,
filling the great thousands of worlds;
they all fall on your body,
as rivers flow to join the ocean.

"The gods rain down parasols, flower earrings,
pearl necklaces, garlands of magnolias,
and garlands of moons and half moons;
yet the offerings do not become mixed together.

"The sky is filled with gods;
not a hairs-breadth of space remains between them.
All render homage to the most exalted of men;
yet you are neither proud nor astonished."

O monks, having greatly praised the Tathāgata seated at Bodhimaṇḍa, the gods of the sky bowed to the Tathāgata respectfully with palms joined and stood to one side.

Then the gods of the earth rendered homage to the Tathāgata, cleaning and purifying the entire surface of the earth, sprinkling it with scented water and covering it with flowers. Offering a fine linen canopy to the Tathāgata, they praised him with these verses:

"Of all places in the three thousand worlds,
only this place is as indestructible as a diamond.
By this diamond nature,
Bodhimaṇḍa is solidly established.
And he has said: 'May my skin and flesh dry up,
may the marrow of my bones dry up as well
before I arise from here
without having attained Enlightenment.'

"O Lion of Men, had you not blessed
all the three thousand worlds,
they would now have crumbled without exception:
so eager were the Bodhisattvas in arriving
that their footsteps have shaken
the tens of millions of Buddha-fields.

"The benefit obtained here by the gods of the earth
has been beautiful and great;
where the most exalted of beings has walked,
even the grains of dust shine brightly.
All the three thousand worlds have become a caitya,
and your body as well.

"We offer you all nourishing food
on the surface of the earth,
and the hundred thousand streams of subterranean water.
All the earth of the three thousand worlds
we offer to you—pray do with it as you will!

"Everywhere you dwell, walk, or sleep,
may we, sons of Sugata, the hearers of Gautama,

discuss the Dharma and listen to the teachings,
thereby making every root of virtue grow.
May we dedicate everything to Enlightenment."

Having greatly praised the Tathāgata who was seated at Bodhimaṇḍa, the gods of the earth joined their palms, bowed respectfully to the Bodhisattva, and then stood to one side.

The Twenty-third Chapter
Praise

Plate 24

त्रपुषभल्लिकपरिवर्तः

།ག་གོན་དང་བཟང་པོའི་ལེའུ།

Trapuṣa and Bhallika

O MONKS, AFTER RECEIVING GREAT PRAISE FROM THE GODS, the Tathāgata, who had become the perfect and complete Buddha, remained seated with his legs crossed, gazing steadily at the king of trees. Nurtured by the joy of contemplation, he stayed for a week at the foot of the tree of Enlightenment, experiencing bliss.

After the week had passed, the devaputras of the desire and form realms brought twenty thousand vases of scented water to where the Tathāgata was seated, and bathed the tree of wisdom and the Tathāgata with the scented water.

Innumerable gods, nāgas, yakṣas, gandharvas, asuras, garuḍas, kinnaras, and mahoragas gathered up this water —and with this scented water which had flowed from the body of the Tathāgata, they anointed their bodies. Returning to their dwellings, they turned their minds toward perfect and complete Enlightenment. None lacked the fragrant water, and none desired any other scent. Furthermore, through the ecstasy of joy and gladness born in their hearts, through respect for the Tathāgata, they henceforth never turned back from striving to attain perfect and complete Enlightenment.

O monks, the devaputra Samantakusuma descended into this assembly and, bowing at the feet of the Tathāgata with joined palms, asked: "Bhagavat, what is the name of the profound meditation which enables the Tathāgata to remain a week without uncrossing his legs?"

And the Tathāgata replied: "This profound meditation is known as Prityāhāravyūha, Adaptation of the Food of Joy. This is the meditation which allows the Tathāgata to remain a week without uncrossing his legs."

Then, O monks, the devaputra Samantakusuma praised the Tathāgata with these verses:

"Your feet are marked by the Wheel of the Dharma;
you are endowed with the splendor
of a thousand sparkling lotus petals;
the diadems of the gods lie at your feet.
I bow to the feet of the one filled with blessings."

Having bowed at the feet of the Sugata,
the devaputra speaks joyously
to the one who removes hesitation,
and who produces complete peace, even for asuras.

"You are the one who creates joy
in the family of the Śākyas,
who brings an end to desire, hatred, and ignorance,
who resolves all questions;
pray, clear away the doubts of gods and men!

"Why do the Buddhas, endowed with the ten strengths,
and with unlimited knowledge,
sit cross-legged for seven days at Mahimaṇḍa?

"Why, Lion of Men, do you gaze without blinking,
your eyes open for seven days,
when your eyes are perfectly pure,
like the hundred-petaled lotus in bloom?

"Is this a vow made by all the lion-voiced
or a vow of yours alone
which allows you to remain for a week
at the foot of the king of trees
without uncrossing your legs?

"Your face shows the ten strengths;
your teeth are beautiful, even, and white;
you have the sweetest scent;
and your true discourse brings joy to men and gods!"

The one whose face is like the moon replied:
"O son of the gods, listen to my words;
I will briefly answer your queries.

"Just as the king who is consecrated by his kin with holy oil,
must not leave that place for a week,
likewise, when the Jinas with the ten strengths
are consecrated, their prayers fulfilled,
they sit cross-legged at Dhāraṇīmaṇḍa for a week.

"Just as a hero looks at the troops of the enemy
completely conquered without a trace remaining,
so at Bodhimaṇḍa, the Buddhas contemplate
the fettering passions destroyed.

"Desire and anger born of ignorance
are like one's enemies and like thieves;
they destroy what is good without leaving a trace.

"Here, the nine kinds of pride no longer have a home,
for I have destroyed them;
I have abandoned all traces of defilement
and produced the highest wisdom.

"Here, with the clear fire of wisdom
I have burned the roots of all the propensities
for performing wrong actions out of ignorance;
I have destroyed the causes of thirsting for existence.

"With the sword of knowledge
I have cut through the noose of faults
and the concept of 'I' and 'mine';
I have cut off the tight bonds of the afflictions
and severed the solid knot of defilement.

"Here, with perfected wisdom
I have destroyed the deceivers, long my masters:
I have destroyed the aggregates,
together with their inclinations.

"Here, I have abolished all discrimination
and wrong ways of thinking, which end in the great hell;
surely they will never arise again
for not a trace remains.

"Here, with the blazing fire of virtue
I consumed the forest of defilement;
the four errors have been completely burned up
and not a trace remains.

"Donning the garlands
made from the branches of Enlightenment,
I have undone the harmful strands
made from conceptualization
and entwined with the thread of perception.

"The sixty-five difficult passages,
the thirty entrapping types of ignorance,
and the forty defilements—
all have been destroyed here at Dhāraṇīmaṇḍa.

"The sixteen omissions, the eighteen elements,
the twenty-five duties, the twenty currents of emotionality,
and the twenty-eight terrors of beings—
all have been conquered through vigor, strength, and valor.

"Likewise, I have here understood
the five hundred great calls of the Buddha,
and also the complete number
of the hundred thousand Dharmas.

"Here, I have destroyed with the flame of knowledge
the ninety-eight proclivities together with their roots;
even new shoots reappearing have been completely razed.

"With the searing sun of wisdom I have dried up
doubt which has its source in uncertainty
and is watered by views
and the rushing current of desire, banked by non-virtue.

"Hypocritical speech, idle talk, and deception,
jealousy, envy, and hatred—all have been abandoned;
today the forest of emotionality has been cut down
and consumed in the fire of discipline.

"Here, the excellent medicine of wisdom
has stopped the quarrels
which lure beings into bad and rocky paths,
and halted all words insulting to the Saints.

"After acquiring the qualities of wisdom and meditation,
I found the end of tears and lamentations,
of groans and afflictions without exception.

"After attaining meditative awareness,
true samādhi and certainty,
I have conquered all heedlessness, pride, and misery,
the knots of sorrow and the stream of desire.

"With the axe of mindfulness I have cut down
the bushes of emotionality
and the trees of existence firmly rooted in concepts;
with the fire of wisdom
I have burned away the last traces.

"Pride and self-esteem,
those powerful masters of the three realms,
I have conquered with the sword of knowledge,
just as the asuras were conquered by Indra.

"With the powerful sword of wisdom
I have pierced the net of illusion
held in place in thirty-six ways,
and have burned it in the fire of knowledge
here at Dhāraṇīmaṇḍa.

"Here, the fettering passions have been rooted out,
together with their propensities
born of suffering and sorrow;
they have been dug up
by the excellent blade of the plow of wisdom.

"Here, I have completely purified
the naturally pure wisdom eye of sentient beings;
with the great medicine of the wisdom eye
I have destroyed the film of ignorance.

"The four spheres of beings
who are burdened with extensive desires
and troubled by the sea monsters of pride,
have been drowning in the ocean of existence.
But I have dried up this ocean
with the rays of the sun of calm and mindfulness.

"Here, the great roaring fire of desire,
fueled by the multitude of sense objects,
smoking with conceptualization,
has been extinguished by the cool water
of the essence of complete deliverance.

"Here, the storm clouds of the propensities,
generating the lightning flash of pleasure,
resounding with the thunder of conceptualization,
have been rent by the strong wind of effort
and entirely dispelled.

"After obtaining the pure meditation of mindfulness,
with the sword of wisdom
I cut down the fearsome foe—
enmity that agitates the mind in the stream of existence.

"Here, after acquiring love,
the best of banners was flown,
and the grotesque army of Namuci was dispersed,
though strong, courageous, and well-supplied
with horses, elephants, and chariots.

"Having mastered the contemplation of what is harmful,
here I reined in the six horses of the senses,
which were inflated with extreme arrogance
and intoxicated with the five qualities of desire.

"After obtaining the meditation of wishlessness,
here I totally and completely banished
desire, hatred, belligerence, and quarrelsomeness.

"After obtaining the contemplation of emptiness,
here, I completely abandoned
all inner and outer forms of pride,
all investigations and conceptualizations.

"After obtaining the meditation of signlessness,
here, I abandoned without exception,
all the pleasures of existence, both human and divine,
even those at the summit of the realms of existence.

"After attaining the three kinds of complete deliverance,
using the strength of wisdom,
I untied all the bonds of existence.

"Here, having seen the causes, I truly overcame
the notions of permanence and impermanence,
of happiness and unhappiness,
of self and not-self and their causes.

"Here at the foot of the king of trees,
using the weapon of impermanence,
I have penetrated the various kinds of karma,
everything rooted in the six senses.

"Here, with the sun of wisdom
I have cleared away the fog
of confusion and ignorance,

of angry and arrogant views,
which have for so long spread such darkness.

"Here, in the ship of strong effort
I have crossed the great ocean of existence,
full of the sea monsters of desire and intoxication,
churning with waves of craving and conceit.

"Having understood what I have understood here,
I burned up desire, ignorance, and conceptualization.
They fell like grasshoppers into a forest fire.

"Here, I have cured the weariness
of misery and emotionality
found on the path of existence
traveled for countless thousands of kalpas.

"For the sake of the world,
I have clearly understood
what all the adversaries have not obtained:
the Immortality that ends old age and death,
sorrow and suffering.

"I have arrived in the citadel of fearlessness
where the suffering based on the aggregates
and the suffering produced by sense desire
will return no more.

"Here, I have understood all the great inner enemies,
and having understood them,
I have completely burned them up;
in the realm of existence
they will no more find a dwelling place.

"Here, I have understood Immortality,
for the sake of which I have given up

many treasures, even my own eyes, and my own flesh,
for hundreds of millions of kalpas.

"Here, I have understood
what the countless preceding Buddhas understood—
those whose soft and delightful language
is renowned in the world.

"Any beings who arise through dependent origination
are empty—thoughts pass in the blinking of an eye;
all is like a mirage, like a city of the gandharvas:
this I have understood.

"The eye with which I see all the world realms
as clearly as I would a fruit held in my hand,
this eye has been truly purified.

"Here, I obtained completely
the memory of preceding lives and the three knowledges;
now I remember countless hundreds of kalpas
as clearly as if awakening from sleep.

"Gods and men burn fiercely with false ideas,
with errors and mistaken views;
but I have drunk the essence of immortality
which is free from error.

"What purpose do the ten strengths serve?
To radiate love to all sentient beings.
Victorious through the strength of love,
I have drunk of the essence of amṛta.

"What purpose do the ten strengths serve?
To radiate compassion to all sentient beings.
Victorious through the strength of compassion,
I have drunk of the essence of amṛta.

"What purpose do the ten strengths serve?
To radiate joy to all sentient beings.
Victorious through the strength of joy,
I have drunk of the essence of amṛta.

"What purpose do the ten strengths serve?
To radiate equanimity for hundreds of billions of kalpas.
Victorious through the strength of equanimity,
I have drunk of the essence of amṛta.

"The ten strengths were acquired
by all the preceding lion-like Jinas,
more numerous than the sands of the Ganges.
And so I also have drunk of the essence of amṛta.

"When the demon approached with his army,
I uttered the vow: 'I will not uncross my legs
until I have obtained an end to old age and death.'
That vow has been kept.

"Having obtained the ten strengths,
I have conquered even ignorance
with the solid and flaming lightning bolt of wisdom.
And so I now uncross my legs.

"I have obtained the quality of the Arhat;
I have destroyed the defilements without a trace.
The army of Māra has been conquered,
and so I now uncross my legs.

"The five clouds of obscurities
I have torn asunder;
I have cut away the ivy of desire,
and so I now uncross my legs."

Then this Moon of Men, arising from his seat,
sat down upon the lion throne,
having received the great consecration.

With thousands of jeweled vases full of scented water,
the hosts of the gods bathed the Friend of the World,
the possessor of the transcendent qualities
of the ten strengths.

With thousands of musical instruments,
hundreds of thousands of gods and apsarases
all joined together to render endless homage.

And so it happened with the devaputras
in the seven days at Dhāraṇīmaṇḍa,
as there unfolded the cause and circumstance and basis
for the Buddha sitting with his legs still crossed.

O monks, endowed with complete Enlightenment, the Tathāgata dwelt at Bodhimaṇḍa for seven days. There I attained peerless, perfect, and complete Enlightenment, and put an end to the beginningless suffering of birth, old age, and death, which comes forth ceaselessly.

The second week the Tathāgata strolled throughout the regions of the three thousand great thousands of worlds.

The third week the Tathāgata gazed upon Bodhimaṇḍa without even blinking. I had attained peerless, perfect, and complete Enlightenment, and had put an end to the beginningless suffering of birth, old age, and death, which comes forth ceaselessly.

The fourth week the Tathāgata took a short walk from the Eastern Sea to the Western Sea.

Now the demon Pāpīyān approached the Tathāgata and addressed these words to him: "May the Bhagavat enter into Parinirvāṇa! May the Sugata enter into Parinirvāṇa! It is time now for the Bhagavat to pass into Parinirvāṇa!"

O monks, the Tathāgata replied to the petition of Māra Pāpīyān: "No, Papiyan. I will not enter into Parinirvāṇa so long as my monks are not firm, controlled, disciplined, clear-minded, confident, well-versed, and abiding in the Dharma and what is connected with it. They must be able to teach the Dharma, making their knowledge known, silencing their adversaries, and with the aid of the Dharma causing them to have faith; they must be able to accompany their teaching of the Dharma with miracles.

"No, Pāpīyān, I will not enter into Parinirvāṇa until the renown of the Buddha, the Dharma, and the Sangha is solidly established in the world; until countless Bodhisattvas have been given prophecies foretelling their attainment of peerless, perfect, and complete Enlightenment. Until my four Sanghas are controlled, disciplined, clear-minded, pure, and aware, and are able to teach the Dharma accompanied by miracles, I will not enter into Parinirvāṇa."

Hearing this reply, Māra Pāpīyān withdrew to one side and remained motionless. Miserable and defeated, his head low, tracing figures on the earth with a stick, he muttered: "He has overcome my empire!"

Then three daughters of Māra, Ratī, Aratī, and Tṛṣṇā, addressed this verse to Pāpīyān:

"Why are you so disheartened, dear father?
Pray, speak. If it is because of this man,
we will bind him with the chains of passion
and control him like an elephant.
We will quickly place him under your power.
Take heart! You will obtain great satisfaction!"

Māra replied:
"The Sugata is the Arhat of the World;
he could not fall into the power of passion.
He has truly gone beyond my kingdom.
This is the reason for my distress!"

Māra's daughters—heedless women—ignored the words of their father even though they knew about the previous actions of the Bodhisattva who had become a Tathāgata. They took on the aspect of youth in its first flower, and blindly approached the Tathāgata. The Tathāgata paid them no heed except to bless them, at which they changed into decrepit old women. Returning to their father, they cried out to him:

"What you said to us, O father, was true;
he is not led by passion,
and he has truly overcome our empire.
How greatly distressed we are!

"To destroy Gautama,
we magically transformed ourselves—
had the Buddha but looked upon us,

his heart would have been broken!
Good father, make these decrepit bodies go away!"

Māra said:
"Nowhere in any of the worlds do I see
the one who could reverse an action of the Buddha.
Go quickly and confess your fault,
and he will give you back your former bodies,
just as you desire!"

Approaching the Tathāgata, the daughters of Māra implored him: "O Bhagavat, forgive us our fault! O Sugata, it was the fault of ignorant women deprived of light, the action of fools. We were confused and misinformed, for we thought the Bhagavat could be moved! Pray, forgive us!"

The Tathāgata replied to them with this verse:

"Seeking to test what is beyond being tested,
you wish to hollow out the mountain with your fingernails;
to work iron with your teeth;
to pierce mountains with your hands.

"For this reason, young girls, I pardon your fault.
It is progress in the discipline of the Dharma
to see and acknowledge a fault as a fault,
and then to succeed in abstaining from it."

During the fifth week, O monks, there came forth a great tempest, and the Tathāgata stayed with the king of the nāgas, Mucilinda. Mucilinda wrapped his coils around the Tathāgata's body seven times, making a shelter with his crest, saying: "Cold winds must not touch the Tathāgata."

From the east came other nāga kings in great number to wrap the body of the Tathāgata seven times with their coils and shelter him with their crests, saying: "The cold winds must not touch the Tathāgata."

From the south, the west, and the north, just as from the east, came nāga kings to wrap the body of the Tathāgata with their coils and shelter him with their crests, saying: "The cold winds must not touch the Tathāgata." Just like Mount Meru, the king of mountains, this group of nāga kings stood fast, raised erect.

And never had these nāga kings experienced such well-being as that which was theirs for seven days and seven nights because of their close contact with the body of the Tathāgata.

When the seven days had passed and the tempest had abated, the nāga kings unwound their coils from the body of the Tathāgata. After bowing with their heads at his feet and circumambulating three times, each returned to his abode. Mucilinda, too, the king of the nāgas, bowed at the feet of the Tathāgata, circumambulated him three times, and returned to his dwelling.

The sixth week, the Tathāgata traveled from the home of Mucilinda to the foot of the nyagrodha tree. Between the abode of Mucilinda and the nyagrodha tree, on the bank of the river Nairañjanā, the carakas, the parivrājakas, the old śrāvakas, the gautamas, the nirgranthas, the ājīvikas, and others saw the Tathāgata and asked if he had spent the week of the tempest pleasantly.

And, monks, the Tathāgata solemnly spoke this joyous discourse:

"Sweet is solitude for the one well-satisfied,
who has seen and heard the Dharma;
sweet is gentleness in the world
and care for living creatures!

"Sweet is the absence of desire,
and sweet the victory over the defilements.
Control of conceit and pride—
these are the supreme happiness!"

O monks, having seen the world tormented, consumed by birth, old age, illnesses, death, suffering, lamentation, worry, and tribulation, the Tathāgata solemnly spoke this discourse:

"This world is afflicted on all sides
by sound, touch, taste, sight, and smell;
though all are terrified by existence,
they desire it still; they seek it still."

During the seventh week, the Tathāgata remained at the foot of the tree of liberation.

At that time, two brothers from the north, clever and learned merchants of great wealth, named Trapuṣa and Bhallika, were traveling from south to north carrying various kinds of merchandise in a great caravan of a hundred fully-laden carts. They had two very clever bullocks, known as Sujata and Kīrti, both fearless: where other bullocks caused trouble or became afraid as they progressed, these two remained firm, as though tethered to a stake. Neither needed the goad of a spur; they were enticed to motion with handfuls of lotuses or with garlands of sumana flowers.

When the merchants approached the tree of liberation, a goddess of the forest halted the carts by means of a charm. The wheels sank in the earth up to the axle; the harness straps came loose, and all of the parts came undone. Despite all efforts, the carts would not move. The travelers were amazed and frightened: why did these obstacles prevent the carts from moving when the way was flat and smooth?

They attempted to lead the bullocks, Sujata and Kīrti, with a handful of lotuses and a garland of sumana flowers, but the bullocks would not advance. Then it occurred to the travelers that if these two would not move, surely there must be danger ahead. Messengers on horseback were sent ahead, but they returned saying they could see no cause at all for alarm.

To reassure them, the goddess made herself visible, saying: "There is nothing to fear." And so the two bullocks pulled the cart close by the Tathāgata. Catching sight of the Tathāgata shining like fire, adorned with the thirty-two signs of a great man, resplendent with the majesty of the rising sun, the travelers were struck with astonishment: "Who can this be? Is it Brahmā come to earth? Or Śakra, master of the gods? Is it Vaiśravaṇa, Sūrya, or Candra? Or is it some god of the mountain or the god of the wind?"

The Tathāgata indicated his saffron garments, and they said: "Since he wears saffron robes, he must be a wandering monk. We have nothing to fear from him." Faith in the monk having arisen, they counseled with each other: "This must be close to the holy man's meal time. We have a little food." So they said to him: "We have some honey, some cakes, and some peeled sugar cane." These they brought to the Tathāgata, bowing to his feet, and circumambulating him three times. Standing to one side, they spoke to him thus: "May the Bhagavat look upon us with kindness. May the Bhagavat take and accept this food."

At this moment, O monks, the Tathāgata thought thus: "Truly, it would not be fitting if I took the food in my hands. How did the former perfect and complete Tathāgata Buddhas accept food?" And he recognized very well that it was in an alms bowl.

Knowing that the time had come for the Tathāgata to obtain the alms bowl, at that very instant the Four Great Kings approached from the four directions. Bringing four golden bowls, they offered them to the Tathāgata: "May the Bhagavat look upon us with kindness; may he accept these four golden bowls."

But considering the bowls unsuitable for a śramaṇa, the Tathāgata did not accept them. Nor did he accept other sets of bowls made of silver, lapis lazuli, crystal, diamond, and emerald.

Then the Guardians offered four bowls of all sorts of precious materials to the Tathāgata. But considering them unsuitable for a śramaṇa, the Tathāgata did not accept them.

O monks, this came to the mind of the Tathāgata: "What kind of bowl was accepted by the former Tathāgatas, the true Arhats, the perfect and complete Buddhas?" And he recognized very clearly that it was a bowl of stone. Such was the thought which occurred to the Tathāgata.

Then the Guardian, the Great King Vaiśravaṇa, said to the three other Great Kings: "Friends! The blue-bodied devaputras gave us four stone bowls, and when we thought to use these bowls, the devaputra named Vairocana said:

" 'Do not use these bowls, but keep them,
for they will be the object of a famous caitya.
There will come a Jina named Śākyamuni,
and you will offer these bowls to him.'

"Friends, now is the time, now is the moment
to offer these vessels to Śākyamuni;
amidst songs and music,
we will bow to him and give him the bowls.

"These stone vessels are indestructible
like the nature of the Dharma;
they are suitable as offerings to him.
Before another takes them, let us retrieve them."

The Four Great Kings approached the Tathāgata, each carrying a bowl. Each was surrounded by his followers and servants, carrying flowers, cassolettes, garlands, perfumes, and scented ointments, singing and playing musical instruments. After rendering homage to the Tathāgata, they offered him the bowls, each filled with heavenly flowers.

O monks, this came to the mind of the Tathāgata: "These four great and pure kings, filled with faith, have offered four stone bowls to me; but to have four bowls is not fitting. If I accept only one bowl, the other kings will be discontent. But if I take all four bowls, I can bless only one for use."

And extending his right hand, the Tathāgata addressed this verse to the Great King Vaiśravaṇa:

"By offering a vessel to the Sugata,
you will become a vessel of the most excellent teaching.
Having given a bowl to one such as I am,
your mindfulness and judgment will never slacken."

O monks, with great kindness, the Tathāgata took the bowl from Vaiśravaṇa. Then the Tathāgata addressed this verse to the Great King Dhṛtarāṣṭra:

"By offering a bowl to the Tathāgata,
your wisdom and mindfulness will never slacken.
After traversing from happiness to happiness,
you will obtain the exalted clarity of a Buddha."

O monks, with great kindness, the Tathāgata took the bowl from Dhṛtarāṣṭra. Then the Tathāgata addressed this verse to the Great King Virūḍhaka:

"By offering a pure bowl to the perfectly pure Tathāgata,
you will quickly obtain a pure mind
and become worthy of praise from gods and men."

O monks, with great kindness, the Tathāgata took the bowl from Virūḍhaka. Then the Tathāgata addressed this verse to the Great King Virūpākṣa:

"By giving a faultless vessel with faith and faultless intent
to the Tathāgata whose conduct and actions are faultless,
the merit of your pure offering is faultless as well."

O monks, with great kindness, the Tathāgata took the bowl from the hands of Virūpākṣa. Having received these bowls, he blessed them, and by the strength of his good will, he made them one bowl. And solemnly he pronounced this joyous discourse:

"In a former existence,
I gave vessels filled with beautiful fruit,
so now the four gods, the great magicians,
give me four handsome bowls."

Concerning this it is said:

After realizing the meaning of Enlightenment,
and gazing on the great tree for a week,
the Lion of Men arises;
moving with the lion's gait,
he causes the earth to shake in six ways.

With the deliberate pace of the lord of elephants,
he walks with measured steps
to the foot of the tree of liberation.
The Muni seats himself, unshakable as Mount Meru,
and devotes himself to meditation, to contemplation.

At that time, Trapuṣa and Bhallika,
two brothers traveling with a group of merchants,
and five hundred ox carts filled with goods,
enter the śāla wood which is in full bloom.

Because of the splendor of the Ṛṣi,
the cart wheels sink instantly into the earth, up to the axle.
A great fear seizes the merchants,
and they take up swords, arrows, and spears.
They wonder who this could be—
this one living like a gazelle in the forest.
And they gaze upon the victorious Jina,
whose face is like an autumn moon
come from behind the clouds.

Putting aside pride and anger, they bow and ask:
"Who can this be?"
And from the middle of the sky,

a god pronounces these words:
"He is, in truth, a Buddha, acting for the sake of the world.

"For seven days and seven nights,
the Merciful One has taken neither food nor drink.
If you wish to calm all fettering passions, offer food to him—
this one who meditates with body and mind."

Having heard these sweet words,
the merchants give homage to the Victorious One
and circumambulate three times around him.
Full of contentment,
the merchants and their companions prepare food
to give to the Victorious One.

O monks, the cowherds then milked their cows, which had been milling about the outskirts of the clearing, and the essence of butter came forth. The cowherds carried this essence to the two merchants, Trapuṣa and Bhallika, saying: "Lord, know that when the cows were milked, they gave forth the essence of butter. Is this a lucky sign or not?"

Some greedy brāhmins at once replied: "This is no lucky sign. You must make a great sacrifice to the brāhmins."

O monks, then a brāhmin known as Śikhaṇḍin, who in a preceding birth had been a relative of the two merchants Trapuṣa and Bhallika, and had been born again into the realm of Brahmā, now showed himself in the form of a brāhmin and addressed these verses to the merchants:

"You made a prayer in former times:
'After becoming enlightened,
may the Tathāgata obtain a meal offered by us,
and then turn the Wheel of the Dharma.'

"This prayer has been fulfilled.
The Tathāgata has obtained supreme Enlightenment.
Offer him food, and after he has eaten it,
he will turn the Wheel of the Dharma.

"It is through a great blessing,
it is under a favorable star,
that the cows have given forth the essence of butter.
It is through the power
of this great ṛṣi's meritorious works."

After thus commanding the merchants,
Śikhaṇḍin returns to his abode,
and Trapuṣa and all the others are filled with joy.

Collecting the milk from all thousand cows,
they extract the cream to prepare a proper meal.

They wash and purify the precious bowl Abucandra,
capable of holding a hundred thousand palas,
and fill it to the rim with food.

With honey and the precious bowl,
they approach the foot of the tree of liberation,
and say to the Teacher: "Pray, accept this offering;
accept from us this nourishing food."

Out of kindness for the two brothers,
and knowing their former prayer,

the supremely enlightened Teacher accepts the offering;
he eats and then tosses the bowl into the sky.

The devaputra Subrahmā catches
the most precious of bowls,
and even today in the realm of Brahmā,
he honors it in company with the gods.

Then the Tathāgata brought joy
to Trapuṣa and Bhallika by saying:

"May the blessing of the gods be with you!
May success follow you always!
May all your affairs go smoothly
and according to your desire!

"May well-being surround you
like a garland around your head.
May glory stand at your right hand;
may glory stand at your left hand;
may glory surround you.

"Whenever business takes you to the East,
may the eastern stars guard you:
Kṛttikā, Rohiṇī, Mṛgaśrārdrā, Andra,
Punarvasu and Puṣya, as well as Aśleṣā.

"May these seven bright constellations,
guardians of the world presiding over the East,
protect you always!

"May their famous king named Dhṛtarāṣṭra,
master of all the gandharvas,
may he, together with the sun, protect you!

"May his ninety-one sons,
strong and learned, all bearing the name Indra,
protect you with health and well-being!

"May the eight daughters of the gods
who reside in the East:
Jayantī, Vijayantī, Siddhārthā, Aparājitā,
Nandottarā, Nandisenā, Nandinī, and Nandavardhanī,
protect you with health and well-being.

"May the caitya named Chāpala, located in the East,
abode of the Jinas, the Arhat Protectors,
and well-known by them,
protect you with health and well-being!

"May the eastern regions be favorable to you,
and may no evil befall you!
May the gods protect you,
and may you return with great wealth!

"Whenever business takes you to the South,
may the constellations presiding there protect you.
Magha and the two Phālgunī, Hastā, Citrā the fifth,
as well as Svātī and Viśākhā.

"May these seven bright constellations,
guardians of the world presiding over the South,
protect you always!

"May their king named Virūḍhaka,
master of all the kumbhāṇḍas,
may he, together with Yāma, protect you!

"May his ninety-one sons,
strong and learned, all bearing the name Indra,
protect you with health and well-being!

"May the eight daughters of the gods residing in the South:
Śriyāmatī, Yaśamatī, Yaśaprāptā, Yaśodharā,
Su-utthitā, Suprathamā, Suprabuddhā, and Sukhāvahā,
protect you with health and well-being!

"May the caitya named Padma, located in the South,
ceaselessly shining with splendor,
and bathing everything in light,
protect you with health and well-being!

"May the southern regions be favorable to you,
and may no evil befall you!
May the gods protect you,
and may you return with great wealth!

"Whenever business takes you to the West,
may the constellations presiding there protect you!
Anurādhā and Jyeṣṭha, Mūla and Dhṛṭhavīryatā,
the two Aṣāṭhas, Abhijit and Śravaṇa.

"May these seven bright constellations,
guardians of the world presiding over the West,
protect you always!

"May their king named Virūpākṣa,
the lord of the nāgas,
may he, together with Varuṇa, protect you!

"May his ninety-one sons,
strong and learned, all bearing the name Indra,
protect you with health and well-being!

"May the eight daughters of the gods residing in the West:
Alambuśa, Miśrakeśī, Puṇḍarīkā, Aruṇā,
as well as Ekādaśā, Navanamikā,

Śītā, Kṛṣṇā and Draupadī
protect you with health and well-being!

"May the western mountain Aṣṭāṅga,
abode of the sun and moon,
grant you the results you desire,
and protect you with health and well-being!

"May the western regions be favorable to you,
and may no evil befall you!
May the gods protect you,
and may you return with great wealth!

"Whenever business takes you to the North,
may the constellations presiding there protect you!
Dhaniṣṭhā and Śatabhiṣān, as well as the two Bhadrapadas,
Revatī, Aśvinī, and Bharaṇī.

"May these seven bright constellations,
guardians of the world presiding over the North,
protect you always!

"May Kubera the king who commands them,
Naravāhana, the king of all the yakṣas,
may he, together with Maṇibhadra, protect you!

"May his ninety-one sons,
strong and learned, all bearing the name Indra,
protect you with health and well-being!

"May the eight daughters of the gods residing in the North:
Ilādevī, Surādevī, Pṛthvī, as well as Padmāvatī,
Upasthitā, Mahārājā, Aśā, Śraddhā, Hiri, and Sri,
protect you with health and well-being!

"May the northern mountain called Gandhamādana,
and the beautiful mountain Citrakūṭa

which is the abode of the yakṣas and bhūtas,
protect you with health and well-being!

"May the northern regions be favorable to you,
and may no evil befall you!
May the gods protect you,
and may you return with great wealth!

"May the twenty-eight constellations,
seven in each of the four regions,
and the thirty-two daughters of the gods,
eight in each of the four regions;

"May the eight śramaṇas and the eight brāhmins,
in the eight types of villages,
and the eight gods who accompany Indra,
protect you everywhere!

"May good fortune be with you as you depart!
May good fortune be with you when you return!
May you have the fortune to see your relatives again;
and may they be happy to see you!

"May the yakṣas, the Great Kings, and the Arhats,
together with Indra, be kind to you.
May good fortune follow you everywhere,
and may you obtain the happiness of Immortality!

"Protected by Brahmā and by Vāśiva,
by those who are completely delivered,
and by those who are without fault,
always treated with kindness by the nāgas and yakṣas,
may you live for a hundred autumns!"

The peerless Guide, Protector of the World,
praises their respectful offerings:

"By this virtuous work, in a future existence,
you will each be a Jina named Madhusambhava."

This is the first prediction
by the Jina, the Guide of the World.
Henceforth, he will predict
that an endless number of Bodhisattvas
will arrive at wisdom
and reach the stage of irreversibility.

After hearing this prediction of the Jina,
well-satisfied and filled with the greatest joy,
the two brothers and their companions,
take refuge in the Buddha and the Dharma.

The Twenty-fourth Chapter
Trapuṣa and Bhallika

Plate 25

अध्येषणापरिवर्तः

།བསྐུལ་བའི་ལེའུ།

Exhortation

O MONKS, WHILE THE TATHĀGATA WAS DWELLING at the foot of the tree of deliverance after his Enlightenment, he withdrew into solitude. Absorbed in this introspection, he thought upon those who live according to the world: "Alas for their condition. The Dharma I have obtained is profound; it is the Dharma of a perfect and complete Buddha. It is peaceful, very peaceful, completely peaceful, full of contentment, but difficult to see, difficult to understand.

"It escapes investigation and is not in the realm of reasoning; it is venerable and can be known only by Arhats, the learned, and the very intelligent.

"It puts aside every aggregate; it clearly sees everything; it has a sure knowledge; it cuts off all sensations; it is absolute and without ground. It has a cool nature, free of all grasping; it does not rise up again.

"It has not been communicated, and it cannot be communicated; it has completely surpassed the six objects of the senses; it is not subject to rules, not particularized, inexpressible; it is ineffable and beyond sound or speech; it cannot be articulated or demonstrated; it cannot be penetrated; it has completely surpassed all imagining.

"It cuts off all emotionality by the path of calm abiding; it is imageless emptiness; it destroys desire and is free from grasping; it is cessation free from attachment; it is Nirvāṇa.

"If I were to teach this Dharma to others, and they did not understand it, how useless and wearisome it would be; having no reason to teach, I will therefore remain silent, and keep it to my heart." At this moment he recited these verses:

"Deep, peaceful, perfectly pure,
luminous, uncompounded, and like nectar
is the Dharma I have obtained.
Even if I were to teach it,
it could not be known by another.
Certainly, I must remain silent in the forest.

"When there are no words, speech is immaculate;
the Dharma is by its nature like space.
Completely free from the meanderings
of the mind and thoughts,
I know how truly amazing, truly wonderful
and superior it is.

"Not with words and letters,
not by language is it understood;
it is understood by those with sharp minds.
The beings who came to the previous Buddhas
heard this Teaching and attained certainty.

"At this place, the Dharma does not even exist;
existence and non-existence do not exist.
For whoever knows successive cause and action,
existence and non-existence do not exist.

"For hundreds of thousands of immeasurable kalpas,
I lived near the former Jinas;
but until there was no self, no sentient being, no existent,
I did not obtain patience.

"It was in the lifetime that I obtained true patience—
when I understood the nature of all dharmas
to be without birth and death, to be self-less—
that the Buddha Dīpaṁkara gave forth my prophecy.

"My compassion for the world is boundless,
and I do not hesitate to satisfy the requests of others.
This multitude has faith in Brahmā—
if he requests it, I will turn the Wheel.

"If Brahmā supports me, like a lotus at my feet,
and implores me to teach the Dharma;
if his request is unreserved and deeply felt;
if beings are well-disposed toward the Dharma
and desire to know it;
then they are ready to grasp this Teaching."

O monks, from the tuft of hair in the middle of his eyebrows, the Tathāgata sent forth a shining ray of light which filled the expanse of the three thousand great thousand worlds with a great golden brightness.

Then the great Brahmā with his crown of hair, knowing through the power of the Buddha the thoughts in the mind of the Tathāgata, realized that the Bhagavat, in his lack of urgency, was inclined not to teach the Dharma, and he thought: "I must approach the Tathāgata and ask him to turn the Wheel of the Dharma."

At once, O monks, the great Brahmā with his crown of hair addressed himself to the devaputras of the Brahma realm: "Friends, though the Tathāgata has become a perfect and completely accomplished Buddha, he is inclined not to teach the Dharma. Alas! This world is lost! Friends, this world is lost! We must approach the Tathāgata Arhat, the truly perfect and complete Buddha, and implore him to turn the Wheel of the Dharma."

O monks, the great Brahmā with his crown of hair, surrounded and preceded by sixty-eight million gods of the Brahma realm, then approached the Tathāgata. Bowing at his feet, they joined their palms and spoke thus to him: "Alas! O Bhagavat, since the Tathāgata who has become a perfect and complete Buddha is inclined not to teach the Dharma, this world is completely lost! Alas! May the Bhagavat have the goodness to teach the Dharma! May the Sugata teach the Dharma! Beings are well-disposed, easy to teach, sincere, and strong; they are capable of understanding the meaning of the Teaching of the Buddha." And at this point, Brahmā recited these verses:

"Having attained the great and sublime
maṇḍala of wisdom
and poured forth light in all directions,

O Teacher, Light of Wisdom, Lotus of Men,
you remain in equipose,
O Bright Sun of Orators!

"After inviting beings to share your noble riches,
and encouraging tens of millions of living beings,
it is not worthy of you, Friend of the World,
to show indifference to sentient beings through silence!

"Beat loudly the drum of the peerless Dharma!
Quickly blow the conch shell of the holy Dharma!
Raise the offering pillar of the peerless Dharma!
Light the great torch of the Dharma!

"May the excellent rain of the Dharma pour down!
May those on the ocean of existence cross over!
May those sick with emotionality be cured!
May peace come to those burned by the passions!

"Pray, point out clearly the path
of peace, happiness, and prosperity,
free of sickness and far from sorrow.
Without a protector, beings stray
from the path of Nirvāṇa.
O Guide, have pity upon them!

"Open wide the gates of complete deliverance;
uphold the way of the Dharma free of confusion.
For the multitude blind from birth,
O Protector, purify the holy eye of the Dharma!

"In the world of Brahmā, in the world of the gods,
in the world of the yakṣas, gandharvas, and men,
truly you alone can end birth and old age,
O Protector, O Moon of Men.

"Together with all the gods, I am your petitioner,
O King of the Dharma;
through this meritorious action, may I, too,
soon turn the Wheel of the excellent Dharma."

O monks, in his concern for the welfare of the worlds of gods, men, and asuras, the Tathāgata consented with compassion to Brahmā's request by remaining silent.

The great Brahmā with his crown of hair, understanding the silent consent of the Tathāgata, sprinkled heavenly powders of sandalwood and aloes around the Tathāgata, and filled with great gladness, disappeared.

O monks, because of Brahmā's repeated requests, and because of the increasing respect for the Dharma in the world, the Tathāgata withdrew into solitude to consider the extremely profound greatness of the Dharma, and the increase in the root of virtue for the world. Deep within his contemplation, the Tathāgata reasoned thus: "Profound indeed is the Dharma which as Buddha I possess; subtle, clear, and difficult to understand, it escapes analytical investigation. It lies outside the domain of reasoning; it is known by wise men and sages; it does not accord with the worldly dharmas and is difficult to see. It puts aside all the aggregates and calms every karmic inclination; it resolves everything by the path of calm abiding. It is imageless emptiness; it destroys desire and is free from desire. It is cessation, it is Nirvāṇa, the perfect and complete Buddhahood.

"If I were to teach this Dharma, others would not understand it, and would make of it a mockery. So I am left with little sense of urgency to teach."

Then, O monks, the great Brahmā with his crown of hair, knowing through the power of the Buddha the reasoning of the Tathāgata, approached Śakra, master of the gods, and spoke thus: "Kauśika, you must know this. The Tathāgata Arhat, the perfect and complete Buddha, in his lack of urgency, is not inclined to teach the Dharma. Alas, Kauśika, this world is lost! This world is completely lost! Alas, Kauśika! This world will be plunged into the deep, deep shadows of ignorance; it will be plunged into darkness because the Tathāgata Arhat, the truly perfect and complete Buddha, in his lack of urgency, is not inclined to teach the Dharma.

"Must we not go and urge the Tathāgata Arhat, the truly perfect and complete Buddha, to turn the Wheel of the Dharma? For without being so exhorted, Tathāgatas do not turn the Wheel of the Dharma."

"Friend, you are right!" Śakra replied. And when they had spoken thus, many gods went with Śakra and Brahmā: the gods who preside over the earth, the gods of the sky, the gods of the realm of the Four Great Kings, the Thirty-three gods, the gods of the Yāma realm, the gods of Tuṣita, the gods of the Nirmāṇarati realm, those of the Parinirmita vaśavartin realm, and the gods of the Brahmā realm, those of the Ābhāsvara realm, those of the Bṛhatphala realm, those of the Śubhakṛtsṇa realm, and several hundreds of thousands of devaputras of the Śuddhāvāsa realm, all manifesting in brilliant colors. Appearing at the end of the night, they shed a shimmering light upon the foot of the tree of liberation. Approaching the Tathāgata, they bowed at his feet, circumambulated him three times, and stood to one side.

Śakra, the lord of the gods, approached the Tathāgata, placed his joined palms to his head, and bowed before him, praising him with this verse:

"Arise, Conquering Hero.
Bring forth the light of wisdom
into the world which acts in darkness,
for indeed, your mind is freed,
just like the full moon delivered from eclipse."

Thus he spoke, and the Tathāgata remained silent.
Then the great Brahmā with the crown of hair
spoke thus to Śakra, master of the gods:

"Kauśika, this is not the way that Tathāgata Arhats,
truly perfect and complete Buddhas,
are urged to turn the Wheel of the Dharma."

And then the great Brahmā with the crown of hair
threw his robe over one shoulder,
placed his right knee on the ground, and bowed.
Joining his palms in front of his forehead,
he prayed to the Tathāgata:

"Arise, Conquering Hero!
Bring forth the light of wisdom
into the world which acts in darkness.
Teach the Dharma, O Muni,
the Dharma which is sought for everywhere."

Thus he spoke, O monks, and then the Tathāgata gave this reply to the great Brahmā: "Profound indeed, O great Brahmā, is the Dharma which as Buddha I possess; subtle, clear, and difficult to understand, the Dharma escapes analytical investigation. It lies outside the domain of reasoning; it is known by wise men and sages; it does not accord with the worldly dharmas and is difficult to see. It puts aside all the aggregates and calms every karmic inclination; it resolves everything by the path of calm abiding. It is imageless emptiness; it destroys desire and is free from desire. It is cessation, Nirvāṇa, the perfect and complete Buddhahood.

"If I were to teach this Dharma, others would not comprehend it, and would make of it a mockery. And so, O Brahmā, these two verses constantly recur to me:

"My profound path goes against the current;
it is difficult to see.
Those blind with passion will not see it;
even hearing it, they would gain no benefit.

"Fallen into the torrent of desire,
beings are swept along by the current.
I underwent great hardships to obtain this Dharma—
how could it help only to teach it?"

O monks, the great Brahmā with his crown of hair, and Śakra, the master of the gods, recognizing that the Buddha would remain silent, disappeared, together with the devaputras, all afflicted and sorrowful.

Three times the Tathāgata had shown his hesitation to teach.

O monks, in the country of Magadha many false, unvirtuous views had been circulating: no longer, they said, would winds blow or fire burn; no more, they said, would the rain fall or the rivers flow. Some said that the harvest would no longer ripen, that birds would fly no more in the air, and that pregnant women would henceforth not give healthy birth.

Then, O monks, the great Brahmā with his crown of hair, knowing the nature of the Tathāgata's thoughts, knowing also these views of the men of Magadha, illuminated the foot of the tree of liberation with a beautifully colored light, and at the close of the night, approached the Tathāgata. Brahmā bowed his head at the feet of the Tathāgata and then threw back his robe on one shoulder and placed his right knee on the earth. Bowing to the Buddha with his hands joined in front of his forehead, he addressed these verses to the Tathāgata:

"Until now among the men of Magadha
wrong teachings, an impure Dharma, has prevailed.
O Muni, you must open wide the door of immortality,
for they are ready to listen
to the stainless Dharma of a Buddha.

"You have done what must be done
to arrive at independence;
you have abandoned defilement,
the manifestation of suffering;
your virtue increases without fail;
you have arrived at the summit of the supreme Dharma.

"Not one in the world, O Muni, is equal to you;
where would one find your superior?
O Great Ṛṣi, you shine in the three worlds
like the mountain abode of the suras.

"Have pity for the miserable beings!
Never are those such as you indifferent;
O Bhagavat, endowed with the strength of fearlessness,
only you are capable of delivering beings.

"May you free all beings, including gods,
including śramaṇas and brāhmins,
from sickness, plagues, and lingering torments.
For them there is no other refuge!

"May the King of the Dharma keep this before his mind—
to teach the Doctrine undiminished, as it is.
With virtuous mind, intent on Immortality,
gods and men have served you for a long time.

"And so I implore you,
you whose skillful effort is beautiful!
Train those whose path has long gone astray.
O great Muni, this multitude, tormented by desire,
aspires to hear what they have not heard;
they seek to extend their understanding.

"Pray, pour forth the rain of the Dharma.
Like a cloud for a parched earth, O Guide,

produce the rain of the Dharma, which quenches thirst!
Long have men been led astray!

"They are traveling through dense brambles of false views.
Pray, show them the clear path, the path free of thorns;
having meditated upon it,
they will be able to obtain Immortality!

"The blind who have stumbled into the abyss
can only find their way to safety with you as their guide—
you, the keeper of the flock, the one with wisdom.
I beseech you to rescue the blind
from the deep abyss of craving.

"How rare the good fortune to be with you, O Muni.
Like the flower of the uḍumbara,
a Jina who is the Guide seldom appears on the earth.
The moment has come, O Protector.
I pray that you will liberate sentient beings.

"In previous existences you thought:
'When I myself have crossed over, then will I free others.'
You have surely arrived at the other shore.
Make true your promise,
you with the skillful strength of truth.
O Muni, dispel the shadows with the torch of the Dharma;
unfurl the banner of a Tathāgata.
It is the moment to make your sweet words heard—
roar like the king of the beasts
whose voice resounds like a drum!"

O monks, the Tathāgata, gazing upon the entire world with the eye of a Buddha, saw beings of different aptitude and types: lowly, ordinary, and intelligent; exalted or base and inferior; acting well or acting badly; easy to purify or difficult to purify; beings with acute intelligence and with sympathetic natures; and he saw them divided into three categories: one set in the condition of error, one set in the condition of truth, and one uncertain. O monks, just as a man at the edge of a pond sees some lotuses under the surface, some at the water level, and some above the water, likewise, O monks, when the Tathāgata examines the entire world with the eye of a Buddha, he sees beings divided into three categories.

O monks, it occurred to the Tathāgata: "Whether I teach the Dharma or not, those set in the condition of error will surely not be able to understand the Dharma. Whether I teach or not, those set in the condition of truth will surely understand the Dharma. As for those not certain, if I teach the Dharma, they will understand it; if I do not teach, they will not understand it." This was his thought.

O monks, gazing upon beings who belong to the third group, the beings of uncertain outcome, the Tathāgata began to generate great compassion. With complete wisdom and self-mastery, the Tathāgata, knowing the request the great Brahmā would make, addressed these verses to him:

"O Brahmā, for those beings of Magadha who have ears,
the doors of immortality are open!
They will listen to the Dharma with faith
and without thought of doing harm."

The great Brahmā with his crown of hair, realizing that the Tathāgata had given his consent, was pleased and delighted. Elated, his heart filled with joy, he bowed at the feet of the Tathāgata and disappeared.

O monks, the gods of the earth called out to the gods of the air: "Today, friends, the Tathāgata Arhat, the perfect and complete Buddha, has promised to turn the Wheel of the Dharma. Out of compassion for the world, to aid and benefit the great multitude of beings, for the salvation and happiness of gods and men, he will turn the Wheel. Friends, the number of asuras will certainly diminish; the gods will arrive at perfection, and many in the world will then reach complete Nirvāṇa."

Having learned this from the gods of the earth, the gods of the air repeated it to the gods of the realm of the Four Great Kings; they repeated it to the Thirty-three gods; and these to the Yāmas, who repeated it to the gods of the Tuṣita realm. The gods of the Nirmāṇarati realm told the gods of the Parinirmita vaśavartin realm, and they finally repeated it to the gods of the Brahma realm. And these last called out: "Today, friends, the Tathāgata Arhat, the perfect and complete Buddha, has promised to turn the Wheel of the Dharma. Out of compassion for the world, for the benefit, aid, and happiness of the great multitude of men and gods, he will turn the Wheel. Assuredly, friends, the numbers of the asuras will diminish; the gods will increase, and many in the world will attain complete Nirvāṇa."

O monks, at once, at that moment, from the gods of the earth all the way up to the realm of Brahmā, a single sound, a single proclamation traveled in just an instant: "Today, my friends, the Tathāgata Arhat, the perfect and complete Buddha, has made the promise to turn the Wheel of the Dharma."

O monks, the four gods of the tree of wisdom named Dharmaruci, Dharmakāya, Dharmamati, and Dharmacāri, bowed at the feet of the Tathāgata and spoke: "Where will the Bhagavat turn the Wheel of the Dharma?" Questioned in this way, O monks, the Tathāgata replied: "At the city of Vārāṇasī, in the Deer Park in the grove of Ṛṣipatana."

The gods replied: "Meager is the population of the great city of Vārāṇasī, and meager the shade of the trees of the Deer Park. There are large and rich cities, opulent, happy, prosperous, and pleasant, filled with men and numerous creatures, embellished with gardens, thickets, and woods. May the Bhagavat turn the Wheel of the Dharma in one or another of these cities."

"Do not speak in this way, O fair-faced ones," replied the Tathāgata. "And why not?"

"Because in Vārāṇasī I previously made
sixty thousand niyutas of koṭis of offerings.
There I have honored
sixty thousand niyutas of koṭis of Buddhas.
There in the great city of Vārāṇasī
the ṛṣis of old have dwelt.
It is a place always praised by the gods and the nāgas,
where people are constantly striving for the Dharma.

"I remember this most beautiful wood, named by the ṛṣis,
where ninety-one thousand koṭis of Buddhas
formerly turned the Wheel.
This place is matchless, calm, perfectly calm,
contemplative, always frequented by deer.
In this most beautiful of parks,
whose name was given by the ṛṣis,
I will turn the holy Wheel."

The Twenty-fifth Chapter
Exhortation

Plate 26

धर्मचक्रप्रवर्तनपरिवर्तः

།ཆོས་ཀྱི་འཁོར་ལོ་བསྐོར་བའི་ལེའུ།

Turning the Wheel of the Dharma

Now, O MONKS, the Tathāgata had completed what he needed to accomplish, what he had to do. He had cut every bond, cleared away all emotionality, purified the defilements and the fettering passions; he had overcome the opposition of the demon Māra and followed all the ways of the Buddhadharma. Knowing all, seeing all, endowed with the ten strengths, he had obtained the four fearlessnesses and accomplished the eighteen pure Buddhadharmas.

Endowed with the five eyes, having looked over the entire world with the completely unobscured eye of a Buddha, he began to reflect: "To whom should I first teach the Dharma? Pure beings, of good nature, easy to train, easy to teach, easy to purify, with little desire, hatred, and ignorance, beings whose consciousness is not obscured, have been greatly deprived because they have not heard the Dharma. To such beings will I first teach the Dharma. And having heard the Dharma, they will understand it and not make of it a mockery."

O monks, then the Tathāgata reflected: "Truly, Rudraka, the son of Rāma, is pure, of good nature, easy to train, easy to instruct, easy to purify; he has little desire, hatred, or ignorance; his consciousness is unobscured; and for lack of having heard the Dharma, he has been greatly deprived. He is teaching his students the ascetic practices which lead to the stage where there is neither perception nor non-perception. Where is he now?" And with this thought, he knew that Rudraka had been dead for seven days.

Bowing at the feet of the Tathāgata, the gods spoke thus: "So it is, Bhagavat; so it is, Sugata. It has been seven days today since Rudraka, the son of Rāma, has died."

O monks, there came to my thought: "It is a great loss for Rudraka, the son of Rāma, that he died without having heard the good Dharma. Had he heard this Dharma, he would have understood it. I would have taught it first to him, and he would not have made of it a mockery."

O monks, the Tathāgata thought again: "What other pure beings are there, easy to train, easy to teach, easy to purify, with little desire, hatred, or ignorance, beings whose consciousness is not obscured, and who have been greatly deprived because they have not heard the Dharma? To such beings will I first teach the Dharma. And having taught them the Dharma, they will understand it and will not make a mockery of the Teaching."

O monks, the Tathāgata thought again: "Truly, Arāḍa Kālāma is pure, of good nature, easy to train, easy to instruct, easy to purify; he has little desire, hatred, or ignorance; his consciousness is unobscured; and for lack of having heard the Dharma, he has been greatly deprived. If he hears the Dharma, he will understand it and will not make of it a mockery."

The Tathāgata reflected: "Where is he now?" And upon reflecting, he knew that Arāḍa Kālāma had been dead for three days.

The gods of Śuddhāvāsa themselves announced this news respectfully to the Tathāgata: "So it is, Bhagavat; so it is, Sugata. It has been three days today since Arāḍa Kālāma has died."

Then the Tathāgata thought: "Alas, this is a great loss for Arāḍa Kālāma—to have died without having heard the good Dharma."

The Tathāgata thought again: "What other pure beings are there, pure, of good nature, easy to train, easy to instruct, easy to purify; who have little desire, hatred, or ignorance; whose consciousness is unobscured, and for lack of having heard the Dharma, have been greatly deprived? If they hear the Dharma, they will understand it and will not make of it a mockery." The Tathāgata considered: "The five who were my disciples were pure, of good nature, easy to train, easy to teach, easy to purify; they had little desire, hatred, or ignorance; their consciousness was not obscured, and for lack of hearing the Dharma, they were greatly deprived. During the time that I was practicing austerities, they surrounded me with solicitude; they will understand the Dharma I teach, and they will not make a mockery of the Teaching."

And so, O monks, it occurred to the Tathāgata to teach the Dharma first to the five disciples.

The Tathāgata reflected: "Where are these five of good family now living?" And the Tathāgata, examining the entire world with the eye of the Buddha, saw them all in the city of Vārāṇasī in the Deer Park at Ṛṣipatana.

And once he saw them, the Tathāgata considered: "I can certainly teach the five disciples the Dharma, and they will quickly understand it." O monks, why is that? Because they are endowed with good conduct and have gathered pure teachings; they are turned toward the path of deliverance and are free from all hindrances.

O monks, having so reflected, the Tathāgata arose from Bodhimaṇḍa and, traveling through the expanse of the three thousand great thousands of worlds in succession, he passed through the country of Magadha and arrived finally at the country of the Kāśikas.

While traveling on Mount Gaya near Bodhimaṇḍa, the Tathāgata was seen at a distance by another mendicant. As soon as he had seen the Tathāgata, he approached him and stood to one side. O monks, this mendicant engaged the Tathāgata in conversation on several pleasant subjects, and then said: "Āyuṣmat Gautama, you shine with the splendor of brilliant gold, like the color of the autumn berry. How clear are your features, so smooth and pure your radiant complexion! The maṇḍala of your face is perfectly pure and clear, like the golden shine left by the ripe fruit of the tāla when it falls from the stem. So pure and smooth are your features, Gautama! So golden the maṇḍala of your face! Like the pure, clear, and radiant color of gold from the Jambu river when fired by the skillful son of a goldsmith, fashioned into a necklace, and wrapped in a cloth of white wool. So clear are your features, Gautama, so pure is the color of your skin, so smooth and golden is the maṇḍala of your face! With whom did you practice brahmacarya, Āyuṣmat Gautama?"

O monks, the Tathāgata replied to the mendicant with this verse:

"In truth, I have no teacher,
and there is no one like me.
I alone am the perfect Buddha,
cool and clear, free from defilements."

The mendicant said:
"Gautama, do you attest that you are an Arhat?"

The Tathāgata replied:
"I am indeed the Arhat of the World.
I am truly the peerless Teacher.
Among the gods, the asuras, and the gandharvas,
there is no one to equal me."

The mendicant then asked:
"Gautama, do you affirm that you are a Jina?"

The Tathāgata replied:
"Whoever has destroyed the defilements
is understood to be a Jina, just as I am,
for I have conquered all the teachings that are wrong.
I am truly the Conqueror, O Upaga."

The other said:
"Āyuṣmat Gautama, where then are you going?"

The Tathāgata replied:
"I am on my way to Vārāṇasī,
and there in the city of the Kāśikas,
I shall emit a light without equal
for the world which is as though blind.

"I am on my way to Vārāṇasī,
and there in the city of the Kāśikas,
I shall beat the great drum of immortality
for the world which is as though deaf.

"I am on my way to Vārāṇasī,
and there in the city of the Kāśikas,
I shall turn the Wheel of the Dharma,
which has never before been turned in the world."

The mendicant replied: "So be it, Gautama. May it be so." And speaking thus, he went toward the south, while the Tathāgata went toward the north.

O monks, Sudarśana, the king of the nāgas, then invited the Tathāgata to take refreshment and to stay at Mount Gaya. Afterward, the Tathāgata traveled to Rohitavastu, and from there to Uruvilvākalpa; from there to Aṇāla, and then to the city of Sārathi; and in all of these places, O monks, the Tathāgata was invited to partake of a meal and to remain. Finally, the Tathāgata arrived at the bank of the Ganges which, at that time, O monks, was overflowing its banks.

O monks, the Tathāgata approached the ferryman in order to cross to the other shore. "Gautama must pay the price of passage," said the ferryman. "Friend, I have no money for passage," the Tathāgata replied, and speaking thus, the Tathāgata crossed from one shore to the other through the sky. Seeing this, the ferryman was full of regret and said to himself: "O why did I not carry over one so worthy of honor! Ah! What a misfortune!" And so speaking, he fell senseless to the earth.

Later, the ferryman reported what had happened to King Bimbisāra, saying: "O King, the Śramaṇa Gautama from whom I asked toll said that he had nothing with which to pay the price of passage. And then he went from one shore to the other through the sky." Hearing these words, King Bimbisāra abolished the toll for all mendicant monks from that time on.

Thus, O monks, after traveling through several lands, the Tathāgata arrived finally at the great city of Vārāṇasī. On his arrival, he put on the outer robes of a monk, took his begging bowl, and entered the city in order to ask alms. After acquiring what he needed for food, after eating what he had received, he went toward the Deer Park of Ṛṣipatana where the five disciples were staying.

When the five disciples saw the Tathāgata approaching from afar, they said to each other: "The Śramaṇa Āyuṣmat Gautama approaches—the lax one, the glutton, the one who has neglected his practice. Practicing mortifications, he was formerly unable to manifest superior knowledge above human teachings; how much less possible for him to manifest special and exalted wisdom now that he takes alms and eats nourishing food. What a lax person; what a glutton! We should not welcome this unfortunate person or rise in his presence; we will not take his monk's cloak or his begging bowl; it is not appropriate to give him a seat, to give him food or drink or a place to rest his feet. We will say: 'There are no other seats than these, Āyuṣmat Gautama. These are the only seats there are.' If he desires to sit down, very well, let him sit." This was their agreement.

The Āyuṣmat Ajñānta Kauṇḍinya did not approve of this in his mind, but he did not speak his disapproval.

O monks, the closer the Tathāgata advanced toward the five disciples, the more ill at ease they felt. Wanting to arise from their seats, they were like caged birds singed by a fire beneath the cage—like birds desiring to fly quickly away to escape the torment of the fire. And so, the five disciples were increasingly ill at ease on their seats. Why? Because there is no person anywhere who, on seeing the Tathāgata, would not arise from his seat. The closer the Tathāgata came, the less the five were able to endure his splendor and majesty; they became agitated on their seats, and breaking their agreement, each arose to honor him. One stepped forward to take his begging bowl and his robe; one prepared his seat; another brought water for washing his feet; and another brought him something on which to rest his feet. "You are welcome, Āyuṣmat Gautama! You are welcome! Pray, sit down, Āyuṣmat Gautama, on this seat prepared for you!"

O monks, the Tathāgata sat down upon the seat. Then the five disciples, after engaging him in conversation on various pleasant and interesting subjects, stood to one side. And together, the five spoke to the Tathāgata: "Āyuṣmat Gautama, your features are perfectly clear. Your complexion is perfectly pure." And so on. "Āyuṣmat Gautama, have you manifested the superior vision of saintly exalted wisdom above human knowledge?"

Thus questioned, O monks, the Tathāgata said to the five disciples: "Monks, do not call the Tathāgata 'Āyuṣmat', meaning 'long-lived'; for a long time now, this state has brought you neither profit, help, nor well-being. Monks, I have made manifest amṛta and the path which leads to Immortality. I am a Buddha, O monks, omniscient, all-seeing, clear and free from the defilements. Master of all the Dharma, O monks, I myself will explain the Dharma.

"Come, listen. Be zealous and listen carefully. I myself will speak and teach; I will instruct and counsel you. When I indicate the true Teaching and instruct you in the true Teaching, you will destroy the defilements and free the mind of these afflictions. You will liberate your understanding within this very lifetime and manifest complete self-knowledge. You will destroy birth and achieve the state of brahmacarya, doing what must be done. You will know no further births. You will have true understanding.

"O monks, did this not come into your thoughts: 'There is the Āyuṣmat Gautama approaching, the lax one, the glutton, the one who has neglected his practice,' and so on. Did you not think: 'If he desires to sit down, then just let him sit'?"

And the instant he spoke, O monks, every mark, every sign marking the five monks as tīrthikas, disappeared, and they found themselves clothed in the three garments of a monk, holding begging bowls, and their heads shaved clean. It was as if they took on the honorable conduct of one who has been a monk for a hundred years; they became quintessential monks, perfect in renunciation.

O monks, bowing at the feet of the Tathāgata, the five monks at once confessed their mistake; recognizing the

Tathāgata as Teacher, they gave him their full love, faith, regard, and respect.

Filled with devotion, surrounding him with attentions, they prepared a beautiful pond of clear and pure water for the Tathāgata.

O monks, when the Tathāgata came forth from the clear water, he thought: "Wherever the Tathāgata Arhats, the perfect and complete Buddhas of former times, have dwelt, they have turned the Wheel of the Dharma." And monks, at the spot where the Tathāgata Arhats, perfect and complete Buddhas had turned the Wheel of the Dharma, a thousand jeweled thrones appeared.

The Tathāgata, out of respect for the former Tathāgatas, circumambulated three of these thrones, and then like a fearless lion, sat down upon the fourth, with his legs crossed. At once, the five monks bowed their heads to the feet of the Tathāgata and sat down before him.

At that moment, O monks, the Tathāgata radiated such a light from his body that all the three thousand great thousands of worlds were enveloped in splendor, and the world which had been covered with the darkness of evil, was bathed in light. He appeared in the world like the sun and moon, which are renowned for their great strength, power, and energy; he appeared like a great magical apparition, outshining the light of the sun and moon, outshining their color, and outshining their glory. Everywhere was wrapped in the splendor of this brilliant flash of light, even those places so dark that beings born there could never even see their hands before their faces. Now, wrapped in this splendor, they saw and recognized each other. And they spoke thus: “Ah! Other beings have been born here. Ah! Other beings have indeed been born here!”

And this region of the three thousand great thousands of worlds trembled in six ways with the eighteen great signs: it trembled, trembled strongly, trembled strongly on all sides; it was shaken, shaken strongly, shaken strongly on all sides; it was jolted, jolted strongly, jolted strongly on all sides; it undulated, undulated strongly, undulated strongly on all sides; it resounded, resounded strongly, resounded strongly on all sides; it echoed, echoed strongly, echoed strongly on all sides; it was lowered on the edge, raised in the middle; it was lowered in the middle, raised at the edge; it was lowered in the east and raised in the west; it was lowered in the west and raised in the east; it was lowered in the north and raised in the south; it was lowered in the south and raised in the north.

At this moment, joyful sounds were heard: fascinating, praise-worthy sounds producing contentment and delight; sounds of which one cannot hear enough, harmonious and soothing. At this moment, not a single being was afflicted, frightened, or upset. The splendor of the sun and the moon disappeared, the splendor of Śakra, Brahmā, and the Guardians of the World disappeared. At that moment, all the beings of the lower realms, born either as animals or in the world of Yāma, were delivered from suffering and filled with happiness. No being felt attachment, hatred, or ignorance, jealousy, greed, vanity, or hypocrisy, anger, malevolence, or meanness. At that moment, all beings had for each other benevolent thoughts, loving thoughts like those of parents toward their children. And from the network of light radiating from the body of the Tathāgata, these verses came forth:

After he had left the Tuṣita heaven,
he entered his mother's womb;
after he was born in the Lumbinī garden,
he was taken up in the arms of Śakra, husband of Śacī.

He took seven firm steps
with the proud gait of a lion,
and spoke with a melodious voice like Brahmā's:
"I am the Principal Being in the world!"

To aid all beings, he gave up the four continents
and became a wandering monk.
And after difficult ascetic practices,
he approached the place called Mahimaṇḍa.

After he overcame the demon and his army,
he gained Enlightenment for the good of the world.
And then he came to Vārāṇasī
to turn the Wheel of the Dharma.

Brahmā and the gods exhorted him
to turn the Wheel of Serenity;
seized with compassion for the world,
the Muni gave his consent.

Behold the one who, faithful to his promise,
has come to Vārāṇasī, come to Mṛgadāva, the Deer Park;
here the Tathāgata, the Glorious One,
will turn the matchless Wheel.

Those who wish to hear the Dharma won by the Jina
through hundreds of millions of kalpas,
let them come in haste.

Very difficult to obtain is the human state,
and the state of a Buddha, even harder;
faith, too, is difficult to obtain.
The eight worldly influences are hard to set aside.
Most important is the opportunity
to listen to the Dharma.

Should you obtain all these conditions:
leisure as well as faith,
the opportunity to listen to the Dharma,
and the coming of a Buddha,
throw off all hesitation!

For hundreds of thousands of kalpas
you have lived in conditions
where the Dharma has not been heard;
today, you have obtained the opportunity,
so abandon all hindrances!

From the earth realm up to the Brahma realm,
this voice exhorts the hosts of gods:
"Come quickly, everyone!
The Guide of the World
will turn the Wheel of Immortality!"

And exhorted by this great divine voice,
the gods abandon their prosperous circumstances
in an instant,
to come before the Buddha.

O monks, in preparation for the turning of the Wheel of the Dharma at Deer Park, the gods of the earth at Vārāṇasī traced the great Tathāgata Wheel at Ṛṣipatana in a supernatural manner; it was beautiful and wonderful to see, wide, extensive, spreading to the distance of seven hundred yojanas. The vault of the sky was decorated by the gods with parasols, victory banners, standards, and tapestries; the devaputras of the desire and the form realms offered eighty-four thousand thrones to the Tathāgata, saying: "After having seated yourself here, may the Bhagavat, in kindness to us, turn the Wheel of the Dharma!"

O monks, at that moment, from the East, the South, the West, the North, from the zenith and the nadir, from all the ten directions, tens of millions of Bodhisattvas who had formerly made Bodhisattva aspirations came and bowed to the feet of the Tathāgata, asking him to turn the Wheel of the Dharma.

And all of those renowned in the three thousand great thousands of worlds for their great power, Śakra, Brahmā, and the Guardians of the World, all bowed at the feet of the Tathāgata and begged him to turn the Wheel of the Dharma: "May the Bhagavat turn the Wheel of the Dharma! May the Sugata turn the Wheel of the Dharma for the benefit of the great multitude of sentient beings. For the happiness of gods and men, and out of kindness for the world, O Bhagavat, pray make the offering of the Dharma! Let fall the great rain of the Dharma! Unfurl the great banner of the Dharma! Blow the great conch shell of the Dharma! Beat the great drum of the Dharma!" Thus did they exhort the Tathāgata to turn the Wheel of the Dharma.

Concerning this it is said:

From the three thousand worlds,
Brahmā and Śakra and the Guardians of the World
come in great number;
they bow to the feet of the Victorious One, saying:
"Remember your former vow, O Great Muni:
'As the first and the holiest,
I will destroy the suffering of all living beings.'

"O Muni, before the king of trees
you conquered Māra with his army;
you attained Enlightenment and the calm of a Buddha,
and the trees of the fettering passions were felled.
The purpose you envisioned for a hundred kalpas
is completely fulfilled.
Looking upon beings who lack a protector,
pray, turn the great Wheel of the Dharma!"

Hundreds of thousands of Buddha-fields
are illumined by the Sugata's splendor;
hundreds of Buddha sons arrive
through the force of supernatural power.
With great quantities of offerings to the Sugata,
they praise the Tathāgata for his great virtues
and implore the one full of compassion:

"Cloud of compassion, lightning bolt of wisdom,
whose intense insight is like the wind,
for thousands of kalpas
beings have been welcomed with a voice of thunder.
The stream of the eight attributes
pours down to quench the thirst of the world.
You who are powerful and steeped in meditation
increase the harvest of liberation.

"For many thousands of kalpas
well-instructed, abiding in Thatness,
you have obtained the remedy
which comes from the Dharma.
You know the conduct of beings,
how the hundreds of sicknesses of emotionality
torment all living beings.
Possessing the remedy of the Jinas,
O Liberator, turn the Wheel of the holy Dharma!

"You have long developed the six Pāramitās;
unequaled, immutable, and complete,
you have accumulated the wealth of the Dharma.
Seeing the unfortunate ones without protector or guide,
share the seven precious things, O Guide,
and turn the Wheel of the Dharma!

"Joyfully you have given up worldly goods:
fortunes of gold and silver, all your beautiful clothes,
flowers, ointments, and cassolettes,
marvelously perfumed powders,
the most beautiful palaces, the most beautiful women,
your kingdom, and your cherished son,
to search for the Enlightenment of the Jinas.
So turn the excellent Wheel of the Buddha.

"Your conduct you have kept intact,
spotless for hundreds of kalpas;
always patient and zealously brave,
Muni, you are well-acquainted
with the best of contemplations,
with omniscience and with insight!
Your desire is perfectly fulfilled;
you who are untrammeled by misery,
pray, turn the Best of Wheels!"

O monks, as soon as this thought was generated, the Bodhisattva Mahāsattva Cakravartin offered a Wheel of the Dharma adorned with precious things from the golden river of Jambu. It was embellished with gems and various ornaments; from its thousand spokes radiated a thousand beams of light; its hub and circumference were decorated with garlands of flowers, nets of gold, a network of tiny bells, a gandhahasta, a full urn, a nandikāvarta, and a svastika. Colored in different hues, it was draped with gossamer cloth. Flowers and divine garlands covered it, and perfumes and aloes scented it. Everything most precious belonged to it, by virtue of a former prayer by the Tathāgata to turn the Wheel of the Dharma. Totally pure, in keeping with the pure mind of the Bodhisattva, it was a fitting offering for the Tathāgata. Well-understood by all the Tathāgatas, this Wheel had perfect balance through the blessings of all the Buddhas. This is the Wheel turned previously by other Tathāgata Arhats, truly complete Buddhas, who offered it now to the Tathāgata.

Then the Bodhisattva Cakravartin, bowing with his palms joined, praised the Tathāgata with these verses:

"When Dīpaṁkara made the prediction for the Pure Being:
'You will be a Buddha, Lion among the lions of men,'
at that moment, this was my prayer:
'When he attains perfect Enlightenment,
may I urge him to preach the Dharma!'

"Countless beings have come here,
holy beings from all ten directions.
Bowing at his feet, with their palms joined,
they urge the son of the Śākya clan
to turn the Wheel of the Dharma.

"All the displays produced at Bodhimaṇḍa
by the gods and the sons of the Jinas
have been set forth
for the sake of turning the Wheel of the Dharma.
The good fortune cannot be measured or expressed.

"The heavens of the three thousand worlds
are filled with gods;
the earth is covered with asuras, kinnaras, and men;
nowhere can the slightest murmur now be heard:
calm and still, all turn complete attention toward the Jina."

O monks, during the first watch of the clear night, the Tathāgata did not say anything. At the midnight watch, he spoke of many things. At the last watch of the night, after summoning the five disciples, he said to them:

"O monks, there are two extremes to be avoided by one who becomes a wandering monk. As a monk, whatever you want can be obtained just by asking, so do not ask for the unnecessary and useless things desired by ordinary people. Your needs are very different. Should you possess harmful things, in the next life you will not develop the state of brahmacarya or interest in the Teachings. You will not attain the absence of desire; you will not be able to stop such negativities; you will not obtain wisdom or perfect Enlightenment or Nirvāṇa. For this is not the Middle Way.

"And then there are those who would mistreat their bodies. By this extreme, one suffers and is filled with distress. And the misery in this life ripens into misery in future lives.

"O monks, having abandoned these two extremes, the Tathāgata will teach the Dharma by means of the path of the Middle Way: right view, right intention, right speech, right action, right livelihood, right effort, right mindfulness, right meditative concentration.

"O monks, here are the Four Noble Truths. What are these four? They are suffering, the source of suffering, the cessation of suffering, and the way that leads to the cessation of suffering.

"And what is suffering? Suffering is the suffering of birth, the suffering of old age, sickness, death, separation from what one desires, and union with what one does not desire. This is suffering. When one desires something and does not obtain what is desired even after zealously seeking it, that indeed is suffering. In short, the taking up of the five aggregates is suffering. This is suffering.

"And now, what is the source of suffering? It is desire for pleasure; it is pleasure which comes only now and again. This is the source of suffering.

"What is the cessation of suffering? The cessation of suffering is being free from all desire—free from the desire which comes forth ceaselessly, the desire for pleasure, the desire which manifests itself again and again, the desire which is always generated, and even desire which is attained. This is the cessation of suffering.

"What is the way which leads to the cessation of suffering? The way is the Eightfold Noble Path itself: right view up through right meditative concentration. This is the truth of the Noble Path which leads to the cessation of suffering. O monks, these are the Four Noble Truths.

"O monks, concerning this Teaching not heard before, by setting my mind on the nature of suffering, I produced knowledge, I produced vision, I produced realization, I produced abundant knowledge, I produced deep humility, and wisdom—and light came forth.

"O monks, concerning this Teaching not heard before, by setting my mind on the nature of the source of suffering, I produced knowledge, vision, and realization; I produced abundant knowledge, deep humility, and wisdom—and light came forth.

"O monks, concerning this Teaching not heard before, by setting my mind on the nature of the cessation of suffering, I produced knowledge, vision, and realization; I produced abundant knowledge, deep humility, and wisdom—and light came forth.

"O monks, concerning this Teaching not heard before, by setting my mind on the path which leads to the cessation of suffering, I produced knowledge, vision, and realization; I produced abundant knowledge, deep humility, and wisdom—and light came forth.

"O monks, suffering must surely be understood. By setting my mind on this, I produced knowledge, vision, and realization; I produced abundant knowledge, deep humility, and wisdom—and light came forth.

"O monks, concerning this Teaching not heard before, the source of suffering must surely be forsaken. And by setting my mind on this, I produced knowledge, vision, and realization; I produced abundant knowledge, deep humility, and wisdom—and light came forth.

"O monks, this cessation of suffering must surely be made manifest. And by setting my mind on this, I produced knowledge, vision, and realization; I produced abundant knowledge, deep humility, and wisdom—and light came forth.

"O monks, the path which leads to the cessation of suffering must surely be cultivated. And by setting my mind on this, I produced knowledge, vision, and realization; I produced abundant knowledge, deep humility, and wisdom—and light came forth.

"O monks, concerning this Teaching not heard before, suffering is completely understood. And by setting my mind on this, I produced knowledge, vision, and realization; I produced abundant knowledge, deep humility, and wisdom—and light came forth.

"O monks, concerning this Teaching not heard before, the source of suffering is abandoned. And by setting my mind on this, I produced knowledge, vision, and realization; I produced abundant knowledge, deep humility, and wisdom—and light came forth.

"O monks, concerning this Teaching not heard before, the cessation of suffering is made manifest. And by setting my mind on this, I produced knowledge, vision, and realization; I produced abundant knowledge, deep humility, and wisdom—and light came forth.

"O monks, concerning this Teaching not heard before, by practicing the path which leads to the cessation of suffering, I produced knowledge, vision, and realization; I produced abundant knowledge, produced deep humility, and wisdom —and light came forth.

"O monks, in this way, I set my mind on the Four Noble Truths, repeating this three times until I had produced true comprehension of this twelvefold cycle.

"O monks, I did not declare that I had accomplished Buddhahood, which is perfect, complete, and unexcelled Enlightenment, until I had repeated the Four Noble Truths three times and had gained true comprehension of the twelve aspects. When I arrived at knowledge, then I attained the truly balanced liberation of wisdom. Having manifested the truly unswerving liberation of wisdom, then O monks, I made this declaration: 'I have attained the perfect and complete Enlightenment of a Buddha. I have generated the vision of wisdom; for me, birth is exhausted. I have practiced brahmacarya, I have done what must be done, and I will know no further existence.' "

Concerning this it is said:

The one with the sweet melodious voice of Brahmā,
with the voice like the song of the kinnaras,
the one exalted by attributes
numbering hundreds of thousands,
the one who for hundreds of millions of kalpas
meditated without pause on truth,
Śākyamuni, self-arising, speaks to Kauṇḍinya:

"The eye is impermanent and non-enduring;
likewise, the ear and nose;
also the tongue, the body, and the mind.
They are by nature suffering, self-less,
empty and hollow;
they are like grass or a wall, non-independent.
They do not even have a self, a name, or life.

"All these dharmas come forth
in dependence on causes;
they are free from the two extremes
of existence and non-existence.
They are like the sky.
There is neither a creator nor one who feels;
only the karma of virtuous and nonvirtuous actions
carries on.

"In this way, suffering arises
in dependence on the aggregates,
and watered by desire, it increases greatly.
By means of the path, one sees all dharmas as equal,
and by means of the Dharma, which cleanses and purifies,
one puts an end to suffering.

"When delusive mental activity is understood,
this complex of production is no more.
The ignorance which brings it forth does not arise;
there is nothing for it to come from.
When the cause of karmic dispositions is removed,
there is no driving influence
drawing one thing after another.
It is in dependence on this driving influence
that consciousness comes forth.

"From consciousness comes forth name and form;
from name and form come forth the six senses.
Contact arises in connection with the six senses;
from the six senses come forth the three forms of feeling.

"Even the smallest feeling, whatever it may be,
proceeds to craving.
From craving and its wake
come forth the mass of sufferings;
from remembered attachment comes forth all that exists;
from the circumstances around existence birth comes forth.

"Old age, sickness, and suffering
have birth as their basis;
as with this net of existence,
the forms of production are many.
Thus for every living being,
through causes and circumstances all things come about.
There is no self or person that is moving from life to life—

"There is no conceptual activity, no conceptualization;
there is only the expression of the way things are.
Knowing the way things are,
there is no more ignorance.
When there is no more ignorance,
all the branches of existence are extinguished;
they do not arise.

"This succession of connected circumstances
the Tathāgata has understood;
therefore, self-arising, he taught himself.
The heap of senses and aggregates
is not 'the Buddha';
Buddha is the understanding of causes, only that.

"The paratīrthikas have no chance to see this.
Debate is empty concerning the Dharma.
It is the perfectly pure beings–
those who have formerly accomplished
the work of a Buddha–
who are the fortunate ones
able to understand this Dharma."

Thus, the Wheel of the Dharma with twelve aspects
has been turned.
It has been understood by Kauṇḍinya,
and so the Three Jewels have been made manifest.

The Buddha, the Dharma, and the Sangha,
these are the Three Jewels.
From being to being the news spreads
up to the abode of Brahmā:

"The spotless Wheel has been turned
by the Protector, the Guide of the World.
The Three Jewels, so difficult to obtain,
have appeared in the world!"

Kauṇḍinya and the other four monks,
as well as sixty koṭis of gods,
purified the Dharma eye.

At the turning of the Wheel of the Dharma,
eighty koṭis of gods from the realm of form
perfectly purified their vision.

Eighty thousand men approached;
their vision was thoroughly purified,
and they were delivered from all wrong paths.

At that instant,
to the farthest reaches of all the ten directions,
there sounds the voice of the Buddha,
sweet and melodious, beautiful and heart-touching.
These words are heard everywhere:
"The One who possesses the ten strengths,
the great leader of the Śākyas,
has come to Ṛṣipatana, and there at Vārāṇasī
has turned the Wheel of the Dharma."

In the ten directions, all the Buddhas become silent.
The attendants of these Munis ask the Jinas:
"Having heard this great voice,
O you who possess the ten strengths of the Buddhas,
your discourse of the Dharma is interrupted.
Please, quickly tell us why you are silent!"

The Jinas reply: "Through great effort,
in hundreds of previous existences,
many hundreds of thousands of Bodhisattvas
have obtained Enlightenment,
but now they stand aside,
for this one who is the Great Benefactor,
the one most purified,
has obtained the final blessed Enlightenment.
He will turn the Wheel of the Dharma three times—
therefore, we remain silent."

Hearing this discourse of the Munis,
hundreds of koṭis of beings generate the power of great love
and enter into blessed supreme Enlightenment, saying:
"By the effect of the power of the great effort of that Muni,
even we can learn the Noble Way.
Pray, quickly grant the world the Dharma vision."

Then Maitreya Bodhisattva spoke thus to the Bhagavat: "Bhagavat, these Bodhisattvas who have assembled from the ten directions wish to hear from the Bhagavat in detail concerning the turning of the Wheel of the Dharma. May the Bhagavat Tathāgata Arhat, the perfect and complete Buddha explain in what form the Wheel of the Dharma is turned by the Tathāgata."

The Bhagavat replied: "O Maitreya, this Wheel of the Dharma is profound, for its depth cannot be imagined. Being non-dual, it is difficult to see.

"Ungraspable by any action of the mind, it is hard to understand. Because it realizes the sameness of consciousness and wisdom, it is difficult to discern.

"Possessing complete unobscured deliverance, it is free of disruption. Because it is free from employing examples, it is subtle. Obtained by vajra-like wisdom, it is quintessential.

"Because what is previous has no ending, it is indivisible. Rid of all error of conditions, causes, and conceptualization, it is difficult to reflect upon. Being the ultimate absolute, it cannot be confused. Like space, it is everywhere.

"Truly, Maitreya, this Wheel of the Dharma is the Wheel of the World, revealing completely its essence and the nature of all dharmas.

"It is the Wheel without birth, without cessation, without origin. It is the Wheel without ground of being; it realizes the way of the Dharma free from delusive mental activity, free from conceptualization.

"It is the Wheel of emptiness, signlessness, and wishlessness; Wheel without ideation; Wheel of solitude; Wheel free from desire; Wheel of cessation.

"It is the Wheel understood by the Tathāgata; Wheel of the pristine Dharmadhātu; Wheel not confusing the absolute; Wheel without attachment, without obscurity; the Wheel which goes beyond the two extreme views linking with what went before; the Wheel clarifying the Dharmadhātu as having no middle or end; the Wheel which does not interrupt the spontaneous action of a Buddha; the Wheel which has no entrance and no final achievement.

"Wheel most imperceptible; not accepting, not rejecting; inexpressible Wheel; Wheel in harmony with its nature; Wheel which penetrates the sameness of all dharmas as one realm.

"Wheel of training all sentient beings, undiverted and constantly blessed; Wheel which is the entrance to the wisdom of the highest truth; Wheel without conceptualization and without duality; Wheel which gathers everything into the Dharmadhātu.

"This Wheel is immeasurable, surpassing every measure; incalculable, outside every calculation; it is inconceivable, unencompassable by the mind; inconceivable, ineffable, completely unequaled.

"Free from all spoken language, it is inexpressible; immeasurable, incomparable, incommensurable, it is like space.

"It is not nihilistic, not eternalistic, not contradicting what went before; calm, extremely calm, Thatness, having its own nature; without error, that itself; not other, not becoming other; speaking the language of all beings.

"This Wheel destroys all of the demons and conquers the tīrthikas; transcends the realm of rebirth and enters the Buddha-realm; it is perfectly known by the venerable Āryas; understood by the Pratyekabuddhas; grasped by the Bodhisattvas; praised by all the Buddhas; indivisible from all the Tathāgatas.

"O Maitreya, such is the Wheel of the Dharma turned by the Tathāgata, and because of this turning, he is called the Tathāgata; he is called the perfect and complete Buddha; Svayambhū, self-arising; Lord of the Dharma; the Guide and the Leader; Guide in all things; Driver of the caravan; Master over all dharmas; Master of the Dharma.

"He is the one who turns the Wheel of the Dharma; the Benefactor of the Dharma; the Lord of offerings; one who makes the best offerings; being whose practices are fulfilled; being whose intentions are carried out.

"He is the Teacher; the one who consoles; the one who reassures; the Hero; the one who has abandoned emotionality; the complete Victor in battle; the one who opens the parasol and unfurls the standard and the banner.

"He is the One who creates light; the being bringing forth clarity; the one who dispels obscurity; the Torch-bearer.

"He is known as the Great King of Physicians; the genuine Healer; the one who withdraws the arrow of misery.

"He has the unobscured vision of wisdom; he sees all; he sees everything; his eyes see everywhere; he illuminates everything.

"He is called the Gate to Everything; and the Completely Good.

"He is known as the one in all ways like the moon: all-gracious, rejecting nothing and accepting nothing in the unstable world.

"He is known as the one like the earth, because his mind is never inflated, never depressed.

"He is known as the Lord like a mountain, because he is unshakable. He is known as the most glorious in all the world, because he is endowed with every good quality. He is known as the one whose head disappears from sight, because he is the most exalted in all the worlds.

"He is known as the one like the ocean, because his depth cannot be fathomed. He is known as the source of the jewels of the Dharma, because he has perfected all the facets of Enlightenment.

"He is known as the one like the wind, because he has no abode. He is known as the one whose thought is unattached, because his wisdom is unbound and free from limitations. He is known as the unswerving Dharma, because he has completely understood all dharmas.

"He is known as the one like a flame, because he has burned away all fetters, abandoned all pride, and reached a state difficult to attain.

"He is known as the one like water, because he is free from all conceptions, spotless in body and mind, and clear of all defilements.

"He is known as the one like the sky, because he has obtained omniscient understanding and knowledge of the sphere of action of the Dharmadhātu—without center and without limits—boundless sphere of wisdom.

"He is called the one who dwells in complete deliverance and unhindered knowledge, because he has abandoned obscured teachings. He is called the one with the body which has completely entered the Dharmadhātu, because he has passed from sight and is the same as space.

"He is called the Highest of Beings, because he is untouched by the fettering passions of the world.

"He is known as the Being of immeasurable intelligence; Teacher of a Dharma beyond the world; Teacher of the World; Caitya of the World; Physician of the World; raised above the world; not clothed in worldly dharmas; Protector of the World; Finest of the World; Most Perfect of the World; Lord of the World; Honored One of the World; the Friend of the World; the one who has reached the shore beyond the world; Lamp of the World; the one who has passed from the world; Spiritual Teacher of the World; the one who renders service to the world; the one who knows the world; the one who has attained mastery over the world.

"He is known as the one worthy of great offerings; worthy of homage; the great Field of Merit; the Great Being; the Holy Being; the Excellent Being; the Highest Being; Unequaled Being; without superior; the Impartial Being; with no likeness; the one always settled in equanimity; dwelling in the equality of all things.

"He is called the one who has obtained the Path; teaching the Path; showing the Path; well-established on the Path;

the one who has gone beyond the demon's domain; who has overcome the sphere of Māra.

"He is called the one who has obtained clarity and the cool quality by passing beyond old age and death; the one delivered from darkness and shadows; delivered from doubt; delivered from hesitation; delivered from the fettering passions; conqueror of doubt and uncertainty; conqueror of hesitation.

"He is called the one free from attachment; the Liberated One; the one entirely pure; he is called the one delivered from desire; from hatred; from ignorance; the one who has destroyed all defilement; the one with no emotionality.

"He is known as the one possessing power; the one whose mind is completely delivered; whose wisdom is very free; who knows all; the Great Elephant; the one who acts; the performer of action; the one who carries the burden; the one who attains his goal; the one who has exhausted all bonds in the round of rebirth; the one who is completely liberated by the wisdom of equality.

"He is called the one who has reached the transcendence of the heroic mind; the one who has attained the transcendence of giving; the one exalted by good conduct; he is known as the one who has reached the transcendence of patience; exalted by effort; the one who has obtained the clear knowledge and contemplation and transcendence of wisdom.

"He is called the one whose prayers are fulfilled; he who dwells in great love; he who dwells in great compassion; he who dwells in great joy; he who dwells in great equanimity.

"He makes full effort to convert beings; he is possessor of unobstructed knowledge of all things; full of confidence; replete with great merit; endowed with great wisdom.

"He is known as the one who possesses pure attentiveness, realization, intelligence; the one who possesses mindfulness; complete renunciation; the degrees of supernatural abilities; the powers and strengths; the branches of awakening; the path; calm abiding and intense insight; he is called the one who has crossed the sea of rebirth; the one who has arrived at the other shore; the one who stands on firm ground; the one who is full of joy; the one who has obtained fearlessness.

"He is known as the one who has cut through the brambles of emotionality; the Puruṣa; the Great Puruṣa; the Lion of Puruṣas; the one who has set aside fear and exasperation; he is called the Elephant; the one without blemish; the one who has abandoned the three defilements; the Sage; the possessor of the three knowledges; the one who has crossed the four currents.

"He is called the Kṣatriya, the kingly one, because he is the only one to carry the precious parasol. He is called the Brāhmin because he has abandoned the wrong teachings. He is called the Bhikṣu because he has broken the shell of the egg of ignorance. He is called the Śramaṇa because he has overcome all the ways of desire.

"He is known as the Pure One because he sees the fettering passions. He is known as the one endowed with strength; possessor of the ten strengths. He is known as Bhagavat; the one who has reflected on the body; King of Kings; King of the Dharma.

"He is called the Teacher who turns the most excellent Wheel of the Dharma; Teacher who shows the unconfused Dharma; the one consecrated with all-knowing wisdom; possessor of the means of highest liberation; and the diadem of spotless great knowledge without defilement.

"He is called the one endowed with the seven sparkling facets of Enlightenment; and the one who has obtained the excellence of all the precious Dharma. He is known as the one who is gazed upon by the circle of noble Śrāvakas and counselors; the one who is attended by the Bodhisattva Mahāsattvas; the possessor of the good discipline; the one well-announced by prophecies.

"He is known as the one like Vaiśravaṇa; distributor of the treasure of the seven noble jewels; the one who gives liberally; the one endowed with the highest happiness; giver of all that is hoped for; Comforter, Aid, and Refuge for the entire world.

"He is known as the one like Indra; the one who bears the vajra of great wisdom; the all-seeing one. He is known as the one whose eyes see everywhere, unimpeded; thoroughly transformed by knowledge, he enters completely into the Teaching, the flowing dance of the Dharma.

"He is known as the one like Candra, the Moon; the one whom beings never tire of seeing; the one whose most pure splendor extends everywhere; the one whose light brings forth joy and delight; the one who seems to gaze upon all beings; the one who appears as a vessel for the thought and intention of every being; the one called the Great Display; followed by hosts of stars—the learners and those finished learning.

"He is known as the one like Sūrya, the sun; the one who clears away darkness and shadows; king of the great banner; immeasurable, infinite, splendid one; shedding great light everywhere; explaining all questions and predictions without confusion.

"He is known as the destroyer of dark ignorance; the one who sees distinctly with the great light of knowledge; the one free of conceptualization; the one illuminating an immeasurable domain with love, kindness, and great compassion; the one shining equally for each living being; the possessor of the maṇḍala difficult to envision, difficult to attain, and profound in transcendent wisdom.

"He is known as the one like Brahmā; traveler on the path of complete calm; the one endowed with all that is needed for great action. He is known as the possessor of the excellent path of activity and wise conduct; possessor of the most holy form; the one who gives unending pleasure to the eye. He is known as the one with senses calm; whose mind is calm; the one who fulfills all the conditions of calm abiding; the one with the eminent abiding calm; the self-controlled one endowed with calm abiding; the possessor of perfect calm and insight.

"He is called the Hidden One; the one well-practiced, with senses subdued; well-trained like an elephant; clear and untroubled like a limpid lake; he who has completely abandoned all obscuring inclinations of the fettering passions.

"He is known as the one endowed with the thirty-two signs of a great man; the Great Being; the one endowed with the eighty secondary marks; the Leader of Men; the one endowed with the ten strengths; possessor of the four fearless affirmations; the eminent Guide of those to be trained; the

Teacher; the one who is replete with all the eighteen Buddhadharmas; the one above reproach in body, speech, and mind. He is called the possessor of the maṇḍala of completely purified knowledge because he is endowed with the best of signs.

"Because he understands the connections and balance of dependent origination, he is called the dweller in emptiness. Because he realizes absolute truth, he is called the dweller in signlessness. Because he is unsullied by emotional entanglements, he is called the dweller in wishlessness.

"Because he halts the stream of conditionality, he is called the one who does not manifest conditioned responses. Because he is unconfused about the wisdom of true reality, he is called the speaker of the genuine reality. Because he abides in the domain of knowledge, described as the sky, the Dharmadhātu, having the nature of Thatness as its characteristic, he is called the speaker of the essence of the nonmistaken.

"Because he regards all things like illusion, mirage, dream, like the reflection of the moon in water, like an echo or double vision, he is called the one who knows the unfettered Dharma.

"Because he causes complete deliverance to arise, he is called the one meaningful to hear and see. Because he strives to train living beings, he is called the one with the meaningful stride.

"Because he has ended the thirst for existence, cutting off ignorance completely, he is called the one who has crossed the fire pit of hell. Because he points out the path to the certain exit, he is called the solid bridge. Because he is unsullied by the deeds of the demon, and has surmounted the obstacles of Māra, and the fetters of passion, he is called Jina, Victorious.

"Because he has gone beyond the realm of desire, he is called the one who has crossed the swamp of desire. Because he has gone beyond the realm of form, he is known as the one who has overturned the banner of pride. Because he has gone beyond the realm of the formless, he is known as the one who has unfurled the banner of wisdom. Because he possesses the Body of the Dharma, and the Body of Wisdom, he is called the one who has gone beyond all the realms of the world.

"He is called the great tree, because he is laden with the fruit of complete deliverance and covered with endless flowers of precious knowledge. He is called flower of the uḍumbara, the rarely blooming lotus, because such come forth but rarely and are seldom seen. Having perfected renunciation according to the Way, he is called cintamaṇi, the king of precious gems.

"He is called the one with the fine stance, because he has long been firm in renunciation, good conduct, and vows, in austerity and brahmacarya, never being diverted from observances, never confused, possessing true firmness.

"He is called the one whose foot is marked with the thousand-spoked wheel, the nandyāvarta, and the svastika, because he has long been a refuge for living beings, not deserting those who have gone to him for refuge, giving complete shelter to parents and teachers, śramaṇas and brāhmins, to the deserving, and to the followers of the Dharma.

“He is called the one with the wide foot, because he has long renounced the taking of life.

“He is called the one with long fingers, because he has long sustained living beings.

“He is called the one with the tall, upright body, because he has long praised the virtues of those who renounced taking life, and has given many beings refuge.

“He is called the one with the soft hands and feet, because he has long honored and served those deserving offerings, never wearying to act for parents, śramaṇas, brāhmins, and teachers, giving baths and massages, giving ointments, oils, and liniments.

“He is called the one with the membrane between his fingers and toes, because he has long skillfully gathered beings with the net of conversion, with giving, kind speech, and helpfulness, with deeds that match words.

“He is called the one who raises his foot, because he has long aimed at noble action, climbing ever higher in virtue.

“He is called the one whose hair on the upper body curls to the right, because he has long circumambulated to the right around parents and teachers, around śramaṇas and brāhmins, and those worthy of offerings, around caityas of the Tathāgatas, applying himself to the Teaching of the Dharma, sharing with others his astonishment and delight, and trembling with joy when he hears the Dharma.

“He is called the one with the limbs of the gazelle, because he has long shown respect, listening to the Dharma, retaining it, reciting it, and skillfully making it known, carefully penetrating it, realizing its letter and its meaning, never showing contempt for a teacher of Dharma, always giving refuge to beings faced with old age, disease, and death.

"He is called the one with private parts enclosed in a sheath, because he has long given all that he could to followers of brahmacarya, to śramaṇas, brāhmins, and others, giving clothing to the naked, never approaching others' wives, praising the qualities of brahmacarya, guarding his modesty and chastity, and following observances.

"He is called the one with long arms, because he has long guarded his hands and feet, acting in body, speech, and mind with love, intent on never harming beings.

"He is called the one like the nyagrodha tree, because he has long followed moderation, being restrained in his eating, distributing medicine to the sick, never harming the unprotected, never scorning ordinary people, giving security to those tormented by fear, repairing ruined caityas of the Tathāgatas and building new caityas.

"He is called the one with the fine, smooth skin, because he has long given to parents, śramaṇas, brāhmins, teachers, and to others worthy of offerings: baths and ointments and clarified butter, liniments of sesame oil, warm water in cold weather, cool water and shade in the heat, soothing amusements, good clothing smooth to the touch, soft beds and soft chairs, offering to the caityas of the Tathāgatas silken banners and cords, and sprinklings of perfumed oil.

"He is called the Golden One, because he has long made a practice of love, setting aside harshness, taking up patience, encouraging all to endure, praising and encouraging those free from malice, adorning the caityas of the Tathāgatas with golden objects of all kinds, golden flowers and vases, inlaid carvings, banners and golden vestments, sprinkling gold dust all around.

"He is called the one with each hair rising distinctly, because he has long attended on paṇḍitas, asking about virtue and non-virtue, about failings in practice and what to depend on, examining what is bad or fair or fulfilling, weighing the teachings with unconfused care, clearing away debris from the caityas of the Tathāgatas, removing the spiders and worms, the dirt and faded flowers, the cobwebs and weeds.

"He is called the one with the seven lofty parts, because he has long shown respect to parents and teachers, to masters and superiors, to śramaṇas and brāhmins, to those worthy of respect, to unfortunate beggars, and to all who approached, giving enjoyment to all, offering whatever they desired: food and drink, bedding, clothes, lamps, shelter, utensils, and medicine, and ponds and wells of fresh water.

"He is called the one whose upper body resembles the lion, because he has long offered obedience, speaking words of welcome and security, and words of peace to parents and teachers, to śramaṇas, brāhmins, and all deserving offerings, upholding the weak, sheltering those seeking refuge, and never scorning or abandoning them.

"He is called the one with broad shoulders, because he has long weighed his own faults carefully, not seeing weakness in others as failings, giving up the source of divisiveness and argument, reciting mantras, and guarding well against extremes of speech and action.

"He is called the one with the well-turned shoulder, because he has long offered welcome and peace, rising in the presence of those deserving offerings, parents and teachers, śramaṇas and brāhmins. Assured in the Śāstras, he cuts short debate; completely trained, he sets ministers and kings on the path of virtue; through meditation, he has comprehended and upheld all the precepts of the Tathāgatas; he has total grasp of all virtuous action.

"He is called the one with the lion's jaw, because he has long given up everything, like a beggar, addressing sweet words to all who approach, despising none, deceiving none, turning none away, fulfilling their desires with gifts and firm support.

"He is called the one with forty even teeth because he has long given up harsh words, and chants which foster divisiveness, eager to bring all into accord, speaking against slander and argument, reciting mantras of conciliation.

"He is called the one with the white teeth, because he has long abandoned the dark side and accumulated the white roots of virtue, giving up the growth of dark deeds while encouraging the white, painting the caityas of the Tathāgatas with a mixture of chalk and milk, giving milk, cooked food, white garments, garlands of sumana, vārṣika, and dhanuṣkarī flowers, and beautiful bouquets of white flowers.

"He is called the one with firm and good teeth, because he has long left off mocking and teasing, giving only joy, guarding his speech, using words which delight, not looking for the weakness and faults of others, greeting all with impartiality and equanimity, teaching the Dharma to the sick, giving firm support for all beings, and never giving them up.

"He is called the possessor of the best elixir, because he has long harmed no sentient being, never scoffing at anyone, caring for the sick, caring for travelers, the deprived, and the weak, giving medicines and remedies, never sad to give, giving all he can.

"He is called the one with the voice like Brahmā's, because he has long given up false speech: cruel, sharp words that wound others, as well as biting and disparaging words. His words are loving and compassionate, joyous, pleasant, sweet, and sympathetic, welcoming and encouraging; they go straight to the heart, delighting all the senses.

"He is called the one with the blue-black eyes, because he has long gazed upon beings benevolently, like a father, giving love to beggars as to an only son, regarding all with compassion, completely free of jealousy, having gazed at the caityas of the Tathāgatas without blinking, with the power of faith, having shown the Tathāgatas to others, welcoming them, upholding them firmly.

"He is called the one with the eyelashes of a heifer, because he has long abandoned base thoughts and feelings, his brow never wrinkled, his face ever smiling, concerned with accomplishing generous intentions, guiding all beings with faith in the best Dharma, seeking continually the presence of Teachers, never hesitating to accumulate virtue.

"He is called the one with the very long tongue, because he has long abandoned erroneous speech, singing instead the praises of the Śrāvakas, the Pratyekabuddhas, and the Teachers of the Dharma, requesting the Sūtras taught by the Tathāgatas, reciting and reading and comprehending them, skillfully conveying the meaning of the Dharma to all beings.

"He is called the one with the unseen diadem, because he has long bowed his head to the feet of his parents, to the feet of śramaṇas, brāhmins, and spiritual teachers, to all worthy of offerings. To the wandering monks he has spoken with just words, giving sweet-smelling oils and shaving their heads, giving beggars colored powders, garlands, and head ornaments.

"He is called the one who has between his brows the circle of hair curling to the right, and the one with the pure and brilliant complexion, because he has long given offerings of all sorts, guiding beings in virtue, not obscuring the rules, and following the teachings of the friends of virtue, encouraging the traveling teachers of the Dharma, honoring the Buddhas, Bodhisattvas, and Pratyekabuddhas, noble Śrāvakas, Dharma Teachers, parents and all worthy of homage, honoring and giving gifts of sweet-smelling oils and butter, lamps and torches to dispel darkness, adorning the images of the Tathāgatas with all the most beautiful things.

"He bears the tuft of milk-white hair between his eyebrows; distinguished by his immense accumulation of virtue, he has encouraged beings to manifest the Thought of Enlightenment.

"He is called the one who has obtained great strength, for he possesses the great strength of Nārāyaṇa.

"He is called the one with the strength of Nārāyaṇa, for he possesses the strength sufficient to rout a hundred koṭis of demons.

"He is called the one who subdues all adversaries, for he possesses the ten powers of a Tathāgata.

"He is called the one with the ten powers of a Tathāgata, for he has the power of knowing what is possible and what is impossible; and having abandoned the ephemeral and lowest vehicle, he possesses and uses untiringly the power acquired from the great vehicle.

"He is called the one who knows what is possible and what is impossible, the one who has given up the ephemeral and lowest vehicle, who possesses and uses untiringly the power acquired from the great vehicle, for he has the power of knowing the complete results and causes of all actions in the past, present, and future.

"He is called the one with the power of knowing the complete results and causes of actions in the past, present, and future, for he has the power of knowing in detail the different degrees of development in the capacities and faculties of beings.

"He is called the one with the power of knowing the different degrees of development in the capacities and faculties of beings, for he has the power of knowing the various dispositions of beings.

"He is called the one with the power of knowing the various dispositions of beings, for he has the power of knowing both complete deliverance and the aspirations of beings without exception.

"He is called the one with the power of knowing both complete deliverance and the aspirations of beings without exception, for he has the power of knowing the paths which lead to various realms of rebirth.

"He is called the one with the power of knowing the paths which lead to various realms of rebirth, for he has the power of knowing the levels of meditation, the deliverances, the samādhis, and the states of calm abiding, as well as the pervasive emotional hindrances, their complete purification, and the total establishment of purity.

"He is called the one with the power of knowing the meditations, deliverances, samādhis, the states of calm abiding, as well as the pervasive emotional hindrances, their complete purification, and the total establishment of purity, for he has the unoriginated knowledge of all past lives.

"He is called the one with the power of knowing all past lives, for he has the power of the divine eye which sees without obstruction the death and rebirth of all beings.

"He is called the one with the power of the divine eye which sees without obstruction the death and rebirth of all beings, for he has the power of knowing that all the defilements without exception have been expelled, as well as all the propensities which lead to rebirth.

"He is called the one with the power of knowing that all the defilements without exception have been expelled, as well as all the propensities which lead to rebirth, for he has obtained the fearless affirmation which cannot be suppressed by heaven or earth, the affirmation that states: 'I am truly a perfect Buddha, manifesting all things.'

"He is called the one of fearless affirmation which cannot be opposed by heaven or earth, the affirmation stating : 'I am truly a perfect Buddha, manifesting all things,' for he has obtained the fearless affirmation which cannot be suppressed by heaven or earth, the affirmation which states: 'I will demonstrate the Dharma which shows the obstacles to Nirvāṇa to be the fettering passions of the grasping mind.'

"He is called the one of fearless affirmation which cannot be opposed by heaven or earth, the affirmation stating: 'I will demonstrate the Dharma which shows the obstacles to Nirvāṇa to be the fettering passions of the grasping mind,' for he has obtained the fearless affirmation which cannot be suppressed by heaven or earth, the affirmation which states: 'Nirvāṇa is obtained by achieving the path of renunciation.'

"He is called the one of fearless affirmation which cannot be opposed by heaven or by earth, the affirmation stating: 'Nirvāṇa is obtained by achieving the path of renunciation,' for he has obtained the fearless affirmation, which cannot be suppressed by heaven or earth, the affirmation concerning the abandonment of all defilements.

"He is called the one of fearless affirmation which cannot be suppressed by heaven or by earth, the affirmation which concerns the knowledge of abandoning all defilements, for he has taught the Dharma with no mistaken words.

"He is called the Teacher of the Dharma with no mistaken words, for he understands the nature of the Dharma, which is inexpressible and without sound.

"He is called the one who understands the nature of the Dharma, which is inexpressible and without sound, for he is indivisible.

"He is called indivisible, for he is able to give blessings in the voice of a Buddha, not bound by the logic of ordinary beings.

"He is called the one able to give blessings in the voice of a Buddha, not bound by the logic of ordinary beings, for he is not forgetful.

"He is called the one who is not forgetful, for he perceives no difference.

"He is known as the one who perceives no difference, for he abides in equanimity, calming the minds of all beings.

"He is known as the one who abides in equanimity, calming the minds of all beings, for he has the evenmindedness which is non-discriminating.

"He is known as the one whose evenmindedness is non-discriminating, for he does not lapse from the samādhi composed of devotion.

"He is known as the one who does not lapse from the samādhi composed of devotion, for he does not shy from effort or break the stream of samādhi composed of effort.

"He is called the one with no diminishing of effort, for he does not turn away from mindfulness.

"He is called the one with no diminishing of mindfulness, for he does not turn away from understanding.

"He is called the one with no diminishing of understanding, for he does not turn back from complete liberation.

"He is called the one with no diminishing of liberation, for he does not turn back from the wisdom vision of liberation.

"He is called the one with no diminishing of the wisdom vision of liberation, for he is endowed with the wisdom that follows wisdom, and all his actions are preceded by wisdom.

"He is called the one whose actions of body, speech, and mind are preceded by wisdom, and who is endowed with the wisdom which follows wisdom, for he possesses the wisdom vision which sees past, present, and future with unobstructed, unoriginated knowledge.

"He is called the one whose wisdom vision of the three times is unobstructed, for he has obtained the complete and unblemished liberation.

"He is called the one who has obtained unblemished liberation, because of his steady skill in influencing the actions of all beings.

"He is called the one with the steady skill in influencing the actions of all beings, for he has skill in teaching the Dharma according to individual understanding.

"He is called the one skilled in teaching the Dharma according to individual understanding, for he has perfected the holy maṇḍala of all the various melodious voices.

"He is called the one who has perfected the holy maṇḍala of all the branches of melody, because he has obtained skill in producing the echo of all voices.

"He is called the one with the voice like a god, a nāga, a yakṣa, a gandharva, an asura, a garuḍa, a kinnara, and a mahoraga; he is called the one who has the melodious tones of Brahmā, sweet as the nightingale, like a song, like a great drum; resounding like the earth, reverberating like the thunderous voice of the nāga king Sāgara; roaring like a lion; trumpeting like the first of the herd; the voice that harmonizes with the voice of all beings; the voice which delights all the pure and vast circles of attendants; the single voice making all voices understood.

"He is called the one honored by the lord of the Brahma realm; venerated by Śakra, lord of gods; bowed to by the chief of the nāgas; respected by the chief of the yakṣas; celebrated by the songs of the chief of the gandharvas. He is called the one whom the chief of the rākṣasas regards without blinking; the one to whom the asuras make prostrations; the one regarded without malice by the chief of the garuḍas; the one praised by the chief of the kinnaras; the one whom the chief of the mahoragas longs to see; the one who is surrounded with homage by the lord of men; the one surrounded with care and concern by the assemblies of Arhats.

"He is called the one who welcomes the Bodhisattvas, the one who causes the Bodhisattvas to celebrate, who makes them happy; the harmonious Teacher of the Dharma; the Teacher of the Dharma which bears fruit. He is known as the one who wastes not a single word, who teaches the Dharma which is always timely.

"Maitreya, this is the turning of the Wheel of the Dharma. The teaching of the shortened form of the Praise of the Qualities of the Tathāgata is finished. Maitreya, to present it in its extensive form, the Tathāgata would need a kalpa or more, for there is no end to his teaching."

Then the Bhagavat uttered these verses:

"Profound, difficult to see, and subtle,
is this Wheel of the Dharma;

neither demons nor paratīrthikas
penetrate its meaning.

"Without ground of being, without activity, without birth,
without origin, empty and solitary by nature;
without acceptance, without rejection
is this Wheel of the Dharma, which has now been turned.

"Without sign or characteristic
is this teaching of the Dharma of equanimity;
this Wheel turned by the Buddha.

"Like magic, like a mirage, like a dream,
like the moon reflected in water, like an echo;
such is the Wheel turned by the Protector of the World.

"For one who enters into the teaching of dependence,
there is neither eternalism nor nihilism;
there is the cessation of all views.
This is how the Wheel of the Dharma is expressed.

"Like the eternal expanse of space,
incomprehensible, shining with clear light,
the doctrine has neither middle nor end.
This is called the Wheel of the Dharma.

"Completely free from existence and non-existence,
without self and without non-self,
the Teaching shows uncreated self-nature.
This is how the Wheel of the Dharma is expressed.

"The absolute expanse is limitless;
its very nature is its very nature;
the Teaching of the Dharma is non-dual.
This is how the Wheel of the Dharma is expressed.

"The eye by its nature is empty;
likewise the ear, the nose, the tongue,
the body and the mind.
They are themselves empty and devoid of activity.

"Such is the turning of the Wheel of the Dharma;
all sentient beings as they have realization
are called Buddha.

"The characteristic of the Dharma, this self-nature,
has not been shown by others;
by myself have I become a Buddha,
thus, self-arising, and endowed with the divine eye.

"He who has obtained power over all dharmas
is called the Lord of the Dharma;
he who knows what is the way of the Dharma,
and what is not, is known as the Guide.

"As many countless beings as there are to be trained,
with perfect discipline, he trains them,
as he himself is trained;
because of this, he is known as the Guide.

"To beings who are lost, he shows the best way;
he leads them to the other shore;
because of this, he is the spiritual Guide.

"Having crossed over the desert of saṁsāra,
I know the ways of gathering beings;
thus am I called the Leader of the caravan.

"With mastery in all the dharmas,
I am called the Jina;
turning the Wheel of the Dharma,
I am called the King of the Dharma.

"The great Donor of the Dharma,
the Teaching and unexcelled Lord of the Dharma,
has indeed made good the sacrifice;
the goal is achieved, the aim accomplished,
and all the blessings are fulfilled.

"Consoler who sees well-being,
Hero who has given up great emotionality,
Victor in all struggles,
the One who is free thus frees all beings.

"Light of the World, shining with knowledge of wisdom,
bearer of the brilliant torch,
destroyer of the darkness of ignorance,

"Great Physician endowed with peerless wisdom,
who cures all emotionality,
skillfully withdrawing the arrow
from the wound of the fettering passions,

"Endowed with all the signs of a Great Man,
adorned with all the secondary marks,
with perfectly beautiful body,
he comforts the miserable.

"Endowed with the ten strengths,
and with total fearlessness,
possessor of the eighteen pure Buddhadharmas,
the great Muni turns the Wheel of the Dharma
of the Great Vehicle.

"It is he who has expressed this Sūtra in short,
and this praise has expressed only a small portion
of the qualities of the Tathāgata.

"For the knowledge of the Buddha
is unending like the vast expanse of space.
One could speak for a kalpa
and not come to the end
of the qualities of the Buddha."

The Twenty-sixth Chapter
Turning the Wheel of the Dharma

Plate 27

निगमपरिवर्तः

།འཛུག་སྡུད་པའི་ལེའུ།

Conclusion

WHEN THE TATHĀGATA TURNED THE DHARMA WHEEL, explaining the Lalitavistara, the eighteen thousand devaputras of the Śuddhāvāsa realm who had asked him for this teaching, those led by Īśvara, Maheśvara, Nandana, Sunandana, Candana, Mahita, Praśānta, and Vinīteśvara, once more assembled. At that moment, the Bhagavat spoke to these devaputras led by Maheśvara and the others:

"Friends, this is the exposition of the extensive Sūtra called the Lalitavistara, the Sūtra which relates the play of the Bodhisattva, the entry into the sport in the domain of the Buddha. It has been related by the Tathāgata for the sake of all; carry it, memorize it, repeat it, teach it carefully and in detail to the Sangha. In this way it will spread the Buddhadharma. Bodhisattvas of the Great Vehicle, upon hearing this aspect of the Dharma, will develop the firmest effort for peerless, perfect, and complete Enlightenment. Beings greatly devoted to this teaching will make fall the torrential rain of the Dharma, and the armies of Māra the demon will be completely overcome. The adversaries will find no further occasion to contend; and, for your part, the virtue that will result from urging others to teach this Dharma will produce great benefit, great fruit, great help.

"Friends, whoever bows with joined hands toward the Lalitavistara, this exposition of the Dharma, will obtain the eight excellent dharmas. Which eight are these? He will obtain an excellent form and great strength, a faithful following, exuberant eloquence, an excellent departure from home, purity of mind, and perfection of samādhi. Above all, he will obtain the great light of wisdom. These are the eight excellent dharmas which he will obtain.

"Friends, whoever procures a position for the teacher of the Dharma desiring to teach the Lalitavistara will obtain eight desirable positions as soon as the teacher's position is procured. What are the eight positions? He will become the chief of merchants and master of the house. He will gain the position of Cakravartin; the position of Guardian of the World; the position of Śakra; the position of Vaśavartin. He will gain the position of Brahmā, and will obtain the lion throne of the one who, as an irreversible Bodhisattva, went to Bodhimaṇḍa, the most excellent of places. Having obtained the perfect and complete purity of a Buddha, he will gain the throne of the one who destroyed the opposition of Māra, the throne of the one who turns the Wheel of the peerless Dharma. These are the eight desirable positions he will obtain.

"Friends, whoever gives his approval, saying: 'Wonderful!' to the one who teaches this exposition of the Dharma, the Lalitavistara, will obtain the eight complete purities of karma with relation to speech. What are these eight purities? By the pure speech which conforms to the truth, one's actions are always in accordance with one's speech. By not opposing the Sangha, one's words are worthy of being followed. By not contradicting appropriate words, one's speech is pleasing. By not being harsh, one's words are sweet and soft. By satisfying body and mind, one's voice is like that of the nightingale. By gathering beings to the Dharma, one's voice is like poetry, overwhelming all sound like the voice of Brahmā. By not giving in to opposition, one's voice resounds like the roar of the lion. By satisfying completely the senses of all beings, one has the speech of a Buddha. These are the eight complete purities of karma with relation to speech.

"Friends, whoever puts this exposition of the Dharma, the Lalitavistara, into writing, takes it up, reads it, honors it, venerates it, renders homage to it, and with thought free from envy, repeats its praises to the four directions, saying: 'Come! Take this aspect of the Dharma, put it into writing, read it, recite it, meditate on it, study it,' this one will obtain the eight great treasures. What are the eight great treasures? By being without forgetfulness, one gains the treasure of mindfulness. By analyzing things well, one gains the treasure of understanding. By understanding the meaning of all the Sūtras, one has the treasure of realization. By comprehending everything one hears, one has the treasure of the Dhāraṇīs. By satisfying all beings with elegant sayings, one has the treasure of eloquence. By guarding the Teachings, one has the treasure of the Dharma. By preventing the interruption of the family of the Three Jewels, one has the treasure of the Thought of Enlightenment. By obtaining patience concerning the uncreated Dharma, one has the treasure of achievement. These are the eight treasures.

"Friends, whoever takes up this exposition of the Dharma, the Lalitavistara, after teaching it well, will complete the eight accumulations. What are these eight? By freeing his mind from greed, one completes perfectly the accumulation of giving. By fulfilling all virtuous intentions, one completes the accumulation of morality. By acquiring unimpeded wisdom, one completes the accumulation of learning the Dharma. By manifesting all the quietudes and samādhis, one completes the accumulation of calm abiding. By attaining realization of the three knowledges, one completes the accumulation of intense insight. By entirely purifying the principal signs, the secondary signs, and the ornaments of the Buddha-field, one completes the accumulation of merit. By satisfying all beings in accord with their desires, one completes the accumulation of wisdom. By not wavering in aiding the complete maturation of all beings, one completes the accumulation of great compassion. These are the eight accumulations.

"Friends, whoever, after reflecting on the way other beings could possess virtues such as these, explains clearly to others this exposition of the Dharma, the Lalitavistara, will obtain by this root of virtue the eight great pure merits. What are these eight? The first of these great merits is that he will become a Cakravartin king. The second of the great merits is that he will exercise control over the realm of the Four Great Kings. The third great merit is that he will be like Śakra, the master of the gods. The fourth great merit is that he will be like the devaputra Suyāma. The fifth great merit is that he will be like Santuṣita. The sixth of the great merits is that he will be like Sunirmita. The seventh great merit is that he will be a Vaśavartin king of the gods. The eighth great merit is that he will be like Brahmā, great Brahmā. Finally, he will become a Tathāgata Arhat Buddha, perfect and complete, having abandoned all the non-virtuous qualities, possessing all the good qualities. These are the eight great merits which he will obtain.

"Friends, whoever listens attentively to this exposition of the Dharma, the Lalitavistara, will gain the eight purities of mind. What are the eight? By destroying all anger, he will obtain love. By giving up all harmfulness, he will obtain compassion. By clearing away all displeasure, he will obtain pleasure. By abandoning desire as well as hatred, he will obtain equanimity. By gaining mastery over all the desire realms, he will obtain the four stages of meditation. By gaining mastery over the mind, he will obtain the four formless stages of meditation. By coming and going in other Buddha-fields, he will obtain the five superior knowledges. By obtaining the hero's samādhi, he will obtain the destruction of all subtle karmic residues. These are the eight purities of mind.

"Friends, wherever this exposition of the Dharma, the Lalitavistara, is found, in village or city, walled city or countryside, in deserted region, courtyard, or vihāra, the eight fears will no longer exist, except through the complete maturation of previous actions. What are the eight fears? The fear of difficulties caused by the king; the fear of difficulties caused by robbers; the fear of difficulties caused by snakes and the fear of starving in a wilderness; the fear of difficulties arising from feuds, disputes, and brawls; the fear of difficulties caused by the gods, and the fear of difficulties caused by the nāgas, the yakṣas, and others. The fear of all harm will no longer exist. These, friends, are the eight fears. They will no longer exist, except through the complete maturation of previous actions.

"In a word, friends, even if the Tathāgata lived for immeasurable kalpas and spoke the praises of this exposition of the Dharma day and night, there would be no end to the praise of the Teaching, as there would be no end to the energy of the Tathāgata.

"And still more, friends—for so great is the morality of the Tathāgata, his meditation, his wisdom, his complete liberation, his immeasurable vision, unlimited in its knowledge of liberation—that whoever understands this exposition of the Dharma, takes it up, reads it, puts it into writing, has it written, penetrates it, teaches it, explains it clearly in detail in the midst of a Sangha with the thought that beings can thus possess the most excellent Dharma, for him and for those he teaches, the increase in merit will know no limits."

Then the Bhagavat addressed these words to the Āyuṣmat Mahākāśyapa, to the Āyuṣmat Ānanda, and to the Bodhisattva Mahāsattva Maitreya: "Friends, I place in your hands the Enlightenment, perfect and complete, which I have acquired completely in the immeasurable space of a hundred thousand niyutas of koṭis of kalpas. I convey it to you by a supreme trust. Take up this exposition of the Dharma yourselves and teach it in detail to others."

Then the Bhagavat, in order to give fuller measure to this exposition of the Dharma, uttered these verses:

"With the vision of the Buddha,
I have seen all living beings.
Whoever pays homage to beings
who have become Arhats like Śāriputra
gains much merit—but even if they honored them
for kalpas as numerous as the sands of the Ganges,
the merit would not equal that of whoever
for one day and night pays joyful homage
with garlands and the like to a Pratyekabuddha.

“If all living beings were to become Pratyekabuddhas,
and one made offerings to them
with great awareness for many kalpas,
giving offerings of food and drink, raiment,
flowers, perfumes, and ointments,
the merit would not equal that of whoever
with a serene mind makes a single bow
to a single Tathāgata, saying:
‘I make obeisance to the Arhat!’
From this, one gains the greatest merit.

“If all living beings obtained Buddhahood,
and one worshipped them
with the most beautiful of human and divine flowers
for several hundreds of kalpas,
the merit would not equal that of whoever,
at the time of the degeneration of the Dharma,
meditates on this Sūtra day and night,
having renounced his body and even his life.
Truly great merit comes from this.

“Whoever desires to render homage to the Guides,
to the Pratyekabuddhas, as well as to the Śrāvakas,
after having produced the firm Thought of Enlightenment,
will always firmly retain this best of Sūtras.

“For this Sūtra which is manifested by all the Tathāgatas,
is the king of all elegant teachings.
The house in which this precious Sūtra is found
is the dwelling of the Tathāgata.

“Whoever gives this transcendent Sūtra,
whoever speaks a single word of it,
will obtain a fine and infinite energy for koṭis of kalpas
and will not stray beyond the letter and the meaning.

"He will be without a superior among the Guides of men,
this being, whoever he may be; there will be no one like him.
The one who, hearing this Dharma, would master it,
will be like the imperishable ocean."

Thus spoke the Bhagavat. All of the devaputras of the Śuddhāvāsa realm led by Maheśvara, all the Bodhisattva Mahāsattvas led by Maitreya, all the great Śrāvakas led by Mahākāśyapa, together with Ānanda, and gods, men, asuras, gandharvas, and everyone rejoiced at the words of the Bhagavat.

The Sūtra of the Great Vehicle, the king of the jewels named Lalitavistara, containing the sacred course of events of all those who practice the state of Bodhisattva, is finished.

The Twenty-seventh Chapter
Conclusion

Glossary

Terms

aggregate	see skandha.
Akaniṣṭha	the highest heaven of the form realm, a very pure abode.
amṛta	magical nectar that can heal, nourish, and transform; nectar of immortality.
apsarases	goddesses residing in the realm of the Four Great Kings.
Arhat	one who has conquered the enemy, emotionality, thus attaining liberation from suffering and rebirth.
Ārya	worthy, noble, exalted, saintly; those who have advanced on the path.
asuras	demi-gods of the desire realm characterized by intense striving for the prerogatives of the gods; the envious or jealous gods.
Avīci	the hell of uninterrupted pain; the lowest and most dreaded of the hells.
āyatana	category used for investigating experience; there are twelve āyatanas, two for each of the six sense functions: eye-visible form; ear-sound; nose-scent; tongue-taste; body-tangibles; mind-mental events.

Āyuṣmat	lit. 'long-lived'; title of great respect.
Bodhi	Enlightenment.
Bodhimaṇḍa	seat of Enlightenment; the place where the Buddha attained perfect Enlightenment.
Bodhisattva	one who seeks Enlightenment for the sake of benefitting all beings; the ideal of the Great Vehicle.
Brahmā	chief of the gods residing in the lowest heaven in the realm of form; often described as the creator of world-systems.
brahmacarya	intense involvement in spiritual training, including the practice of continence, chastity, and various austerities.
brahmavihāra	see Numerical Lists—four unlimiteds.
brāhmin	a member of the highest of the four traditional Indian varṇas; the educated, priestly class.
Buddha-eye	the unobstructed knowledge of the Buddha; see Numerical Lists—five eyes.
Buddha-field	the sphere of influence of a particular Buddha; may include one or more vast universes, each containing three thousand great thousands of worlds.
caitya	a monument containing holy relics, built in one of many traditional shapes representing the enlightened mind of a Buddha.
Cakravartin king	a great ruler reigning with righteousness over all kingdoms in the world.
continents	four regions inhabited by humans in the desire realm of a world-system: Pūrvavideha in the east; Jambudvīpa in the south; Aparagodāna in the west; Uttarakuru in the north; see world-system.
desire realm	the lowest of the three realms that make up a world-system; inhabited by hell beings, pretas, animals, humans, asuras, and the lower gods.

devaputra	a god residing in one of the six heavens in the desire realm.
dharma	individual things, elements, or phenomena; the truth, the true law, the Teaching of the Buddha is called 'Dharma.'
dharmadhātu	the realm of the Dharma.
dhāraṇī	lit. 'that which bears the meaning'; formulas that enable us to remember essential points of doctrine; meant to be memorized and recited.
dhātu	category used for investigating experience; there are eighteen dhatus, three for each one of the sense functions: eye-visible form-seeing consciousness, etc.; cf. āyatana.
Dhṛtarāṣṭra	one of the Four Great Kings; ruler of the East and lord of the gandharvas.
divine ear	capacity to hear sounds both human and divine, near and far; see Numerical Lists–six superior knowledges.
divine eye	capacity to see the death and rebirth of all beings; see Numerical Lists–five eyes and six superior knowledges.
emptiness	the absence of any inherent self or entity; śūnyatā.
form realm	one of the three realms that make up a world-system; inhabited by the higher gods; the realm between the desire realm and the formless realm.
formless realm	the highest of the three realms that make up a world-system; inhabited by the highest gods.
four assemblies	the communities of monks, nuns, laymen, and laywomen that practice the Dharma.
Four Great Kings	rulers of the lowest heaven in the desire realm and guardians of the world; the four are Dhṛtarāṣṭra, Virūḍhaka, Virūpākṣa, and Vaiśravaṇa.
Four Guardians	see Four Great Kings.

gandharvas	lit. 'scent eaters'; celestial musicians residing in the heavens of the desire realm.
gods	beings residing in one of the heavens in the three realms; a form of existence characterized by increasingly refined pleasure and happiness that last a great length of time but are impermanent.
garuḍa	a great bird, enemy of the nāgas.
Great Vehicle	the Mahāyana, the way of life which leads to the realization of Buddhahood for the benefit of all living beings.
Indra	see Śakra.
Jambu River	river of rose-apple nectar, whose source is Mount Meru, the center of a world-system.
Jina	conqueror; a title of the Buddha.
kalpa	a very long period of time; the creation, evolution, and destruction of a world-system each require twenty kalpas, and are followed by twenty kalpas of emptiness; a great kalpa is the entire period of one such world-system's arising and passing away.
karma	any action of body, speech, or mind of ordinary beings; former actions which condition present and future experience.
kinnaras	beings with bodies partly human and partly animal, residing in the desire realm.
koṭi	a very large number.
krośa	a distance of approximately 2.5 miles.
kṣatriya	a member of the second of the four traditional Indian varṇas; the warrior class.
Kubera	see Vaiśravaṇa.
kumbhāṇḍas	vampire-like beings residing in the desire realm.
land of Jambu	Jambudvīpa, the 'rose-apple' or southern continent; the region of a world-system where the Buddha takes his final birth.

Lesser Vehicle	the Hīnayana, the way of life which focuses exclusively on one's own liberation from suffering.
Mahāsattva	lit. 'great being'; refers to great Bodhisattvas or to the Buddha.
mahoraga	a serpent-like being residing in the desire realm.
maṇḍala	a symbolic diagram; a meaningful configuration of elements related to a center.
Māra	chief of the gods of the highest heaven in the desire realm, and so lord of the whole realm of desire; also known as Namuci, Pāpīyān, or the demon Māra; the tempter of the Buddha.
merit	the momentum generated by wholesome thought, speech, and action, which accumulates to support spiritual development.
Mount Meru	the mountain at the center of a world-system, ringed by chains of lesser mountains and lakes; see world-system.
Muni	a sage; a title of the Buddha.
nirvāṇa	final liberation from suffering.
niyuta	a large number.
nāgas	powerful serpent-like beings residing in the desire realm, inhabiting bodies of water and often guarding great treasure.
Pratyekabuddha	a follower of the Dharma who attains his liberation without a teacher; Pratyekabuddhas only appear in a period when there is no Buddha.
pretas	miserable ghost-like beings residing in the desire realm; also called hungry ghosts; see six realms.
pure Buddhadharmas	(1) eighteen Buddhadharmas, special characteristics of the fully Enlightened Buddha; (2) the collection of Buddha qualities which includes the ten powers, the four fearlessnesses, the three equanimities, and great compassion; see Numerical Lists.

rākṣasas	malicious demons residing in the desire realm.
renunciations	a set of four intentions: to prevent that which is non-virtuous from arising; to leave behind all that is non-virtuous; to produce that which is virtuous; to maintain and perfect virtues which have arisen.
ṛṣi	seer; practitioner of traditional Indian disciplines who has gained psychic powers; the Buddha is often called the Great Ṛṣi.
Śakra	chief of the Thirty-three gods; also known as Indra or Kauśika.
saṁsāra	the cycle of birth, death, and rebirth within the six realms of existence, characterized by suffering, impermanence, and confusion.
Sangha	see the Three Jewels.
Śāstra	a commentary which explains religious teachings; a Buddhist Śāstra is a commentary on the Teachings of the Buddha.
siddha	lit. 'accomplished one'; a master of psychic powers or siddhis; in the Buddhist tradition, the highest siddhi is Enlightenment.
six realms	destinies or kinds of existence into which sentient beings are born, according to their past actions; they include: gods, humans, asuras, animals, pretas, and hell beings; the last three are especially miserable and are known as the three unfortunate realms or the three lower realms.
skandha	lit. 'heap'; aggregate; category used for investigating experience; the five skandhas are form, feeling-tones, perceptions, karmic dispositions, and consciousness.
śramaṇa	a monk or religious mendicant.
Śrāvaka	lit. 'listener'; a disciple of the Buddha; a follower of the Lesser Vehicle.
Śuddhāvāsa	the highest level of the form realm, having five heavens, characterized by great purity.

śūdra	a member of the fourth and lowest of the four traditional Indian varṇas, or classes.
Sugata	lit. 'well-gone'; one of the titles of the Buddha.
Sūtra	a discourse spoken by the Buddha.
Tathāgata	lit. 'thus-gone' or 'thus-come'; one of the titles of the Buddha.
ten directions	the four cardinal directions, plus the four intermediate directions, plus the zenith and nadir; often used to mean everywhere.
ten powers	ten special powers of the Buddha: knowing the possible and the impossible; knowing the consequences of actions; knowing the capacities of beings; knowing the dispositions of beings; knowing the aspirations of beings; knowing the paths that lead to various realms; knowing the obscuration and purification of all the contemplations, meditations, deliverances, concentrations, and absorptions; knowing former lives; knowing death and rebirth of beings; knowing the defilements are exhausted. Bodhisattvas have a different set of powers also known as the ten powers.
Three Jewels	the Buddha, the Dharma (the Buddha's Teaching), and the Sangha (the community of those who follow his Teaching); the Three Jewels are the refuge for those aspiring to Enlightenment.
three lower realms	see six realms.
three realms	the desire realm, the form realm, and the formless realm; together these three comprise a world-system; see world-system.
three thousand great thousands of worlds	1,000 × 1,000 × 1,000 worlds, i.e., a billion (a thousand million) worlds; each world is an entire Mount Meru system; see world-system.
three unfortunate realms	see six realms.

tīrthika	an adherent of extreme views such as nihilism or eternalism, not according with the Middle Way of the Buddha.
Tuṣita	the most pleasing of all the heavens in the desire realm; abode of the Bodhisattva before his final birth into the human realm; the present abode of the future Buddha Maitreya.
two accumulations	the growth of merit and wisdom which lead one to the path and ripen into Buddhahood.
ūrṇā	a small tuft of hair between the eyebrows; one of the thirty-two marks of a great man.
Vaiśravaṇa	one of the Four Great Kings; ruler of the North and lord of yakṣas; also known as Kubera.
vaiśya	a member of the third of the four traditional Indian varṇas; the agricultural and mercantile class.
Veda	the ancient sacred scriptures of traditional Indian culture.
Virūḍhaka	one of the Four Great Kings; ruler of the South and lord of kumbhāṇḍas.
Virūpākṣa	one of the Four Great Kings; ruler of the West and lord of nāgas.
world	see world-system.
world-system	the environment of the six realms of beings; includes the four continents where humans and animals reside, arrayed around a central axis known as Mount Meru; most of the hell realms are beneath the continents; upon the peak of Mount Meru dwell the Thirty-three gods and the Four Great Kings; above Meru range the heavens of the rest of the desire realm and those of the form realm; the formless realm has no specific location.
yakṣas	beings of the desire realm, inhabiting trees and mountains; usually benevolent.

Yāma gods	celestial beings residing in a desire realm heaven, characterized by their freedom from strife; ruled by the devaputra Suyāma.
yojana	a distance of approximately ten miles, equal to four krośas.

Cosmological Lists

tridhātu	khams gsum	three realms
kāmadhātu	'dod-pa'i khams	desire realm
rūpadhātu	gzugs-kyi khams	form realm
ārūpyadhātu	gzugs-med khams	formless realm

ṣaḍgati	'gro-ba rigs drug	six realms of beings
deva	lha	gods
manuṣya	mi	humans
asuras	lha-ma-yin	jealous gods
tiryayoni	dud-'gro	animals
pretabhuta	yi-dvags	hungry ghosts
narakāyika	dmyal-ba	hell beings

kāmadeva	'dod-khams-kyi lha	desire realm gods
cāturmahārāja	rgyal-chen bzhi	the Four Great Kings
trāyastriṁśa	sum-cu-rtsa-gsum-pa	the Thirty-three
yāma	'thab-bral	the Yāmas
tuṣita	dga'-ldan	the Tuṣitas
nirmāṇarati	'phrul-dga'	the Nirmāṇaratis
parinirmita vaśavartin	gzhan-'phrul dbang-byed	the Parinirmita vaśavartins

rūpa-dhātu	gzugs-kyi khams-kyi lha	form realm gods
brahmakāyika	tshangs-ris	gods of the first level of meditation
brahmapurohita	tshangs-'khor	
mahābrahmā	tshangs-pa chen-po	
parīttābhā	'od-chung	gods of the second level of meditation
apramāṇābhā	tshad-med 'od	
ābhāsvara	'od-gsal	
parīttaśubha	dge-chung	gods of the third level of meditation
apramāṇaśubha	tshad-med dge	
śubhakṛtsṇa	dge-rgyas	
anabhraka	sprin-med	gods of the fourth level of meditation
puṇyaprasava	bsod-nams skyes	
bṛhatphala	'bras-bu che	
śuddhāvāsa	gnas gtsang-ma	

arūpyadhātu	gzugs-med-pa'i khams	formless realm
ākāśānantya	nam-mkha' mtha'-yas	endless space
vijñānānantya	rnam-shes mtha'-yas	infinite consciousness
ākiṁcanya	ci yang med	nothing whatsoever
naivasaṁjñānāsaṁjñā	'du-shes med 'du-shes med min	neither perception nor non-perception

tryakuśala mūlāni	dug-gsum	three defilements or three poisons
rāga	'dod-chags	desire-attachment
dveṣa	khong-khro	hatred-aversion
moha	ma-rig-pa	ignorance

trayaḥ vimokṣadvāra	rnam-par thar-pa'i sgo gsum	three doors to deliverance
śūnyatā	stong-pa-nyid	emptiness
animitta	mtshan-ma med-pa	signlessness
apraṇihita	smon-pa med-pa	wishlessness

trividyā	rig-pa gsum	three knowledges

The fourth, fifth and sixth of the six superior knowledges; see six superior knowledges.

catuḥ smṛtyupasthāna	dran-pa nye-bar-bzhag-pa	four applications of mindfulness
kāya	lus	body and physical world
vedanā	tshor-ba	feeling
citta	sems	mind
dharma	chos	dharmas, Dharma

caturogha	chu-bo bzhi	four currents
kāmarāga	'dod-pa la 'dod-chags-pa	desire for sense-objects
bhavarāga	srid-pa'i 'dod-chags-pa	desire for existence
avidyā	ma-rig-pa	ignorance
dṛṣṭi	log-par lta-ba	wrong views

catuḥ pratisamvid	so-so yang-dag par rig-pa	four exact knowledges
dharma	chos	all forms of the Dharma
artha	don	characteristics and intention
nirukti	nges-pa'i tshig	regional usage of language and interpretations
pratibhāna	spobs-pa	eloquence

caturvaiśāradya	ma 'jigs-pa bzhi	four fearlessnesses
dharmābhisambodhi	chos thams-cad mngon-par-rdzogs-par byang-chub-pa	due to having fully known all dharmas
āsravakṣayajñāna	zag-pa thams-cad zad par mkhyen-pa	due to knowing all impurities have been extinguished
antarāyikadharma	bar-du-gcod-pa'i chos-rnams gzhan-du-mi-'gyur-bar nges-pa'i lung-bstan-pa	due to having correctly described obstacles to emancipation for others
nairyāṇikapratipada	nges-par-'byung-ba'i lam de-bzhin-du 'gyur-ba	due to having shown how to enter the path which leads to deliverance

catur ṛddhipāda	rdzu-'phrul rkang-pa bzhi	four foundations for supernatural power
chanda	'dun-pa	willingness
vīrya	brtson-pa	effort
citta	sems-pa	intentiveness
mīmāṁsā	dpyod-pa	investigation

catur dhyāna	bsam-gtan bzhi	four levels of meditation
The first level is accompanied by:		
vitarka	rtog-pa	observation
vicāra	dpyod-pa	reflection
prīti	dga'-ba	pleasure
sukha	bde-ba	joy
The second level is accompanied by:		
prīti	dga'-ba	pleasure
sukha	bde-ba	joy
The third level is accompanied by:		
sukha	bde-ba	joy
The fourth level is accompanied by:		
upekṣā	btang-snyoms	equanimity

catuḥ saṁgrahavastu	bsdu-ba'i dngos-po bzhi	four means of conversion
dāna	sbyin-pa	giving
priyarādita	snyan-par smra-ba	kind words
arthacaryā	don spyod-pa	helpfulness
samānārthatā	don mthun-pa	consistency between words and deeds

catur āryasatyāni	'phags-pa'i bden-pa bzhi	four noble truths
duḥkha	sdug-bsngal	suffering
samudaya	kun-'byung-ba	source of suffering
nirodha	'gog-pa	cessation of suffering
mārga	lam	path that leads to the cessation of suffering

samyak prahāṇa	yang-dag-par spong-ba bzhi	four renunciations

see Terms—renunciations

apramāṇa	tshad-med-pa bzhi	four unlimiteds
maitrī	byams-pa	love
karuṇā	thug-rje	compassion
muditā	dga'-ba	sympathetic joy
upekṣā	btang-snyoms	equanimity

pañcaskandha	phung-po lnga	five aggregates
rūpa	gzugs	form
vedanā	tshor-ba	feeling
saṁjñā	'du-shes	perception
saṁskāra	'du-byed	karmic dispositions
vijñāna	rnam-par-shes-pa	consciousness

pañcacakṣus	mig lnga	five eyes
māṁsacakṣus	sha'i mig	physical eye
divyacakṣus	lha'i mig	divine eye
prajñācakṣus	shes-rab-kyi mig	wisdom eye
dharmacakṣus	chos-kyi mig	Dharma eye
buddhacakṣus	sangs-rgyas-kyi mig	Buddha eye

pañca abhijñā	mngon-shes lnga	five superior knowledges

The first five of the six superior knowledges; see the six superior knowledges.

pañcendriya, pañcabala	dbang-po lnga, thobs lnga	five powers, five strengths
śraddhā	dad-pa	faith
vīrya	brtson-'grus	effort
smṛti	dran-pa	mindfulness
samādhi	ting-nge-'dzin	concentration
prajñā	shes-rab	wisdom

ṣaṭ pāramitā	pha-rol-tu phyin-pa drug	six perfections
dāna	sbyin-pa	giving
śīla	tshul-khrims	moral conduct
kṣānti	bzod-pa	patience
vīrya	brtson-'grus	effort
samādhi	bsam-gtan	concentration
prajñā	shes-rab	wisdom

ṣaṭ abhijñā	mngon-shes drug	six superior knowledges
ṛddhyabhijñā	rdzu-'phrul-gyi bya-ba	supernatural abilities
divyaśrotrābhijñā	rna-ba shes-pa	divine ear
cetaḥparyāyābhijñā	pha-rol-gyi gzhan sems shes-pa	power of penetrating the thoughts of another
pūrvanivāsānusmṛti-abhijñā	sngon-gyi gnas rjes-su-dran-pa shes-pa	knowledge of former lives
divyacakṣus	lha'i mig	divine eye
āsravakṣayābhijñā	zag-pa zad-pa shes-pa	knowledge that the impurities and defilements are extinct

sapta bodhyaṅga	byang-chub yan-lag bdun	seven branches of awakening
smṛti	dran-pa	mindfulness
dharmapravicaya	chos rab-tu rnam-par-'byed-pa	investigation into dharmas
vīrya	brtson-'grus	effort
prīti	dga'-ba	joy
praśrabdhi	shin-tu sbyangs-pa	refinement and serenity
samādhi	ting-nge-'dzin	concentration
upekṣā	btang-snyoms	equanimity

aṣṭa āryamārga	'phags-pa'i lam yan-lag brgyad	eightfold noble path
samyagdṛṣṭi	yang-dag-pa'i lta-ba	right view
samyaksamkalpa	yang-dag-pa'i rtogs-pa	right intention
samyagvāk	yang-dag-pa'i ngag	right speech
samyakkarmānta	yang-dag-pa'i las-kyi mtha'	right conduct
samyakājīva	yang-dag-pa'i 'tsho-ba	right livelihood
samyagvyāyāma	yang-dag-pa'i rtsol-ba	right effort
samyaksmṛti	yang-dag-pa'i dran-pa	right mindfulness
samyaksamādhi	yang-dag-pa'i ting-nge-'dzin	right concentration

aṣṭalokadharma	'jig-rten chos brgyad	eight worldly dharmas
lābha, alābha	rnyed, mi-rnyed	gain and loss
sukha, duḥkha	bde, mi-bde	happiness and sadness
praśaṁsā, nindā	bstod, smad	praise and blame
yaśa, ayaśa	snyan, mi-snyan	fame and disgrace

daśākuśala-karmapatha	mi-dge-ba'i rtsa-ba bcu	ten bad paths of action
trīṇi kāyaduścaritāni	lus-kyi nyes-par-spyod-pa gsum	three faults of body
prāṇātipāta	srog-gcod	killing
adattādāna	ma-byin-len	stealing
kāmamithyācara	'dod-pas log-par-g•yem-pa	sexual misconduct
catvāri vagduścaritāni	ngag-gi nyes-par-spyod-pa bzhi	four faults of speech
mṛṣāvāda	rdzun-du smras ba	lying
paiśunya	phra-ma	slander
pāruṣya	tshig-rtsub	harsh speech
sambhinnapralāpa	ngag-'chal	idle talk
trīṇi manoduścaritāni	yid-kyi nyes-par-spyod-pa gsum	three faults of mind
abhidhyā	brnab-sems	craving
vyāpāda	gnod-sems	ill-will
mithyādṛṣṭi	log-lta	wrong views

daśabhūmi bodhisattvasya	byang-chub-sems-dpa'i sa bcu	ten stages of the Bodhisattva
pramuditā	rab-tu-dga'-ba	the Joyous
vimalā	dri-ma med-pa	the Immaculate
prabhākāri	'od byed-pa	the Light-giving
arciṣmatī	'od 'phro-can	the Radiant
sudurjayā	shin-tu sbyang dka'-ba	the Invincible
abhimukhī	mngon-tu gyur-pa	the Realizing
durāṁgamā	ring-du song-ba	the Far-reaching
acalā	mi g•yo-ba	the Immovable
sādhumatī	legs-pa'i blo-gros	the Beneficial
dharmameghā	chos-kyi sprin	the Cloud of Dharma

pratītyasamutpāda nidāna	rten-cing-'brel-bar yan-lag bcu-gnyis	twelve links of dependent origination
avidyā	ma-rig-pa	ignorance
saṁskāra	'du-byed	karmic dispositions
vijñāna	rnam-par-shes-pa	consciousness
nāmarūpa	ming dang gzugs	name and form
ṣaḍāyatanāni	skye-mched drug	six senses
sparśa	reg-pa	contact
vedanā	tshor-ba	feeling
tṛṣṇā	sred-pa	craving
upādāna	nye-bar-len-pa	grasping
bhava	srid-pa	existence
jāti	skye-ba	birth
jarāmaraṇa	rga-shi	old age and death

saptātriṁśad bodhipakṣa	byang-chub kyi sum-cu-rtsa-bdun	thirty-seven wings of Enlightenment
catuḥsmṛtyupasthāna	dran-pa nye-bar-bzhag-pa bzhi	four mindfulnesses
catuḥsamyakprahāha	yang-dag-par spong-ba bzhi	four renunciations
catuhṛddhipāda	rdzu-'phrul rkang-pa bzhi	four foundations for supernatural power
pañcendriya	dbang-po lnga	five powers
pañcabala	thobs lnga	five strengths
bodhyaṅga	byang-chub yan-lag bdun	seven branches of awakening
āryamārga	'phags-pa'i lam yan-lag brgyad	eightfold noble path

Acknowledgements

Dharma Publishing acknowledges the kind permission granted by the following museums and individuals to reprint thangkas of the Buddha from their collections.

Plate A Courtesy of the St. Louis Art Museum; W. K. Bixby Fund.

Plate B Copyright ©1971 by the Metropolitan Museum of Art, New York; Mrs. W. Murray Crane Gift Fund.

Plate 1 Courtesy of the Freer Gallery of Art, Smithsonian Institution, Washington, D.C.

Plate 2 Copyright ©1971 by the Metropolitan Museum of Art, New York; Mrs. W. Murray Crane Gift Fund.

Plate 3 Copyright ©1971 by the Metropolitan Museum of Art, New York; Mrs. W. Murray Crane Gift Fund.

Plate 4 Cliché Musées Nationaux, Paris.

Plate 5 Dudjom Rinpoche.

Plate 6 Courtesy of the Brooklyn Museum, New York; gift of Mr. Arthur Wiesenberger.

Plate 7 Copyright ©1970 by the Metropolitan Museum of Art, New York; gift of Joseph H. Heil.

Plate 8 Courtesy of the Brooklyn Museum, New York; gift of Mr. Arthur Wiesenberger.

Plate 9	John Gilmore Ford.
Plate 10	Cliché Musées Nationaux, Paris.
Plate 11	Cliché Musées Nationaux, Paris.
Plate 12	Copyright ©1971 by the Metropolitan Museum of Art, New York; Mrs. W. Murray Crane Gift Fund.
Plate 13	Courtesy of the Brooklyn Museum, New York; gift of Mr. Arthur Wiesenberger.
Plate 14	Cliché Musées Nationaux, Paris.
Plate 15	Dudjom Rinpoche.
Plate 16	Courtesy of the Brooklyn Museum, New York; gift of Mr. Arthur Wiesenberger.
Plate 17	Copyright ©1970 by the Metropolitan Museum of Art, New York; gift of Joseph H. Heil.
Plate 18	Copyright ©1971 by the Metropolitan Museum of Art, New York; Mrs. W. Murray Crane Gift Fund.
Plate 19	Cliché Musées Nationaux, Paris.
Plate 20	Copyright ©1970 by the Metropolitan Museum of Art, New York; gift of Joseph H. Heil.
Plate 21	Tibetan Nyingma Meditation Center.
Plate 22	Dudjom Rinpoche.
Plate 23	Courtesy of the St. Louis Art Museum; W. E. Bixby Fund.
Plate 24	Cliché Musées Nationaux, Paris.
Plate 25	Sergei Daikoff.
Plate 26	Cliché Musées Nationaux, Paris.
Plate 27	Dr. Frederick Adler.

Index

brahmacarya 362
brāhmin
class 36
predictions by 98–99
Buddha
descriptions of 639–659
nature of 135–136, 634
play of 532–533
Buddha-fields, names of 443ff
Buddhahood, attainment of 524
Buddhas
of the ten directions 443ff, 636
previous 10, 256–258, 427

caitya 339, 409–410
Cakravartin king 30–34, 99, 150–151, 153, 209, 318, 324
seven precious treasures 30–34, 151, 153
causes and conditions 263–266
Chandaka 142, 143, 183, 205, 316ff, 339, 342ff, 350–353, 361
constellations 584–588
contests with Śākyas
archery 231ff
feats of strength 229ff
mathematics 223ff
writing 221ff
Cyutyākāraprayoga, teaching of 53

Daṇḍapāṇi 215ff, 231
Deer Park 35, 607–608, 614, 617, 622
demons, army of 463ff, 506ff
dependent origination 518–524, 633–634
desire
faults of 259–260, 487–490, 492–495
like poison 366ff
objects of desire 320–321
three examples concerning 376–378
Devadatta 219–220, 229–230
devaputras
decorate road to Bodhimaṇḍa 417ff
discourage Māra 500–502
guarding Bodhimaṇḍa 422ff
helping the Bodhisattva depart 306–308, 329ff
praise Buddha after Enlightenment 537–555
request teaching of Lalitavistara 9–11, 12, 667
serving the Bodhisattva, 77–83
wishing to nourish the Bodhisattva 403
Dhāraṇīmaṇḍa, see Bodhimaṇḍa
Dharma
Bhagavat's lack of urgency to teach 593–596, 599, 601
consent to teach 605
doors of 55–64
four gates of 273–274
of a perfect and complete Buddha 593–595, 598, 601
Dīpaṁkara 258, 267, 279, 539, 595, 627
divine eye 131, 516ff
dream
Bodhisattva's 297
Gopa's 293–296
Māra's 459–461
Māyādevī's, see Māyādevī
Śuddhodana's 283

Śrī Vaiśravaṇa